The Quirky Landlord's Romp, Wrangle, & Warble

Clancy Rohring

ISBN: 1530509572

ISBN 13: 9781530509577

Library of Congress Control Number: 2016904192

CreateSpace Independent Publishing Platform

North Charleston, South Carolina

My Motif

Is anyone's life typical? I doubt it. To prove that it isn't, I report excerpts in my life, especially these last two years, 2014 to 2016, to illustrate how good life is for me; not without challenges, but nothing overwhelming so far.

Pope Frances, a hopeful man like our President Obama, told congress, September 24, 2015, choose "people over profit." In my book, people, I finally realize, have been the most important element in my romp, wrangle and warble of a journey. In fact, again and again I have been more influenced by the persons in my life than all the books, newspapers, magazines, and some film I have dug into and eaten voraciously.

These persons didn't necessarily all love me, I assure you. Nevertheless, their calling card seemed to pump up my heart or deflate it; sometimes they do or did both. Barbara Streisand sings, "People who need people...are the luckiest people in the world."

That's me. I'm lucky so I reach out in search and sing, in spite of conflicts internal and external, debate, and tragedies that require a tough stomach. And just maybe the troubles I've seen you ain't seen yet.

Is it futile to hope? Some of my people merely rely on the bottom line or spend wit and energy to manipulate it using loopholes or false information. Trump is surely proof that money alone doesn't build character. According to him he doesn't need people, can do without twelve million or more. You see, he did it all by himself. Paved roads and police protection had nothing to do with it and. of course, food stamps and school lunches enables employers to hire cheap. Our bankruptcy laws stepped up to somehow save his fortune.

Deporting the Hispanics would cause an extreme labor shortage and inflation. We would need a wheelbarrow of dollars to buy a loaf of bread or a burrito or a head of lettuce out of Salinas. Columnist Kathleen Parker wrote on New Year's Eve, 2015, "Donald Trump is White Man's last stand." She means they're uncomfortable with the diverse world that is; surely not as easy to predict, case, or cash out.

I do realize that I'm just a peon. I'm okay with it. According to a Canadian AI student, "Carnegie Mellon's Artificial Intelligence (AI) center has more than one hundred PhD researchers." I hope, ultimately they make life better for all of us, not just the one percent.

Part One

Fragments of The Now

Pinched

In late November of 2014, I knocked on Jed's door and gave him the following letter. He read it and didn't look too happy.

From: Clancy Rohring To: Jed Hildebrog Re: Rental fee

My expenses for operating my home are up $160.00 per month. Not my fault…Not your fault. So it is necessary for me to raise the rent for the coming year 2015, $50.00 (fifty dollars) per month. I realize that is a hefty sum and I duly regret having to do so. Have given it lots of thought.

So Jed, as of January 1, 2015, please pay me $550.00 per month. I have no problem with you or your lifestyle. You are a wonderful person. I know very few persons who could take your place. I am comfortable with you in my home. Please do not take this rate increase personally.

I have been told that it is courteous to give a renter at least a 30-day notice when a rent payment increase is involved. So I am submitting this in writing to you on Saturday, November 22, 2014. Sincerely, Clancy Rohring 11/22/14, 10:05 AM

He merely said, "I'll check with friends for lower rent elsewhere and ask my bank to examine my account to see if I can manage the increase."

The letter was a gamble because I wanted Jed to stay. But a one-bedroom now costs $750 per month and studios are about $650 without fridge, range, washer/dryer, porch for a smoke, etcetera. Jed loves the squirrels and the blue jays, even the crows in the back yard. Fortunately, less than one week later he assured me that he would be able to handle the rent hike when he gave me December rent in November, ahead of time.

Due to an unfortunate event Tuesday, December 2nd, I lucked out with the timing of my letter.

At my age, by the act of gravity or whatever, some areas of my body, such as the stomach, sport a layer of droopy flesh. The sag has lost its resilience, its bounce back, its muscle. I tend to treat it at times as squeezable when getting into a pair of jeans. Since it was freezing outside, I intended to wear a new vest, purple with a warm, fuzzy lining, over a lavender sweater. I had lost five pounds so hoped for looks, but mostly warmth. I could get into my grey wool slacks I made years ago, when I weighed less.

Because the slacks have a metal zipper on the left side, I figured it would execute the squeezing necessitated by what I knew would be a tight fit. So I proceeded to pull up the zipper, which met much resistance, one-third of the way. "Ouch!" I hit some skin. I quickly pulled the zipper back down to avoid it. Not giving up, I tugged again to move it forward. Sucking in took all my strength; with one last pull – "Ah!" I've almost got it to two-thirds, just above my hip bone, "It hurts." What's strange, I didn't realize when it happened, when I did it. A hunk of me was caught in the zipper. "Hell!"

Finally aware, I pushed down to undo the damage. The zipper wouldn't budge. It's stuck biting into a piece of my skin. I can't leave it this way. This is serious stuff.

I knocked on my renter's door. Jed weighs like three hundred pounds – don't have an official count – so naturally his hands are stronger than mine. He is strong enough to shut off the water so my garden hose won't leak. Recently he helped a disabled friend of his bolt down a toilet with a wrench.

"Jed, my skin is stuck in my zipper. Can't move it. Can you try? To undo it."

Calmly, Jed moved out of his doorway, reached around me to turn on the hall light in the ceiling. Then he took hold of the zipper and tugged. To no avail. "Let me try with the pliers," he said. He reached for them on the round table at the end of his bed. He didn't even have to search for them in all that clutter of sauces, a box of wine, Sangria – (his current favorite), more CDs and junk. He tends to let the cans and bottles accumulate before finally disposing of them. He took hold of the sturdy hook on the zipper. It didn't give. "No, that won't work."

"Let me get my good scissors. They're stiff to use, but strong," I said. "Cut the zipper out."

"I need a better light. Let's go to the kitchen," Jed directed. I grabbed my scissors I keep next to my sofa bed and we headed downstairs. The kitchen has six huge lights in the ceiling, a light I can turn on over the island between the kitchen and living room, and the 24-hour-light in the range hood.

With not much space to work with (the cloth and zipper were tight against my body) Jed cut on the stomach side, then the other side. "It'll destroy your pants."

"Gonna have to."

His action released the pressure of the garment against my stomach but the zipper remained lodged, gripping my skin. It was getting scary. "Your doctor is going to have to cut you out," Jed warned.

I cringed. "Cut the zippers," I said. He tried. The scissors didn't make a dent, not strong enough to cut metal.

"I have it – let me find my wire cutters," he came up with.

I found that suggestion encouraging but a last resort. We went back upstairs. His walls are filled with shelving with small boxes that serve as files for tools and CDs, a steamer, Foreman grill, stainless steel pans, every size for the oven, and of course his computer, always on, and his music recording equipment.

He records the live performances for several bands when they come to town. He just did one in Newberg the night before. To be friendly and alleviate the do-or-die urgency I felt, I asked him about his trip to Newberg. "It was at my friend's house. His next door neighbor, a notable mandolin player who was the first mandolin artist to be admitted to the Berkleley School of Music in Boston, performed with a Banjo player," Jed mentioned, while looking for his wire cutters. I feared he wouldn't find them. How could he in all this?

Jed located them in a short time, keeping my anxiety under control. Doctors use knives, scalpels, not metal cutters. Relieved, I was so afraid he wouldn't find them, but he always finds what he's looking for in all that stuff in his room. He found them.

"That's them?" I asked. "They're the size of cuticle scissors. I expected my rose clippers, at least. Got a big day planned. Meals on Wheels and Cherry Blossom bridge today." I don't know if I was optimistically planning ahead or actually giving up the ghost when I saw those itty-bitty wire cutters. He did say wire, not metal.

Amazing. The cutters worked. Jed cut the zipper right above the jammed spot. "It's still stuck," I uttered. Just then the zipper pulled apart. The grip, the pressure, subsided. Ah, released from prison. "Yay, you did it. What if you weren't here? I would have had to go to my clinic. But doctors use knives not wire cutters, I imagine."

Back in my room, in a change of mood, I left the waistband pinned so the slacks did not fall down. They just enjoyed a gaping hole at the hip. I took off the flannel shirt and t-shirt I usually sleep in and tried on the sweater and new vest. Long enough, they both covered the gaping hole in my pants adequately. I left the wool slacks on, read the day's Clark county *Columbia* on line, brought to boil left over coffee on the top of the stove (I'm not a modern day microwave addict), split a pink grapefruit in half and scored it with a butcher knife that has a great point, and opened and stirred a Tillamook coffee-flavored Greek yogurt, my favorite. I took my Centrum vitamin after the meal, as if nothing had happened...pursued business as usual.

That man is so resourceful. What would I have done if he wasn't here? I'm glad I raised his rent before this potential disaster or, yes, ridiculous situation my vanity brought about. I wouldn't have the nerve to do it now. Just last week my TV quit. Of course, I thought, have to buy a new one. But I told Jed about it. After all he is a computer tech, laid off from Portland State University in the budget crunch of 2008. He investigated – found the light out on the cable box. I had dropped the remote on its face – turning it off? Complicated? Simple!

Is this proof of my contention that life is loaded with minor conflicts and hopefully resolutions? Is it worth sharing?

I told my friends at bridge. They couldn't quit laughing. "Belongs in The Quirky Landlord," Gerard said. But when I mentioned it to A.J., my eighty-six-year-old friend, who recently lost her husband, a WWII vet, she sounded shocked, "Your renter IS A MALE, isn't he? How awful!"

People asked about the "hurt" they imagined. The "hurt" was not primary. My immediate concern was my "freedom."

LIFE IS ASTONISHING, AT TIMES...SIMPLY WONDERFUL! My life includes bridge, my son and his family, brother and sister, friends, my son's newspaper, The *Columbian*, roses, beer, ideas, writing, my granddaughter's volleyball games, my grandsons' football, basketball and now soccer for the little one, the Ducks and Portland State Vikings football, Senator Merkley, Governor Brown, and Congressman Blumenauer, and especially, Obama, Seattle Seahawks, Portland Trailblazers, *Bloomberg Business Week*, *Foreign Affairs*, and local free papers; my favorites being: *Asian Reporter*, *Mid County Memo*, *The Skanner*, *El Hispanica*, and *Portland Tribune*. *Willamette Weeks*'s investigative reports make it a winner too. Some people I take for granted, in my stride, in my spare time: neighbors (my favorites – the first generation immigrants), and my renter, Jed Hildebrog.

Jed has turned out to be a major factor in releasing me from my fate I have illustrated in *The Quirky Landlord*. I not only can count on him to pay the rent (he pays early), is good company – up to date with current affairs, sports and politics (he likes Bernie) – and food and drink and music, of course. He helped me transmit *The Quirky Landlord* to CreateSpace, installed my modem for internet and a new faucet in my downstairs bathroom. Recently he steam mopped my hardwood floor in the living and dining rooms and the tile in the rest of the first floor. He has family he cares about. Even his passion or obsession for food is mostly intriguing rather than one that causes me to lose my appetite.

This morning I slept in. I plan to join my bridge group of four fellows hoping to see if Tully needs a substitute. He spent almost four months in South France, just returned. I had a great chat with Tully last Wednesday at Mountain View Athlete Club, when I took the potato salad with my mother's salad dressing (miracle whip, cider vinegar, chopped Gherkin pickles and French's mustard). I felt sheepish about it because I was supposed to use Pat O'Reilly's Irish potatoes from his garden. But they were white new potatoes which would not absorb my dressing, so I used Russet and white onions but did add extra hard boiled eggs like Pat suggested. Pat is dissatisfied with his version of potato salad dressing and said he would try mine.

Tully is very up-to-date on France, and Europe in general. I admitted to him I had learned to read French in undergraduate school but couldn't speak it and "can't comprehend a word of it spoken." He related how he spoke enough French in an introduction, to ask strangers to speak it slow enough, so he could engage back and forth with them.

Tully is a short fellow, always in motion. He makes comments of his passion and admiration for his wife. He mentioned their early years of marriage, where their first child was born, serving a mission for their Lutheran church in Madagascar. I said, "Your wife must be adventurous and innovative."

He said, "Not really. Fragile, petite, and easily frightened."

Rei Takachi, a friend and a bridge partner, called me last night just before 10 PM and apologized for the late call. Rei, Ito, and Trudy play bridge at my house every other Thursday 2:30 PM to 5:30 PM; so late, because Trudy, a corporate airline reservationist who works out of her home, isn't off work until 2 PM. We play three games, six hands each, then switch partners. The park bureau's East Portland Community Center is closed next week for maintenance so the regular Tuesday afternoon bridge, managed by Blake, a retired attorney, is cancelled. Rei wanted to play. "Ito has been invited by Joan and Marge to Joan's home to continue the game, so can we drum up a game on Tuesday at your house or mine? Is Gerard or Barton available?"

"Barton is enamored with Marge so I bet he has plans. But I'll call both of them. Haven't seen Gerard for so long. I told him I'd type his book but, fortunately, he found someone else. I should touch base. Barton was rude to me last time I played against him – but maybe he just had bad cards. For once in my life I had barn burners. Hee Hee!"

Rei is amazing. She had warned me Wednesday PM before our game last Thursday that she had to be in Lake Oswego at her daughter's new home for a county inspector, to okay the new gas line her daughter ordered for her range, and was concerned she would be late for bridge. She made it on time because she quit waiting for him. He had just given her a date for the entire day, no two-hour or even four-hour window.

After leaving messages for Gerard and Barton for a possibility of bridge next Tuesday, I got on the bus shortly before 9:00 AM for Mountain View Athletic. This is the first Friday I would not be the fourth for bridge with Brock, Tzok and Paul– three old time, very serious tennis players and bridge players. Since Tully is back in town, he is the fourth on the court for doubles and their bridge game. Pat O'Reilly just plays as fourth hand on Wednesdays.

Thursday at 5 PM Brock informed me that Tully was now back on schedule for Friday's bridge game. I had played in Tully's place all summer, in fact, almost four months. I told Brock that Tully use to beg off about 10 AM and let me take his place. "Maybe he'll still do that?"

Brock said, "Never know. Worth a gamble."

So I arrived at 9:30 AM and took two chocolate chip cookies with my coffee. Neil, Katy's husband, is a retired postal inspector. The two of them are addicted to giant ship tours anywhere and everywhere. Katy is a blond beauty, a retired, doting grandmother, looks thirty-five, who plays tennis. She looks like a model for tennis wear. Neil lifts weights, has for years, in spite of the fact he is slight of build and maybe only five foot seven or so, boasts of a tough, New Jersey waterfront heritage, and bakes cookies and brownies every Friday, mostly for the tennis players. He puts them on a table available close to the door to the courts and us extras for bridge.

The place is loaded with tennis players, a lot of old timers, at least in the early mornings, but not a lot of enthusiastic bridge players. I find that old timers hesitate to learn bridge even if they would like to. But to defend old timers, I recall in college lots of acquaintances expressed a desire to learn bridge but hesitated in the same way. My mother used to say, "Once a dud, always a dud, whether you're twenty or seventy."

The television on the south wall between the windows looking out on the swim pool is always on the tennis channel. The bridge players often share outstanding plays and players they have seen. The many tennis buffs coming and going is a side show I enjoy. The kaleidoscope of tennis shoes – some so unique, not all Nike and the usual brands, even from

Union of South Africa – and skirts and shorts for every style, regardless of the size of the player - arrive in east Portland via the internet.

The extra tall, slender, blond, lead tennis pro, of Scandinavian descent, stays very quietly in the background. When it's time for the floor tarp to be scrubbed he leads the crew to operate the heavy machinery to do so. With eight double indoor courts it takes an entire day of no tennis. In the same consistent but low key fashion he coordinates court times, assesses skill categories, and organizes tournaments. In his spare time he restrings tennis rackets. Always learning new things I found out that the handle on tennis rackets differ in circumferences. So it is necessary to be sure the owner/player has sufficient, correct, and comfortable grip on his chosen racket relative to the size of his hand.

A month ago, Martin, a beloved fellow, passed away suddenly, after a release from an overnight in the hospital. His wife Bia, Chinese, is also a tennis player, a crack one. Martin was so grateful to her adult children. He had recently told me, when he was a fourth in our bridge group, "They give me outstanding gifts, this iPhone for my birthday. They know how much I love their mother."

On a Monday, his church in Beaverton was filled, including all his tennis cronies. One of them, a handsome, outgoing fellow, white hair, strong jaw, with a wife partner who is just as talented and energetic as he is, Walt, gave one of the eulogies. It brought tears to the usually tough, still serious but aging athletes, Grace told me.

Grace, a retired nurse who comes to the Gresham location out of Oregon City, offered me a ride to the funeral. I could not take her up on it. At the time I was volunteering at East Portland Community Center on Mondays at KP duty. Shortly after that I was replaced by a developmentally disabled fellow in training for meal service. Until Robin, who is bilingual, became manager I did liaison with the old time Chinese, Vietnamese and Russians to troubleshoot for them. I spoke for them at a City of Portland budget hearing to retrieve their Wednesday and Friday bus passes, to attend Meals On Wheels for a special Asian menu prepared often times by Asians. In any event I was comfortable in not attending the funeral because I am not a tennis player. These men and women have been friends and associates for many years. In fact I find the game very strenuous. I'm a swimmer. I did say a prayer for Martin's family.

I asked the fellows if Pat happened to share the potato salad, in a plastic container, with them. I had put it in a Victoria's Secret shopping bag. I told them, "A friend gave it to me. It isn't mine. I have never shopped there, honest." I included loads of napkins and plastic forks but only two paper plates.

"That's the best potato salad I've ever had," Paul said, "but don't tell my wife that!"

"Sounds like my wife," Tzok said, "She accuses me of things I have no memory of – dreams them up – just to complain."

"They tore the two paper plates in half for four plates and the potato salad slopped over," Tully said.

"I only had two paper plates left in my kitchen," I further explained.

Tully got up out of his chair. "You came at a good time, Clancy. Bad hands all morning. I'll let you struggle with them."

"Thanks, Tully. When you were gone I was first string on the team for a while. Now I'm second string again, benched, although Tzok considers me a third stringer."

Now my partner, Tzok Zanger, second generation from Germany, long married to a registered Daughter of the American Revolution is a very demanding partner. I'm damned if I do, damned if I don't. It doesn't matter how I bid my hand, Tzok would have done it differently. He's impossible if we fail to bid a slam, but unknowingly make one and get a star for not doing so. He will never forget or forgive. He goes into a rage at me regardless, at times scares the hell out of me. Most of all, he seems to be bothered by my registration as a democrat. He often has said, "Your only problem is you're a liberal."

At the same time, I join in the game hoping for his ultimate approval somewhere down the line, hoping someday he'll see my worth and give me his okay. For me, I have respect for his achievements in his profession and a mutual love for his expertise in roses. He is also passionate about his family. I do suspect that problems cropping up for his children and his precarious health explain some of his short temper. He did tell me he pays a fortune for health insurance. Last year he had a second scare with cancer on a leg but it was short-lived. I have no way of telling him that I care what happens to him and his.

Tzok thinks I have it so good maybe because I tend to share only the good and great happenings in my life. I don't share what I worry about except to my doctor. I pray. I am optimistic. I hope. And fortunately I have confidence in my loved ones to handle the really awful challenges of these times, maybe because of their capacity to do so in the past. I have no lasting pain, physically. But I behold and get burdened with other's pain, which I can take and shake off because it's not happening to me, at least at the now.

I don't tie up in bridge with anyone else except Tzok, and possibly Blake, who is just the opposite; whereas Tzok goes into an emotional tirade, Blake who is hard of hearing, avoids all expressions of approval or disapproval, the stone face of poker.

No such problem with Brock and Paul. Paul is married to a devout Mormon, was a Pop Warner football coach for years, and flies electronic model planes he builds. Now I wonder if he'll advance to drones? He's always with it and plays a clever, heads-up game; he always finds a way to make a good hand a winner. Good looking, friendly, and outgoing, many people, both men and women, give him greetings.

Brock, an engineer, has a patent on a photo system that clocks the end of horse races, used at Portland Meadows. He has replacements for both hips, so he is especially grateful for his health and the ability to play tennis. Since he is extra tall, with daddy-long-legs he tells fun stories of his efforts to play hockey in college, one time flying into the team bench flat on his stomach. At 64 he still has a son in college. He recently fell off his motorcycle when a motorist went out of his turn at a 3-way stop, required by a temporary detour, on his way home. Fortunately, a policeman was on the scene.

Brock has been the one that coordinates most of the card games and sees that I am involved. So far he and I share our interests from radon to computers to people. He directed the major federal study of Radon in the 1980s and 1990s in the region, a side effect of a major geological event, the Missoula floods. In a more serious vein he actively follows the latest physics-related mathematical theorems and follows them on line on his phone. That's out of my bailiwick. Strangely he was an underclassman when I taught at Centennial high school in 1964. His brother, who lives in California, was in my U.S. History class. His family is real close. His father is retired from the Navy. His mother, deceased, was from Czechoslovakia. An officer in Viet Nam and a scholarship student at Brown University, I think of Brock as a good friend, easy to be candid with. In spite of being a republican he's a great guy.

I have brought some of my favorite roses for Tzok; the most recent – my five-petal Altissimo, a glorious red climber. It was a magnificent solo. He took it home. The next day he told me their home always has three bouquets; at the entry, on the dining table and on the kitchen table. Tzok was and still is an executive in the international rose market. A graduate in Marketing from Oregon State University, still in his seventies, he advises on rose patent disputes, usually in Amsterdam. He later told me he gives the annual report on the latest innovations in the rose industry to the International Horticultural society.

There's not a large belly or any flab to be seen among these amazing seniors. Even the ones born extra large are "fit as a fiddle!" Health is very important to them. They pay over one hundred dollars per month for access to the courts and the tennis program.

I'll admit, the people I compete with in bridge and pinochle have become extra special to me at this time in my life, in addition to family and other more normal activities. Special enough that I want to put them down on paper. They give meaning somehow and challenge in life as it has come to be. In these pages I will probably relate to: my son, his wife, my grandchildren, my doctor, other friends in my writing and political world. I realize in a book there is to be one giant conflict and a resolution.

In my everyday world there are, often times, more than one conflict and maybe a resolution, of sorts. Pan Am people had a wise saying, "Play it by ear."

I informed Rei that Barton, Gerard, and I will be at my home for bridge with her, Tuesday, noon. Noon means I better get to cooking something. I was happy that I could deliver on her hopeful suggestion.

Which is More Fickle? Roses or People?

I got ready for the 2014 Portland Rose show to celebrate the annual Rose Festival. I had to set up and deliver my flowers 6:30 to 9:30 AM, Thursday, June 5th, this year for the two-day show. This is an exciting event for me. I prepare for it most of the year.

In the week prior, I had my hair cut – ended up with bangs too even - I prefer them spiked. Already summer weather, so I had a pedicure for sandals. Vivian, the Vietnamese proprietor of Global Nails, remembered my favorite polish, metallic green. She exercises her podiatrist skills, quickly removes the pain of an ingrown toenail on my big toe, left foot, for a bargain price.

Last year, I won ten ribbons and a trophy for a single-stem shrub rose spray, Carefree Spirit, red with a white center. The trophy, a huge cut glass dish four inches deep and a smaller deep dish (perfect for chips and dip), for the shrub category, was donated by Seven Dees Nursery on Powell Boulevard. Rich Baer said the spray "was perfect." With lots of 70-plus-degree weather, facing west and south, my rose bushes had been blooming for more than a week. Some were coming close to "peeked."

For two years, Trish, who had been a next door neighbor to my con-do, packed my roses in her 1990 Buick (a heavy auto, rides smooth): two buckets in the trunk and two in the back seat. She delivered me to the ice arena at the Lloyd Center. After I set up single stems and/or three stems in mostly Division II for floribundas and multiple sprays, but some in Division III, shrub and climber categories, Trish would deliver them to the proper number at each table, further designated by color categories such as dark red, medium red, orange-red, etcetera. Trish and I had a first rate team effort going. She loves roses too. We are required to use the Rose Associations vases and water which I feel is a good thing, a necessary control.

Tuesday morning, June 3rd, two days before the show, Trish called to cancel this year. She and her husband had moved to NE Portland several months ago. She was going through a divorce, and having car trouble. So I asked my son, who had offered. I hesitated to do so because he works long hours, has three children to get to school, 16, 11, and 5, and has to travel I-205 from Vancouver to my home. He can't distribute my entries to the table, which saves time for me to arrange them, since he has to report to work at 8:00 AM.

That same Tuesday afternoon was bridge day at East Portland Community Center. Strangely enough, Glenda – an aggressive old timer, who moves firmly, says she is a Master Gardener, and dyes her short, sparse hair dark red--approached me. "Isn't the rose show coming up?" she asked.

"It's this weekend. My friend can't help me this year, just told me she can't, going through a divorce, so I will have to have my son take me," I said.

"Can I help?" Glenda offered.

"If you can take me, and then, stay and deliver them to the tables – that would be great."

"What time?" She was ready to move away, go to another bridge table. Always in a rush.

"The usual – pick me up, six o'clock, Thursday, June fifth, day after tomorrow."

"Six o'clock, this Thursday."

"I'll call my son to cancel," I said, as she pushed off.

A load off me. Glenda drives a late model small black pickup.

That day at bridge, as she has been doing so for several months, Glenda shouted, "Quiet, everybody. Can't hear the bids," or some such thing, several times during the afternoon. This leads me to believe she's becoming hard of hearing, but she hasn't mentioned it. She takes her bridge seriously, and plays lots of duplicate. She's become what I call a bridge snob, a know-it-all.

What put me on edge, even more, is an event I'm suppose to forgive and forget. Three years ago Glenda offered to cut and display my roses for the September 2011 Portland Rose Show so that I could visit my brother in California that weekend. I typed a list of possible categories, and color numbers, but there were only a few possibilities. The most outstanding was my shrub, Lady Elsie May, which was glorious that year. She actually admitted that a Rose Association representative, a gentleman, told her when he saw hers that "Lady Elsie May would definitely be a contender." She said she got there late and there were no vases available that fit the stems.

To complicate further she is aggressive and complex. When I first met her she had a line of brassieres and pushed for a time to "fit me with one". It took several "No way," to get her to back off. Later, she told me she was going to bid on an extra large, barn-like, two story house around the corner from me. "My dream is to run a boarding house for fellow veterans," she said, but changes rank and duties, dependant on the audience such as noncoms versus former officers, as to what she did in the military; seemingly which story she can get by with at any given time. The house finally sold and is a half-way house for ex-cons. And finally, Glenda is freely very touchy, feely, and huggy with many of the old duffers. Startled at first, they usually end up wanting more. Again it depends on the group. I've never seen her operate in that fashion with staid upper crust types, like at an exclusive duplicate bridge operation.

Recalling this, I called Glenda's phone number Wednesday evening, to verify. It said, "The party at this number is not available." I started cutting at 7:00 PM. This time there were lots of three stems per bush. I made a list of the categories on sticky notes and posted them on the bucket I put them in. Once in the house they didn't require much trimming. Surprisingly, they weren't dropping petals, but some of the leaves did entangle with so many stems. Shortly, I filled four buckets. To keep their faces up, I left all the kitchen lights on; six on the ceiling and one in the adjoining dining room plus a 24-hour one in the range hood. I have 28 rose bushes: 18 flori-bundas, 1 Hybrid Tea, 2 Grandifloras, 2 climbers and 6 shrubs. My condo neighbors let me use community space. By 11:00 PM, I turned in, watched the news then David Letterman, to take my mind off the project.

5:10 AM, up with the alarm. Put on my face, had some yogurt. Always dressing for the temperature, I put on my purple/red dress pants with purple and red polyester blouse. A red cashmere cardigan Maddi, my bartender friend at Cleary's, gave me, finished the outfit. Ready for six o'clock. At 6:30 I dialed Pam's number – not available. At 6:45 I dialed it again. Then called my son and left a message. He called right back. Could be here by seven-thirty.

At 7:05 the phone rang, "Where in the hell are you?" Glenda shouted, "I've been at the Lloyd center since six AM...Isn't your son going to bring you?" I tried to talk back. She hung up.

For some reason I wasn't surprised or taken back. It seemed to be part of a normal routine, to be expected. I had fair warning, a sizable amount of it.

Got there at 7:50. Only bud vases were left and giant jars. The slight-ly larger vases usually available for three-stems were all gone. My three-stems wouldn't fit in the buds but got lost in the large jars. All the foliage stuffed the jar and the blooms barely showed on the top. Disaster. To complicate, I had prepared 25 displays (one stem or three stems in a vase) and that took what little time was left.

"She must be hard of hearing," I had tried to explain to my son.

I persisted. Put my address label on each card, wrote the name of the rose, the Roman numeral for the display division, and the number of the color. Poked a rubber band through the top hole on the card, stretched the band to pull the card up through the bottom of the jar, or better yet, to save time, put the card on the jar at the mouth, which is smaller than the bottom, before filling the container with the roses. I carried it to its destination.

The last straw. The women's bathroom was closed for cleaning. It's quite a walk, as it is far from the ice arena. I opted not to take the elevator to the third floor, for another bathroom, to save time. Not too much later, I wet my pants. If I had worn black or dark jeans, it wouldn't have been so obvious. In purple/red slacks my incontinence announced itself to God, and all his people, as I made twenty-two trips to the arena, to place my submissions.

I returned the next day, June 6th, my seventy-seventh birthday, in another outfit, of course, to view the damage. There was a massive turn out of spectators and entries. Newly retired baby boomers have joined the association in great numbers just recently. The blossoms were magnificent. No trophy, of course, but I saved face: one blue ribbon first place for *Ludwigschafen an rein*, a deep pink floribunda with 45 petals, the rose bush that was suppose to be a *Robusto*. I purchased it as *Robusto* at Fred Meyers and planted it in the ground. When it bloomed I knew it wasn't a *Robusto*, which has huge dark red flowers.

I counted its 45 petals. The number of petals and *Ludwig*'s deep pink and daisy-like form is unique; my research found it listed in the American Rose Association catalogue, so I decided to keep it. It won the novice trophy, my first year of participation. Two honorable mentions for *Walking on Sunshine*, a medium yellow floribunda, (introduced just two years ago), and *Nearly Wild*, a medium pink floribunda, a sweetheart of clusters with only five petals each.

My roses weren't at fault. It was my fault. I failed to read the signs. What the hell. I lugged two huge vases with my roses to my first rose show and caught the number 71 bus for the MAX at 6:05 AM.

An irony! Retribution was in order. Glenda didn't speak to me at the next two Tuesday bridge gatherings, but there are eight tables, 32 players. Nora, a regular at Gresham duplicate bridge, asked me to be her partner, Thursday, June 19th, 12 noon. I had only played duplicate two times before. Glenda was playing there, with a male partner, Gerard, a friend of mine, who swears my book should be a movie, due to the stark characters in it. "It's good to see you," she uttered, as she rushed by. She also hollered for the players to quiet down, just once, that time.

On my email that night, were the results of the duplicate games. Nora and I played East/ West. We tied for second place. Glenda and her partner ended up last, out of the ten East/West couples. For the hard of hearing, I must write it down. One doesn't have to hear as much to play duplicate bridge because they use placards for bidding rather than speech.

I can't wait for the September rose show. My son's van is better than a taxi and he is willing and able and always on time. But my special gift, hopefully to him and his family, is a self-sufficient, independent, and mostly happy mother and grandmother. So, naturally, I hate to ask him to give me a lift.

Dr. Nik:

Catch up:

Sunday, 2 PM, at a funeral house in Gresham, was very special. Trudy, my friend, gave me a ride – she plays bridge every other Thursday with Rei and Ito at my house. Rei's husband, (his name means "broadminded"), was a retired, emeritus professor at University of Hawaii, a PhD out of University of California, Berkeley, died of cancer of the liver and pancreas. The service was directed by her Buddhist minister. A Korean veteran, Oshi Takachi was given military honors at the ceremony. The room was packed and a scrumptious buffet was served afterward.

Rei's family came to Portland from Japan in 1895. She has shared at times her life with her parents and siblings: three sisters (the oldest born with cerebral palsy), and three brothers with doctorates in science, math, and psychology, still working in their professional positions in their eighties. During the war they lost their farmland when they were interred in a camp in Idaho. Three years old, as the time, Rei is the only one of her family who remembers the number printed on her arm.

She attended Reed College and met Oshi while getting her Masters in chemistry at Cal. She put her husband through graduate school as a researcher and analyzer of patents at Shell Oil. At the time she did not speak Japanese, only English. Shell provided classes in Japanese so she could research in both languages. In Honolulu she wrote speeches for the Japanese Consulate and served as an interpreter. Rei has won awards for her productions in calligraphy, including those awarded in Japan. On her living room walls are life size, very sensitive, revealing and loving portraits Rei has painted in oil of her mother, and in charcoal of her father, who made his living after the war as a gardener at a local college.

Rei moved them back from Hawaii in 2003, when Oshi was diagnosed with Alzheimer's. Fortunately they both had long-term insurance. He was active until 2005, then she attended him for seven years in the house she grew up in southeast Portland. She and I joke about our homes in "felony flats." She had put the proceeds from the sale of their home in Hawaii in a condo in downtown Portland. She does not rent it out but makes it available to visitors and family friends.

By 2012, the responsibilities as his caretaker became overwhelming and she placed him in Assisted Care. Her husband called for her all night long and pushed and shoved at the caretakers. She visited him daily, giving him a bath and shaving his face. He became what was termed as violent, so they sent him to a hospital for evaluation. The care center refused to take him back, so she found a caretaker in Clackamas whose philosophy is to establish a close, caring relationship with each patient. He suggested to Rei that she quit her daily visits, that she pull away and let his new relationship replace hers.

When I first met her in 2012 at East Portland Community Center's Cherry Blossom Senior Bridge on Tuesdays, she shared with me that her psychiatrist told her she "had no friends and should get some." We became fast friends. I admire her greatly.

Of special note – we once talked over the phone of our mother's influence in our getting married. Then she said, "I was caretaker for so long it made me question what I felt about him which gave me awful doubt, awful guilt." I realize that comment was due to the punishment of those final years.

Yesterday, Rei, without tears, greeted people who raved about her husband's professional accomplishments. He was recognized by international organizations and universities in his field, chemical agricultural. Acquaintances in Portland thanked him for his contributions to a community garden at their church and the safe and orderly mushroom hunting expeditions he advised. The minister pointed out that Rei had shared "not once did Hiroshi get angry with me." She had told me he "often told me I was smarter than him."

When departing this heartwarming gift on that ice bound Sunday afternoon, Trudy and I told her how thankful we were that we came to the celebration. Many photographs had been displayed and a video of their lives, accompanied by her favorite songs, such as "It's a Wonderful Life" and the Hawaiian anthem revealed how happy and handsome he was and what a beautiful couple they were. "I know why you married him, Rei, it was due to an irresistible physical attraction."

November, 2014 – I write this because you said a friend had taken you to Urban Farmer when I told you my brother and his wife suggested it for dinner at The Nines, where they were staying to attend a friend's fiftieth wedding anniversary in Portland, so I thought you'd find the evening interesting.

P.S. Regarding Urban Farmer – A fellow writer, Lindsay Mohlere, 65, who took the photo for my book cover, gives me a ride home from writing class on Wed nights when he's not hunting Elkor pheasant. His loving wife refers to me as "your girlfriend," for fun since I'm thirteen years older than him. Early on we discovered we both have roots in Montana. Both had tales to tell about political machinations on family members. His, a Lieutenant Governor, assassinated right before election, my father lost his job when his party lost the election. He gave me a ride downtown to The Nines so I could dress up in my lavender wool plaid, long dress with powder blue winter sweaters and Chinese coolee flats.

I met my brother and his wife, Luke and Kris, at the eighth floor lobby on time at 5:30PM. They were dressed in jeans and navy windbreakers but Kris loved my outfit. They ordered a cheese plate and wine. I had a Bud Light. We sat in one of those all metal and glass private, still-cage-like, spaces. With the high ceiling and the glass like ice made it even more cold and uninviting, especially on that cold night with east wind giving out a 19 degree chill factor. I showed them photos of my special immigrant neighbors from Costa Rica, Bosnia, Ukraine, Ethiopia, and Saigon, all condo owners who pay their bills. I also have bizarre fellow travelers on the bus where a pretty girl proudly posed for me with her "self-designed" peacock blue and other exotic colors hairdo. On the Green MAX, on the way to my granddaughter's volleyball game, I found four middle-eastern fellows in long white gowns and stark red and white head garbs, strumming mandolins and singing.

Fortunately, Luke's wife, Kris, had invited my son, Herb and his family. Since it was so cold out we took a taxi to meet them at 6:30PM at Jake's

Crawfish at 10th & Stark. Turned out to be a great evening. Jake's was warm and full of bustling and uninhibited people.

Jake's provided an abundance of choices with a choice of prices. Luke's wife is a real looker and mother of four children. He doesn't approve of her blond dye job, makes her look like his daughter or his mistress. (She is fifteen years younger.) She also wins tennis tournaments in her category at their tennis club. She roots for Djokavic. Kris usually does a fun job of jiving with the male waiters. Her fun got cut short. Our waiter was a female this time, whereas Jake's is noted for male waiters.

A friend of mine's first job out of college was as a waiter at Jake's. He was nervous about being hired. He was soon fired. He dumped a full glass of beer off the perennial little round tray down the back of a fellow dressed up for the symphony.

The waitress said halibut is out of season so I had sole (2 pieces) like Pan Am used to deliver. I'd prefer my brother spend his money on something other than an eight ounce for sixty dollars. Kris took one look at the Urban Farmer menu and didn't like it. She said, "Has lots of words I've never heard." They usually go to Jake's or a small little-known Italian place downtown. A friend had recommended Urban Farmer – I'm glad they avoided It. My renter had downloaded the menu for me. He was familiar with all the terms and suppliers mentioned. I had been dreading it after a peek at the menu and had decided to have the pork – it was the cheapest, least complicated, and most familiar that I could find. You said a friend took you there. Tell me, doc, what, if anything, did I miss out on?

Luke and Kris complained of being cold the entire time. "California is never this cold." Thank goodness I was dressed for the weather. Luke had planned to rent a car but decided not to drive in the ice, so my son and his family took me home. Luke wanted to order a taxi for me. I half-heartedly said I could take MAX but I'm glad they found what to do with me with four of Herb's family in their back seat. Kind of chancy. Herb rarely breaks a rule.

But that brings up an important story that he insists was the "first and last time I was deceptive," that is, broke the rules. How he met his wife. A friend of his at Parkrose High, Catherine, the daughter of a doctor, had transferred her junior year to St. Mary's Academy because her father didn't approve of the fellow Catherine was dating. For the junior prom at St. Mary's, Catherine asked Herb if he would pretend to be her date, meet her father, and then take her to the prom so she could be with her chosen fellow there. Herb agreed to it.

The only motivation I can figure that tempted Herb to be so deceptive is that in Junior High he played an old man and his friends insisted Herb should become an actor. I'll have to ask him, "Really why did you do it?" some time, when he has time to reminisce, maybe in his seventies. At the dance, Herb met the girl, Mary, part Hispanic, and spent the entire evening with her. Probably their first connection was they were both serious about sports. Afterwards, they went to a party on a yacht in the Willamette River and to breakfast at another student's home in Portland Heights. When he arrived home at 6 AM he said to me, "I've met the one, Mom."

Those hospitals and insurance companies mislead people. They push that the hospitals "share." The saleswoman at Providence led me to believe that you, of course, practice at Providence, too. I apologize. No doctor other than you has exchanged more than two statements with me. No wonder I am so grateful to Dr. Nikolas. God bless you and yours.

My friend Gerard has told me that Rei has pointed out that her husband did not have Alzheimer's. Instead, he had a frontal lobe condition that caused him to turn very angry, although he never turned on her. "At night he would seem so attacked by whatever that he would beat at the walls. To remove herself from the noise, at times she would escape to the automobile to get sleep for the night." Years of sessions with two therapists, she felt enabled to cope. Gerard loves to play bridge with her saying, "She laughs easily and makes comments that get all of us engaged. She is so happy. I thought she was fifty when I first saw her, so asked myself, what is she doing with us old timers?"

Rei has had more than one unfortunate experience with doctors. Recently she was diagnosed with what she figured was a nervous shut down of her eyelids, "Psychosomatic." An expert's prognosis was, "You're going blind." She lived with that for six months when a second diagnosis said, "No such thing." The further away she gets from care giving the less she "gets long blinks."

Dokteur, you're a class act. Last time I saw you I related my current mood, "I don't like how I look today."

You casually commented, "Don't look in a mirror, then."

Your advice never includes sympathy. You're not inclined to be diverted by nonessentials. I like that. You're not an old timer yet who likes to share ailments. When I recall your wiseacre retort I chuckle and share the story with others who laugh with me.

Per your advice I walked a ways down Division to the Gelato store operated by a "real Italian." I had three flavors: strawberry, cherry and espresso. Great treat! Thanks. Shops on that street get write ups often in the news. Have you tried Salt n'Straw ice cream? President Obama did when he came to Portland. Will do, next summer.

Odd Outcomes From A Nightmare - Which is the Real Nightmare?

At 5:40 AM I awoke to go to the bathroom and then went back to sleep. I dreamed of making caramel apples for my-six-year-old grandson to thank him for his thank you letter for my card with six dollars to him for his sixth birthday in March. It wouldn't take. The caramel kept running off. I admit it. This was my very first effort at them. A perfect set-up for a dream. For real, I never would attempt caramel. A frustrating downer.

Next I waited for the bus to go to writing class. The bus didn't come. On my cell phone it said the bus was skipping this scheduled time. It began to pour down rain. Without my umbrella I got soaked. Had a paper bag with my manuscripts and an open purse; like horses' feedbags, they sopped up the water. (I forgot that the purse has a zipper, which I've never used.)

I went to a cheap motel and asked for a room, to dry off, salvage my manuscripts, and avoid catching cold. 6:30 PM, already too late to call anybody. Class began at 6:00. How irresponsible, derelict of me. No heat. I requested another room. They explained "in daylight saving time we don't turn on the heat until sundown." I'm in the month of April, 2015, Pacific daylight time. People are griping about it. Not me. Many want to return to an "ideal, natural" time that never existed.

Can't salvage the damage. Suppose to read tonight. Will the professor kick me out of the class? Give me an "F"?

I woke up. It's 7:16 AM. It's only Sunday, not Wednesday, Easter Sunday, 2015. My son will pick me up for a brunch at their house with a gathering of at least twenty-six, mostly family, some friends, at 11:30 this morning. I have three bottles of wine to take this time, whereas I usually bake something; a Sangria from Spain, a Pinot Grigio from Italy and a White Riesling out of Monterey County (California needs all the help we can give their agriculture these days). I looked out the bedroom windows to the east. The sun is shining. I looked for scratch paper to write the dream down. This is the first nightmare I ever tried to record. I usually bypass, that is "forget," dreams and nightmares, maybe because they're not real important to me; maybe to a psychiatrist, but not to me. I'm fortunate. I remember what's important to me. But there's a moral to this fable.

If real, I would be able to take shelter at my neighbor, Les Schwab. And I know where every bathroom is between home and Vancouver, Washington. Further, I don't use paper sacks to house my manuscripts. Portland has an anti-plastic bag resolution so I faithfully use Fred Meyer heavy duty cloth bags. Where was my real life in my dream?

I was at an unfamiliar bus stop, on an unfamiliar street, waiting for an unfamiliar bus; as if I had retired, like so many dreamers do, to an unfamiliar place that only has sunshine going for it (they put pressure on its water resource) and for a promise of companionship, tons of people just like them. Here's looking at wrinkles and walkers, responses of "Huh? What did you say?" and utterances of regret, "I use to remember everything." And of course, most everyone can deliver a detailed rendition of their latest medical diagnosis.

I'm not making fun of the deafness. I'm appalled at it, at the extent of it. I'm stating a fact. It's a chronic one, largely ignored by the medical profession. I realize there are schools for the deaf that treat (I'm guessing) at the most twenty-five percent of those afflicted. If we can have internet on cell phones for the masses, why can't we have hearing devices that alleviate the rampant deafness among our elderly? The hearing aid industry has long been recognized as an inept rip off. Personally I pay close attention to any research regarding hearing in legitimate tabloids like *Bloomberg Business Week* or *The Economist*. I dutifully post notes about it in my address book, just in case.

A friend of mine, a sixty-nine-year old nurse who teaches nursing, still looking for work (she wants to work and is qualified to do so), watches the overabundance of pharmaceutical advertisements on television "for all the side effects, to become informed, up-to-date." Whereas, I switch channels as soon as those ads start in; that goes for Cialis, as well. Yuk! Now, there's a pill for women who "have never had a thought about sex in my life," said the blond beauty of twenty-six on the television advertisement. In fact I vaguely recall small children in the background.

I have to query: "Where in physical contact does sex begin? With hands? A kiss? A certain smile? A look? "Just whistle!" Is an area in the brain missing a gene? Some persons would surmise, "Maybe God meant her to be a nun." Why do they run their ads where they know the audience is mostly over sixty-five? Of course, in the twenty-first century, another great way for pharmaceuticals TO CREATE URGE THEY CALL NEED (market) and make more money.

The flu vaccines are late this year again and another shortage of them is again predicted, worse than the year before. From time to time I understand the clinics run short, that is, can't get delivery from the certified makers, of the most common strain for measles and diphtheria, as well. Recently the very tragic whooping cough reared its ugly head big time, which can be curtailed by vaccines for infants.

For fun, lots of organized mind-numbing games like Bingo and Bunko. For the gutsy gambler types, there's Texas Hold 'Em and free bus trips to casinos, in pursuit of the continuation of the life-like thrill of winning and losing, a so-called reality-trip. A fellow I know bragged that he bought a new TV for his wife for six hundred dollars, a year's winnings from Double Pinochle games he organized at a Moose Lodge on Wednesdays and a bar and grill on Saturday mornings at breakfast time.

A columnist with the Clark County *Columbian*, in Washington, wrote an article recently as to how the citizens somehow seem to assume that work is not the way to riches anymore. They now figure that the only way to wealth is to win a lottery. How much is put into those lotteries that could have been saved and put to good use? The more common answer these days is, not enough to make a difference in their lives.

Personally, I need to find a way to reduce my blood pressure, which went up when the Republicans won a majority in the House and, again, insisted on their impractical, six-year-old Ryan budget, which ignores the reality of the now. My emotional trips are dependent on family, friends and the latest "ugly" coming out of the hateful, negative, doomsayer Republicans, who'll say and do anything to hang on to their money, which President Bush gave to the wealthy by extreme tax cuts when he was anxious to get his hands on all that surplus accumulated by the Clinton administration. So, naturally they are fearful of losing their power, if they ever let the truth of history reach us.

In fact I'll never forget how his Secretary of the Treasury, Paul O'Neill, who had been the CEO of ALCOA, opposed the tax cut, so President Bush fired him and took us to war, which put us further into debt. It's interesting to watch large serious corporations, non-defense industries, of course, beginning to abandon that party, so outraged by their extreme statements; statements that are merely predicated to keep the religious right and the rednecks in their fold and Texas on the march. Trickle-down ideology is corrupt.

I am especially concerned about persons who have what they consider a lot of money. I know they worked hard for it but they wrongfully assume they are the only ones who worked hard. They lead themselves to believe they are a target of the effort "to get the rich one percent – individuals and corporations – to pay their fair share;" the extremely rich due to loopholes such as write offs for losses and off shore shelters, which these "successful hard workers" have no access to. And what totally breaks them is the struggle now their offspring suffer in spite of their efforts to help them. This final blow destroys their spirit, so they turn cynical and blame the government, especially any government programs for the poor. They lead themselves to believe that the poor is their enemy, not the rich who own ninety-nine percent of production of wealth in the world.

Yes, they need to scapegoat and choose the only target the media, controlled by the one percent, chooses for them, government, and the taxes that support it. So now we have persons running for office who are anti-government and it seems the only thing these people know how to do is shut down government and ultimately get rid of it unless we give them TOTAL CONTROL OF IT. The only "yes" vote they can muster is the one that raises their government paycheck, operating expenses, and benefits.

How foolish of those "hardworkers" to identify themselves with the now famous one percent. The two-income households, the middle class, are struggling. Cost of child care. Cost of education. Cost of housing. Cost of transportation. Cost of students' sports and other activities, including equipment, time and travel, instability of their company or industry. Now, outrageous shenanigans and gross inaction persist where some of these problems use to get listened to and addressed.

Analysis of the nightmare: In real life I am optimistic and hopeful. Why am I a pessimist in a dream? Have the fear mongers gotten to me, too? March hires are down, potholes up.

MY HOROSCOPE TODAY, Wednesday, April 22, in The Clark County, Washington *Columbian*, (I try to read it every day usually just after 6 AM when it comes on the internet) seemed to predict my day forthcoming.

Confrontation doesn't bother you as much as it does some, and you can use this talent to your advantage. You don't mind playing bad cop to someone's good cop if it keeps the peace in the end." From The *Columbian*'s "Your Horoscope" by Holiday Mathis of Creators Syndicate Features, page D2.

Wednesdays are especially loaded with activity, which I look forward to. Before 9 AM I caught the bus on Division for a possible bridge game as a fourth with fellows at Mountain View Athletic: Tzok Zanger, Paul Maboro, Brock Norther, and Pat O'Reilly. The bus stop is right across from the main entrance of the huge building which includes racket courts, covered tennis courts, an Olympic-size pool, lots of saunas and hot tubs. Out back are tennis courts and a new swim pool, popular with the young people in the summer time.

The parking lots on both the east and west side of the main building looked full as usual. The reception desk in the morning is always manned by Trevor, a handsome and happy black, in excellent condition, whose easy smile, a happy to see you one, swipes my number I keep on my key chain, which matches my photo on the PC. He's also responsible for the chemical content of the pools at all times.

Instead of getting coffee today, I moved directly down the hall, down six steps toward the tables that sit in front of the windows in the corner that look out on the tennis courts and the swim pool. I saw where Rose is leading the seniors in exercise for Water Aerobics. She is also a bicyclist and leads tour/exercise groups both out of this location and one of their other outlets. She always remembers my name. The Gresham Chamber of Commerce meets here once per month. Their leftovers such as grapes, bananas and muffins are available to all passersby.

My friends greeted me, but it was easy to see that they were in the middle of a game so I didn't offer lots of news which is usually my habit to do so. The Friday night prior, I attended The Wayne Morse Gala, where Governor Brown, Senator Merkley, and the female senator from Minnesota, Klobuchar, spoke, and was anxious to tell them about it, especially the unlimited wine, both red and white, donated by Willamette Vineyards, I could drink at our table. Tzok and Pat's coffee cups were empty so I picked them up, Tzok's in the right, Pat's in my left hand, and headed back to the snack bar next to reception, poured from a canister of French Roast into each one, conscientiously remembering which is whose cup – then headed back to their table.

Paul has made a recent trip to emergency and now is taking antibiotics for pneumonia. He's normally in top notch health and consistently plays a smart game of bridge, but I have anticipated that maybe he would appreciate being relieved from a three hour game today. I ask, "Is anyone leaving at ten? I can play until eleven fifteen?"

Paul said, "I'm in need of a shower. That'll take a while. Do you want to take my place until I get back?"

"Go ahead and deal. I have to get a cup of coffee. Be right there," I said.

"Hurry," Brock urged. "Tzok is going again to Europe and wants to take a big win with him. We're ahead of them so far so beware, Tzok, your partner, is mighty hungry."

I hustled the short distance to the coffee bar, than took my seat. My hand was waiting for me.

"Where are you going this time, Tzok?" I asked. "Amsterdam, again?"

"No. Hamburg."

"That's an industrial port city. Where are the roses?"

"A few miles inland. Two huge rose growers."

"On the Elbe river?" I asked

"Kordes is in Elmshorn, on a small tributary of the Elbe, tricky to pronounce, starts with a K."

"Lavaglut is a Kordes rose. My doctor's favorite, that I take to him. Dark red. So perfect, dependable, I wish I had two of them."

"Let's play." As usual he got impatient with the small talk.

I don't forget that Tzok is an expert. He seems to expect that respect and adoration from me at the bridge table. I make an effort to abide by his expectations.

That morning, Tzok and I continued to suffer nothing hands. For the fourth time in a row I was dealt a hand with only one point in it – a lone Jack. This time, Pat, on my left, dealt and opened one heart. My partner, Tzok, passed. Brock, on my right, jumped to indicate also an opening hand and bid three hearts. It was my turn. It takes thirteen points to open, at least six points usually to support my partner's bid. I was fed up and this is party bridge, a partly social occasion where one is allowed to, once in a while, give vent to their emotional changes, so-called moods, relative to what the cards do to one. So I said, "There ought to be a law against hands like this. I pass."

Tzok came unglued. Angrily, he retorted, "You talk too much." This insult was a new one. He hadn't said this one before. Other assessments of me by Tzok include: "You can't bid, you've got to learn to listen, but you play beautifully." "I consider you and Bob (another extra bridge player) in a training mode." Often he has said, "The only thing wrong with you is you're a liberal."

There is another consideration that I am sure is a factor – but left unsaid. I was given membership on a special senior rate, and although much of the early morning tennis gang are seniors my age, they pay through the nose. I suspect that they don't have much tolerance for us newcomers on special rates.

The table is close to the pathway to the entrance to the courts, so tennis players sometimes tarry at it and us to say hello. Tzok has friends he engages with as well. When I talk to a passerby, especially an old friend from the fifties, Red Randle (now very grey), he never avoids to comment, "Quit talking and play bridge."

What he was angry about my admission to a "zilch hand," my nothing hand, is that my comment readily gave our opponents free reign to bid to their heart's delight and let our opponents know Tzok's better hand would be the one to finesse. Mine would definitely be a nonfactor and, above all, Tzok likes to try and fool them.

Of course, Tzok goes all out to win every game, or at the least, set the opponents. I, too, have gone all out to set my share of opponents. He wants to win at all costs but, in my defense Tzok also vocally complains about a string of lousy hands dealt to him. At other times, he brags about a long stretch of victories, always claiming skill, never acknowledging the role of "luck."When he makes a mistake he gives his excuses, which turn out to make his partner the goat. His partner's bid or play invariably caused the defeat. In other words I've never heard Tzok admit to a bad play on his part. A stark incidence I'll never forget is when he said of Brock, "You're so anal, Brock." Brock didn't flinch at that one. Brock never fails to be a gentleman, rarely reveals feelings other than his concerns regarding his physical condition. He does make comments regarding his pain.

This time I refused to bow, kowtow. Usually I take his barbs in silence or pretend to ignore them as if I didn't hear him. But this time I sassed back, "So do you. I'm not the only one who likes to talk."

He made no further comment.

The very next hand we bid and made slam. Honestly, I don't recall who did what on that one. I usually think team – don't tally up my so-called credits, my occasional tour de force. And I do admit when I "played it badly." But at least it made him smile and even laugh, for once. A win makes Tzok exceedingly happy. I thanked him for letting me play and ran to catch the bus to go to lunch at Meals on Wheels at Gresham Senior Center.

I use to volunteer at MOW, and still offer when they need a hand, but no need for me recently. When put to work, some people with limitations gain great personal satisfaction for getting to help out, clearing and cleaning tables and dishes, for instance. Other volunteers are experts at what they do--delivering trays to tables of those with mobility issues, washing dishes or chopping vegetables, brewing coffee-- and have done so for many years. The centers are very dependent on both.

The volunteers who drive their own vehicles to deliver to the elderly in homes and apartments are often recently retired. Most of them just do so once or twice per week. In addition to the hot meal, they will take bread, rolls, buns and bagels, and even desserts donated by Fred Meyer, Safeway, and Grocery Outlet, Franz, Dave's Killer Bread and French's bread outlets, and current newspaper issues like the Portland Tribune or Gresham Outlook.

James is a tall, handsome black, and the Chef who goes the extra mile. He makes soup and salads every day, even though they're not on the menu. He purchases broths on his own and uses leftover vegetables and beans. Fridays, he does clam chowder. Often there is butter for the rolls or slices of bread. For our pinochle group, after lunch on Friday, he brings desserts for the players at our four or five card tables, leftovers from the meal. He is a minister at a church in North Portland and gets to know most of the regular visitors.

As usual, James made the rounds around the tables and grabbed the bobble (he calls a bun) at the crown of my head, as he approached our table number fifteen, which looks out on the Blue MAX tracks and several warehouses on the other side of them.

Mike Eno, a retired dentist, just turned eighty, and Chinese, who also helps distribute produce when it is donated by local farmers such as onions, cabbage, potatoes and apples, looked up from the book he was reading to ask James, "What kind of fish is it today?"

"James said, "What do you mean?"

"Farm raised or wild?"

"Manufactured."

Mary, a little, friendly lady with thick, blond, short hair that grows too fast (she has trouble keeping up with it), is a nurse and very serious about nursing at 69, but between and betwixt looking for one more job or retiring, mostly because she too is a victim of the overwhelming cost of an extended illness. That of her husband's, who died after a long time in great and costly pain, left her broke, although after many years of what she feels was a good life. He left her with wonderful memories and three children with grandchildren.

Ralph (from Romania under "that awful" Ceausescu) at eight, raised seven kids as a realtor, now struggles just a little bit with speech due to a stroke on his right side and me, all laughed.

Mike didn't. When he was practicing dentistry, he golfed at the Columbia Edgewater golf club as a member. His wife suffered a debilitating and expensive illness before she died. He no longer plays golf but reads serious books about the economy, with usually the word MONEY in the title. Many of them predict doomsday, although he insists he votes across party lines. Mike admits to a few annual poker games with his old cronies.

Don is the glue, so to speak, for our group. Retired as a truck driver from Fred Meyer, he moves from table to table and knows everyone's name and history. In his nineties, even his son, a teacher, is retired. Don often announces when each table can go up to the counter and grab a tray and choose their dishes for lunch, photographs each newcomer and puts their picture on the wall, and donates a sheet cake and ice cream to celebrate birthdays each month.

Recently Don sits at the table where Joe, a great Mexican personality, who tells stories which make good looking Jane, also ninety, who still mows her lawn, rakes leaves, trims bushes, and walks her dog every morning and Don laugh often. Joe always raises his sport style, but yet traditional hat with his left hand when I arrive and says, "Good morning." He told me one time he taught himself English to keep a job in construction but cannot read. In my view Joe is extremely intelligent – speaks with perfect English diction and grammar. At that time he asked me where he could take a class to learn to read. I told him I had no idea. In prior immigration surges in our history there were lots of literacy classes. Now, they're not so readily a known.

Another Hispanic couple, Estella and Alberto, were well known in the Spanish classical guitar world as performers. Just recently he is not able to play his guitar anymore, cannot recall the chords, still he's a congenial man with the handsome body and face of a popular musician. Estella worked for a heating company as a secretary all those years, and sang, danced with castanets, whatever the crowd could absorb, evenings and weekends. She is gorgeous, her hair still dark, and some of her costumes are now worn for everyday at lunch. She was comfortable on stage.

We saw them for the last time last week as they have found a permanent residence close to some of their family to retire at a lower rent in Silverton, northwest of Salem. They had to move. Their apartment in Gresham was going to be "improved." A government agency helped them locate it. She is good and helpful to him and takes the lead, as she is gifted not only with beauty but energy and intelligence. She speaks Spanish but her education from the time she was three was in English. More recently, with a daughter, she worked as a foster parent for many years, while Alberto tried to make a living in Mexico. He struggles with English. In my day musicians led a precarious life to pursue their love of music. Many of them are part of the poverty that legitimately prevails. She gave me their promotions card. Only the phone number is current. She hopes it will remain so.

MY REVIEW of THE GROW, A Novel, by Lindsay R. Mohlere. I took an emotional trip of outrage, fear, and then hope, with The Grow by Lindsay R. Mohlere, a fellow who has interfaced with the good, the bad and the ugly his entire life but does not claim to be all of the above. He gives us two original characters (tough to like) who the good guys and the bad guys both fear and despise, rightfully so, and two naive, but unpredictable personalities out of ER, who are redeemed by happenstance. Finally, there's a hero and a heroine, good people, each battered by forces of fate, I can identify with and root for.

The hunter expertise of Creek, one of Mohlere's many pursuits in an action packed lifetime (although he has more time and energy left, yet), illustrates the wild and complex aura of the Wallowas of Eastern Oregon and Southwestern Idaho. Loaded with curiosity, I skipped supper, started the book at 5 PM and finished it at 2 AM ...not disappointed, kind of astounded. He took me to places I have not been and to people I did not know existed. He exposed me to a reality of motives, habits and mindsets mere photos fail to reveal. For instance, on the highway out of Klamath Falls, Oregon, a moving camera couldn't do justice to the deer slamming through Mouse's windshield and lodging in the back seat. No way. A classic, Lindsay. Did it maybe actually happen? Your fiction commands its people and events to be for real, true. Thanks for the sheer satisfaction, Lindsay. You consistently make the journey I take with you worth the effort. Clancy Rohring, Penname 3/18/2015 2:07 PM

Lindsay and his wife had a wonderful book signing party at their home in Cherry Park in southeast Portland. It was a beautiful Saturday afternoon, an open bar including Manhattans and hors d'oeuvres, smoked duck on toasted sourdough. The dining room doors reach out to a huge private patio with a swimming pool enjoyed by lots of their friends.

I met his wife for the first time. "I can see why you're Lindsay's girlfriend," she said smiling with warmth in her cool voice. She's in real estate, very slender and attractive, could pass as one of those beautiful news announcers, so fresh looking as if they're just out of college, on CNN or FOX (they're the only thing attractive about FOX in my opinion). She also swears by Makers Mark, like Lindsay does, and made the Manhattans out of that bourbon.

He signed my book, "It's a real pleasure to call you a friend."

He's absolutely an amazing fellow, more than a survivor...he thrives. Many people put demands on him. He's important to loads of person's lives, including mine, I have to admit. I always try to learn from people who are able to do things I cannot do – especially, those who do well at what I also yearn to be good at. I'm especially grateful because he photographed me, without question, in my black Adiddas shorts and Nike's, cleaning a toilet, for the cover of my book, *The Quirky Landlord*.

There are those dependent on him for scouting out where the Elk, trout, duck and pheasant are, and lead their crew, usually his friends, to promising hunting grounds. In his spare time he is a certified referee for young and upcoming boxers, including some who aim for the Olympics. He is a listener and a mentor for them. A graduate of Washington State University, his first job was as an academic counselor at Pacific University. He has owned and managed a communications business in Hawaii, and served as a cook, dependent on a Betty Crocker cook book, on a ship hauling a string of huge barges loaded with construction equipment in Alaskan waters. Recently, to help a friend and for the exercise plus the camaraderie, he worked on a branding crew processing 800 new calves on a ranch in Montana.

He is absent from our Wednesday night writing class in October for sure, and the class misses his stories and critiques of our stories immensely. He is always kindly, takes time with those who need the time to explain it, and totally nonpartisan; open-ended to any and everyone's effort to express themselves.

So I have the deepest respect for his person, although my very first reaction three years ago was what a beautiful hunk of humanity. I especially love to look at him when he has just had a haircut and shave. He lets all that go when he's trekking through the wilds or up a mountainside looking for springs, one of his favorite haunts. I don't like all that wool.

Back when I found a great t-shirt marked down for three dollars at Fred Meyers. A very hairy, wild looking fellow holding up a string of dead ducks says, "I love duck hunting, it's in my blood." I almost didn't buy it because it was extra/extra large and would hang on Lindsay. He loved it although I've never seen him wear it. I wonder if his fellow duck hunters have got a glimpse of it? Maybe that shirt is why his wife calls me "his girlfriend."

Due to his many skills and occupations he identifies with a huge cross section of human effort. One time he shared with me that as a kid he wanted to box more than anything at that time. So he identifies closely with his young boxers.

I had occasion to think twice about that and had a change of heart regarding my initial interpretation of why kids want to box and emailed it to my friend, Lindsay. I had to express that I realized there are a number of motives that make us want, not just one. So I dug into myself.

FOR LINDSAY FROM CLANCY R: "Get out of the ghetto," An outworn cliché I'm too much of an economic determinist sometimes. "That's the reason they want to box!" My version: An oversimplified human motive.

The urge or passion or desire to box? To get their anger out of their system? Or fear of failure?

Want to excel at something, boxing comes natural? Just to expel their excess energy? Obsessed with it? That's all they lead themselves to believe they've come to know? Money might have very little to do with the why! That burden of energy caused by a human's need to express oneself. Hear me! See me! Root for me and my expertise, my unique being! Love me! After all, it is a spectator sport. Or simply, defend yourself from a bully!

Sometimes I get lazy, merely assume, especially when confronted with that which I know little of, with only a small pocketful of memories of fight movies when I was a kid. Loved Rodeo movies. I consider myself still a Tomboy – identify with men and the once male-dominated endeavors.

Strangely enough I don't try to compete with them but try very hard to be part of their team, a necessary one. Here I have not tried hard enough to see the intricate, unique experience of another, especially of a friend. Need your patience until I catch up.

You should write a story of your youth and your need or desire or uncontrollable urge to Box, and now, to write. You're bursting out with serious stories to tell. So am I, although I don't know how earthshaking. I use to make up stories, now I'm loaded with telling what I saw and who was with me that made me think or care about what someone else out there might find touchable, willing to reach out for.

My independent urge – My Way -- gets in the way of the professional requirements of the so called art. Nietzsche said for man to excel, he must remain in search of the truth. A never ending pursuit for me, but I'm limited by my human foibles as well. My mother used two terms to describe me: "Bull in a china shop." "The Princess and the Pea."

Working a minimum of 65 plus hours per week 1984 to 1997, to keep the ship afloat, because my husband, wishing for earlier times in history, muddled by his futility and lack of optimism, was saddled with his twisted assumptions, including: "Takes money to make money."

"It's who you know, not what you know." "What appears to be is more important than what is." "Fate and supply and demand rule the market place. It's out of our hands."

So on July 4, 1995 when my mother died, (she had said I was her best friend), he had the gall to say, "You have no friends." I was allowed no time to spend much social time with anybody. My fellow employees shared their lives with me. She had helped to keep him afloat as well and became terribly disillusioned regarding his person before she died. Up in heaven she knows the whole story finally, thank goodness. I kept mum about my ridiculous marriage because of my son. She was a devout Catholic and opposed to divorce.

Once she said, even in the 1990s, "Don't get pregnant."

No chance of that. I never shared with her or anyone the fact that I never slept with him from 1987 to 1997, year I divorced him. In 1987 he removed $2,000 from joint checking, our son in college, and avoided to explain it, per usual. I opened a separate account, and paid all the bills from then on, except his expenses. I bought a used Ford for him in 1994, for $7500.00. He hated it and, I think, intentionally wasted it. Or he just didn't have the money to have it repaired.

He was diagnosed with severe arterial sclerosis when he was thirty-five and kept it secret from me and untreated. So no explanation for his increasingly questionable mind sets. But somehow he managed to buy long term care insurance for himself, again on the sly, and of course, succeeded in hiding the condition of his health. About that time, I recall my fellows discussing that "Men are more likely to go into denial."

I wrote an entire story of the drama that evolved as a result of such an incompatible relationship, but I don't think I will ever publish it. It's too remorseful – other than thirty-seven years wasted. But not entirely. I was gifted with an amazing son and his family – worth the sacrifice made to grow up with him. My life has been one great romp, wrangle, and warble – search, destinations and adventure, challenge, discovery and people, and joyful song. What's motivating my burst of urgency now is my quandary: "Are my seventies to be my Last Hurrah?"

Cheers, Clancy

I shared that with Lindsay, a very special friend, whose story telling I admire greatly to let him know what a strong lady I am. He knows I'm not subjected to the whims of a female merely panting to be laid, like some of the women in his stories, but not entirely devoid of ego. Hank Gradfohl, a fellow married to a best friend, twenty years ago, used to critique my writing. He had been a Naval Systems Engineer, then got a law degree but struggled in real estate on commission.

Later he complained about his wife's behavior towards him (their marriage was going out the window due to economics). In a conversation over the phone I gave my hackneyed comment for further discussion, "My dad told my mom that 'a stiff prick has no conscience."

Hank, a devout Catholic and Villanova alum retorted, "If that be the case, a wet cunt has no conscience, either." I hadn't heard that one before so gave him a good laugh of approval in return. I too shared with him my struggle with a relationship required by my deep commitment to the well being of my son (who loved his father) complicated by my mom's faith.

Marriage, among the rich, wheel and deal to protect their wealth in existence and that of the future. Shouldn't the poor be encouraged to do the same to protect the fruits of their labor? I see marriage as an economic contract, a partnership before the law. As an attorney, Hank confirmed to me that the courts (and people in general) are more likely to believe the male rather than the female. "The female is accused of hysterics, and the illogical, often."

Dr. Charlie White, History Emeritus, at Portland State University, pointed out to me five years ago, at Professor Brooke's funeral that the exclusive and powerful Arlington Club "has just barely, reluctantly allowed one token female." Charlie has a long history of boosting his female students into much success in their chosen professions. He helped me open doors. I love him like family, too.

When Hank's wife shared with me her divorce as final, she was devastated weeks later by Hank's sudden death caused by a brain tumor, but leaving a one-hundred-thousand-dollar Navy-related insurance policy which she couldn't collect. (It went to his sister). I told her, "I have the best of all possible worlds." Fortunately I was employed at the time, not just one job but two.

It seems I tend to build relationships with people in their struggle years. For some, is it a continual struggle?

As an adventurer, Lindsay has seen much violence both in nature and among human beings; yet, as a writer he is loaded with compassion for human destinies, so I trust him explicitly. He does not exploit – he merely exposes, like an artist who can illustrate. The only thing we owe each other in friendship, that is, is honesty. I feel no need to give him guarded responses.

I've never been accused of being possessive, do avoid wanting and fantasies, do know how fleeting meaningful encounters can be. My major goal for my son was his independence, including that from me. I gave him basics and options for making decisions very early.

If Lindsay was a son, I would feel fortunate to claim him. When we depart I shake his hand and say, "I luv ya." In this era of hugging there's been no occasion to hug…no great triumphs yet to celebrate. He says he loves me too. He has shared with me his deep love for his mother. When departing, my son always says, "I love you." So I keep up!

Even though I play for keeps, nevertheless I recognize the role of the performance of change in need, on all of us, so I retain what's unique and wonderful in those few special people who reach me. My memory serves me well. It provides complexities to quarrel, plus much joy. I feel blessed for those who have shared with me and made me feel necessary – at critical times in their lives. And probably mine.

Maybe life is nothing but a series of boxing matches! Real friendships are excerpts of sparring events. An ideal relationship is where a sparring match occurs and a person opens up – reveals real self – unafraid to. That never happened in my marriage. Rather, I was met with deception, six corners of silence – shut down – so I quit boxing and escaped to the couch. No subject was a safe one. There was no sparring in my marriage, only deafening silence. Can you imagine me giving up, not uttering another word? For sure, I did it. I was in that much pain. Maybe it's as simple as that. I continue to seek sparring partners.

Part Two

Excerpts of The Never Forgotten

Kickin' Butt

Part 1.

From 1987 to 1997 I worked one and a half jobs. My full time included advertising with newspapers, then in 1992 Marketing Coordinator for Oregon/Washington Group, a division of ARAMARK. My part-time job with ADDI Corporation (Ask, Decipher, Determine Information Corporation), a political and market research firm, was named such to avoid the overworked term "research."

The list of clients was long and impressive. Every field of economic endeavor was represented, from forest products and the health industry to real estate developers. It included majors in the region such as Intel, Alaska Airlines, Port of Portland, Weyerhaeuser, Bank of America, Wells Fargo, The *Columbian*, Portland Public Schools, System of Higher Education, Portland Development Corporation, Tri-Met, and many more.

Of significance, lots of projects by Tim Hibbetts, a statistician in contract with the Republican Party, ran his political surveys via ADDI. I vividly recall my exposure to his first one – an anti-gay push to promote a local minister going political at the time, Lon Mabon.

To illustrate the reach of this start-up, listed as one of the 100 companies in Oregon to work for, the utility category represented by ADDI involved Portland General Electric, Northwest Natural Gas, Seattle Light, Washington Water Power, Pacific Gas & Electric, Pacific Power and Light, and Nevada Power, as well as small, little-known energy and telephone outfits. The focus of much of that research: to canvass customers in the early evening and weekends in ten western states, for opinions regarding customer service contacts; acquire total household income, to determine what rates the traffic will bear; opinions regarding controversial pending legislation, and information about water rights and tough relations with local Indian tribes to be sure that the utilities side of the story be told.

Their song and dance, strangely enough, was invariably presented in the form of a question! With extra help from a load of appeals to their emotions and value system, the questions, not giving many options, persuaded the customers to support the company's point of view. The final outcome told the study that the majority of the respondents concurred with the company's objectives; "You're absolutely right, I agree with you." The usual percentage of those interviewed, who refused to answer or would say, "I don't know," served only to keep the standard deviation above questionable levels.

In the early days what put ADDI on the map was the introduction of revolutionary Windows 3.0 May1990 by Microsoft. For three years ADDI had recruited designated professionals in hi-tech as well as random citizens, for "hands on" tryouts of the nascent Windows PC program. For $30.00, plus travel time and expenses, Microsoft paid willing participants to put in 50 minutes on their computers located in Zip Code 97005 at ADDI's offices. I felt the feedback contributed in major to the product's ultimate success, which indeed fulfilled Microsoft's claim "user friendly." Ultimately, we interviewers on the project felt a sense of historic contribution. We were also active for the tech breaker, Windows '95, but I did not participate on that one.

I also worked yearly on Intel's "Annual Impact of Technology on the Region" study. Not only did the survey ask communities in proximity to Intel's operations and campuses for feedback but, more so, approached areas far and wide for results of hi-tech equipment on their quality of life and lifestyle, and effects on their transportation. At that time many people seemed totally unaware or naive of any changes in equipment or advances in the routine of their daily lives. (The calm before the storm.)

I worked five to nine in the evening Tuesday-Friday, ten to six Saturdays, and twelve to five Sunday afternoon. I started at six AM in my daytime job, afforded by flexible hours. These surveys were slated for the public opinion division. A strictly business-to-business market research full house operated daytime, but I was unfamiliar with the clientele or focus. My expertise with political surveys was recognized and I was given the title of Senior Political Interviewer. Reviews stated that on open-ended questions, that is, essay questions: "I comprehended their responses and recorded them accurately." If the content of a survey offended me, I was allowed to work on another category.

When there wasn't a political project scheduled, I often did surveys mostly in utilities, media, and education; especially, for Northwest Natural Gas, contacting people on their customer list about recent contact with their customer service. The last time I did a NWNG survey served to complicate my life and challenged my judgment foremost. The survey immediately posed questions as to its structure and lack of positive intent.

The usual gas company surveys promoted a positive image for their personnel. The always short questionnaires were intended to make the customer "feel good" about their company. It routinely queried about the most recent exchange the customer had had with gas company personnel.

The survey was highly flawed. It simply wandered and floundered without purpose. For one, after the recipient answered the question, the questionnaire repeated the same question not once but again and again. This routine persisted for more than forty-five minutes, whereas their previous surveys were ten to twelve minutes. To say the least, it tried the patience of the respondent and irritated the hell out of most. The repetition was obviously insulting. Some hung up. More than one gulped, "Sounds like my gas company! Have they gone haywire?"

When we called a Northwest Natural Gas customer, we almost always explained that we were calling on the company's behalf. This time we were still calling from a customer list, and although it was supposedly a NWNG questionnaire, we were instructed not to inform the respondent that the call was on behalf of their gas company. This survey seemed only to infuriate those interviewed.

My fellow interviewers became restless and aware of discrepancies. They also were getting hung up on during the survey which was far out of the ordinary.

I related the discrepancies to Anthony, the supervisor responsible to listen to our interviews, using all the tact I could muster.

"This survey turns people off. For one, it's repetitive – doesn't go anywhere. They ask me if this is Northwest Natural Gas. Naturally I say, 'To remain impartial we are never told who the client is.' Then some say, 'What's their problem with me? I've had no problem with them. Why are you asking me these stupid questions over and over? I already answered you. Don't you stay told?'"

In his late thirties, he was always stern and hush hush, a real fraidy cat for his part time job. But dear Anthony was afraid for our jobs too. His full time accounting job was with a small bank. As a bachelor he was paying off college loans and buying a house with a garden. We talked roses. He distinguished them by fragrance, whereas color is my thing.

The wonderful thing about him was his in-depth capacity to grasp the power politics, in the organization of what he called the "turnover that keeps execs happy." Anthony once explained, "R.I.F., reduction in force, keeps the front door open and swinging to and fro to keep wages at entry level." Most of the employees were college students, or professional persons looking for work in their field. But Lulu, Operations Manager, with a Masters in Mathematics, was always pleading, "I need bodies." At the same time she failed to curtail an impulsive mean streak. When I was first hired in 1987, a wonderful Operations Manager, a recent graduate from Reed College, hired me. At that time employees included many students from Reed. Shortly he went on to graduate school at Cornell in upstate New York and the nature of management changed.

So Anthony stepped ever so lightly and kindly when evaluating the Interviewers (us peons) efforts on the phone. Bless his heart. Although he had no power to recommend raises or promotions, he recognized how limited, but still instrumental he was to help us keep our jobs. Posing an uncompromising façade, he was warmhearted and humane within. "It is not our function to question. We must merely ask the questions," he routinely reiterated, but with a new wrinkle or fold of pain on his forehead, his brown hair receded prematurely. Was it due to this wacky, yes foreign, project?

Anthony had no idea how I was completing the difficult survey, so he had no reason to believe that I was not cooperating with what he attempted to pass off as just the usual routine, when things were all but. To make quota as well as alleviate pain for their loyal customers, I would skip questions that were especially repetitive. My routine was chancy because if he listened closely he might be able to track. The questions were so redundant that a listener would have trouble determining exactly where I was. Anthony had so many to listen to he would not hang in from beginning to end with us trusted veterans. As usual, eight hundred of these awful things were ordered.

I didn't tell anyone, especially Anthony, what I intended to do. It was so obvious that maybe I didn't need a second opinion. Sunrise, my friend and respected fellow worker, was away from ADDI on a three month job in Newberg, pulling up deleted information from a hard drive for discontinued accounts who want to reactivate; "fun, tricky stuff," Sunrise called it. If she had been on the same assignment, she would have empathized.

I wanted the Market Research department at the gas company to be in possession of this particular questionnaire, so as to compare it to their usual surveys. In less than two minutes it destroyed their good will with the customer. ADDI had a standing policy – "Never remove a survey from the premises." I had actually taken some of Hibbetts' Republican surveys because I couldn't understand how very tricky they were – negatives instead of positives – yes meant no and no somehow ended up yes.

This situation required action. Who was out to get Northwest Natural Gas?

First I tried to make contact with the president of the gas company, Robert Ridgely, a well known Republican lawyer, out of Stole-Rives, the largest law firm in the Northwest. For years he had been on the Board of Directors for Portland Public Schools. I got as far as an administrative assistant. I told her of my suspicions. I strongly suspected that the survey was being done for somebody else, an enemy of Northwest Natural Gas. She didn't seem to grasp what I was talking about. I merely wanted her to give me an address to mail it to. She failed to respond to my minimal request

My major objective was to get the evidence to someone at the gas company that would comprehend its significance. I took a copy to the corporate office on NW Second in downtown Portland. The security man at the entrance pointed out the customer service mailbox where I could leave my information. I reluctantly did so, since there was no other alternative, but wrote an explanation detailing why I questioned whether the current project was actually authorized, by their marketing research department. I made another effort to be sure it got to the right people, and mailed a second copy, Attention: Marketing Department.

I got no feedback, but ADDI was investigated in 1998 and went out of business. Later I suspected that this survey was commissioned by Enron. They bought Portland General Electric and tried to buy out Northwest Natural Gas, who balked. Thank goodness, and the rest of Enron is a well documented story. Among other things Enron used the PGE employee 401-K accounts to pay towards its loans to buy the electric company. I know former PGE employees who lost their retirement savings at that time.

To avoid doing anymore so-called NWNG surveys, I took a few weeks off. At about that time NWNG became Northwest Natural. When I returned to sign in for more work, I was called into ADDI founder, Peter Rutherford's office. Fuming at me angrily (I couldn't understand a word he muttered), he kicked me out without explanation. At that time there were unfamiliar people in some of the offices, leading me to believe an investigation was underway. The final upshot: In 1998 my full time job ended. In looking for work I found out I couldn't get a recommendation for my ten years at ADDI, so I ceased to list them on applications. Even though I had gained very great working knowledge of a variety of businesses, mostly west of the Rockies, but couldn't claim how I gained it.

ADDI was founded by Peter Rutherford, born wealthy in an old family in Dunthorpe, had actually been a history teacher or a principal at an exclusive yet public school at one time. In the early days of the firm, he had the prettier college women sit on his lap at social events until someone clued him in. He thought of himself as loving and lovable. Employees couldn't understand why he kept kissing his brother on the lips at a summer picnic.

Totally harmless, of some interest, his wife was a stick of a creature, a pencil front and center – now you see her, now you don't - - with Mimi Eisenhower bangs on a tiny face. Seriously, she made me uncomfortable; a starving concentration camp survivor came to mind. Moreover, I was concerned that she was extremely ill. She was breakable, not cuddly. "A mere twenty mile wind gust would blow her over," someone said. I only saw Mrs. Rutherford one time but couldn't erase the memory. I didn't want to believe what I saw. Sometime later I thought of Bulimia or anorexia, so maybe there's hope for her.

Yes indeed, Peter was often the center of conversation among the mostly young employees of the firm. Of course, my situation caused me to identify with my fellow employees, rather than my bosses, who were usually critical of management. I never regretted my actions or second guessed the decision I made to get that survey back to the people at NWNG.

In fact I didn't give it much thought until now, when I decided to report my actions nineteen years later in print. Sunrise and I started at $4.25 per hour at ADDI in the late 1980s and ended up at a whopping $9.00 per hour in 1997. No bonuses. Once in a great while, pizza. Less has changed than we're led to believe in the time that has passed. I have great doubts that Peter Rutherford has yet to pay his debts or suffer any real consequences for his actions. In my last year there he had made several project managers so-called partners, shareholders in his corporation. There was a project manager for the category, utilities. So potentially Peter could have avoided direct responsibility for the fraudulent contract.

In retrospect, is it possible that ADDI reported to ARAMARK, my full time employer, my whistle blower actions? The new CEO, as I described in *The Quirky Landlord*, was a barracuda, her shenanigans inexcusable.

My Group Manager had nothing to do with my removal from the team. She isolated him...kept him on a wild goose chase in Denver trying to justify to their managers that reduction of wages of designers, patternmakers and custom power sewers of ARAMARK's latest acquisition of an elite operation, to that of washer attendants and wardrobe inventory clerks company-wide. She used my manager's hungry comptroller and male-dominated newlywed and naïve – just out of college, always barefoot because her feet hurt, probably due to her excess weight (but she was told that her little pudgy feet were cute) administrative assistant to bump me. Typical Machiavellian maneuvers – divide and conquer. After she let my manager go, a final blow to the NW Group, the CEO got dumped finally, in less than three years. She had taken the company public, cut the value of our 401-K by more than fifty percent. Eventually the owners retrieved their prior control at a loss, not only for them.

Part 2.

I missed my smoke breaks with Sunrise at ADDI Corporation. In fact I have fond memories of the many people there, especially women. Some came and went, but nevertheless contributed. Some of the most memorable included a woman in her forties. After being diagnosed with multiple sclerosis, she quit her job as a curator at the Smithsonian Institute in Washington, DC, divorced her husband, and moved to Portland, Oregon. She felt ADDI was the perfect job for her to enable her to sort things out.

Another, about that same age, was an English professor at a local college who was let go. She befriended me and we shared our mutual bad marriages. But she exposed me as an economic determinist. She said I rejected my husband because he didn't bring in any income. She claimed she didn't mind that her husband didn't work. "That isn't why I have fallen out of love with him," she insisted. "I don't resent being the bread winner. I've always held good paying jobs." I've often wondered if she was able to continue finding "good paying jobs." If not, would she still be willing to support her husband?

She was also an artist and drew portraits in pencil of numerous employees. Once she sketched me while I worked on the phone. To be honest, I didn't recognize myself in her drawing, but I didn't make a big deal about it. Of course, I'll never really see how others see me. But I'll still keep making an effort to get them to see me the way I see myself.

Another attractive blond in her thirties was married to a Jewish fellow. They owned a house with a historical designation in Ladd's addition, which included strict specifications regarding any repairs and replacements. It outlawed add-ons. They were required to merely retain or restore the origins of the dwelling, which they found expensive as well as frustrating. But it turned out her husband was solidly committed to the house, so retained their mortgage on it. Under no circumstances would he consider other options. It was a dilemma for her in that she waivered back and forth in her critique, at one time of his Jewish faith and another time at his passion for the house. After about a year and a half on the job, she was fired outright for breaking a rule of the company. The rest of us were never informed of which rule, we were kept in the dark. Of interest, she never protested the decision or explained it to us and dropped out of our lives, as other former fellow employees did.

A new employee, Charidee, an attractive, five foot eight inch African-American, a Portland State student, joined us on break. Her last name was Thompson, but this was a time when first names predominated and one rarely knew another's last name.

"The f**kin' teach, calls herself a professor, a f**kin' poem she read, she shouldn't have – that f**cker in it the word, nigger she said it, the f**kin' racist – I was so f**kin' – I told her, I was absolutely f**ked. F**k her!"

Charidee was wound up. She couldn't explain anything, couldn't say a complete sentence without several F you's. A graduate from Jefferson High School's Performing Arts Department and a singer, she had a deep contralto, soulful voice that had soothed us listeners. Now she had urgently disrupted us by her foul mouth and awkward effort to explain her outrage.

Once we got Charidee to identify the poet as T.S. Eliot, we tried to explain to her that the teacher didn't use that language; rather the poet used that language, writing out of a much earlier time in history. "To study the poet's work the teacher didn't dare change the poet's choice of words," I tried to explain.

Nia Lichter, just graduated from Reed College with a degree in languages, said, "The teacher didn't dare change the offensive word or leave it out. That isn't allowed in scholarship. How would you like it if someone said they were quoting you and left some of your words out or changed what you exactly said or wrote?"

"You don't get my f**kin' point. She shouldn't have read the f**kin' thing."

I said, "Charidee, to appreciate the now and things like civil rights laws, T.S. Eliot was way before the March on Washington. He's typical of what was acceptable at the turn of the century; a white, unsophisticated, sheltered man who thinks he's worldly, who never had much contact with blacks, probably not much exchange with a large array of people, including people like us. We talk differently. We belong to the late twentieth century. As the saying goes, we have to study the past and how people thought in those days so as not to repeat their mistakes."

Sunrise, who was taking two classes per term at Portland Community College in the daytime, so she could work at night, said, "My boyfriend and roommate, Josh, is a black. He hurts when he is treated like a nigger or called one. You gotta shake it off! He says, 'Just consider the source.' They want to upset you, to cause you to lose your cool...make you do and say rash, maybe even dangerous, things – like threaten somebody. If you do that, act out angry, you put them in the driver's seat – give them even more control over you than they already have. Keep your best foot forward. Don't let them know they're getting to you. Pretend like they don't exist. Ignore them – no matter how tough it is to do so!"

"Why bother with ignorant people loaded with hate. What a waste of time," Nia said.

"Walk away and keep looking for good people like us," I said. "You don't want to rewrite history, do you? Like they try to do in Texas!"

It was time to return to work. The three of us, Nia, Sunrise, and I, shared our concern for Charidee on the job, due to her seeming inability to express herself without her use of slang. It turned out the job was perfect for her. Since she had to read verbatim the survey questionnaire under supervision, it assisted Charidee in learning to communicate in complete sentences without swearing. We decided it served as a positive conditioning mechanism. It turned out we were accurate in our hypothesis.

At times I gave her a ride home to the NE Williams and Knott area. Charidee spoke lovingly of her father, who lived in New York City who she was very close to. She had made a recent trip to visit him and fell in love with the city. She lived with her mother and a sister in a two-story house that was expensive to heat, but she pointed out that her father was generous to the family and proud of her.

Charidee completed college and went on to law school and got her degree. I know this because she came back to work as a part time supervisor in 1997, while she studied for the State of Oregon Bar exam. That's as far as I got to go with Charidee, but she learned to let her anger roll off her back and, yes speak in complete sentences void of the four-letter words she was so comfortable with coming out of high school. People never cease to amaze me.

Sunrise and Josh lived with her mother, a psychologist with the state of Oregon, in a daylight basement home in Tigard off 99W, just east of Bull Mountain Road. With a slight but troublesome scoliosis condition, pretty and bright Sunrise attended PCC part time while looking for a solid full time job. Five foot seven and slender, she admitted shopping the "sleaze market" for DVDs and "toys," etcetera, to stimulate their sex life. She became morose at times when her birthday and the holidays came around. When she was ten her father, a highly recognized Human Resources executive, abandoned the family, including a younger brother, and moved to San Francisco for a top position, taking his secretary with him.

She loved her father and sometimes blamed herself for his actions. 'Could it have even been the lump on my upper back?' she asked me one time. Sunrise swam regularly in an effort to exercise her back and shoulders to subdue the pain. She would report to work after a swim, twist her wet, extra abundance of hair in a large knot on top of her head without tools, just tied up with more of her hair. This hairdo displayed her sculptured hair line and white Irish face – somewhat longer and narrow (like a Modigliani model), with puckered, pursed, perfect lips (devoid of a silicone injection), ending in a pointed chin above a poised neck. With her long muscles, like that of a swimmer, she moved gracefully.

A master interviewer, typing responses at 80 words per minute (I only typed 65 wpm), she was getting straight A's in tough courses: Biology, Chemistry and Anatomy. Sunrise and I many times vied for top producer on a project – based on number of interviews completed per hour and quality of information gathered. In Focus group recruitments, like the home builder from Colorado who needed to interview people in the Portland metropolitan market who would buy homes in the area, over five-hundred-thousand dollars, which we would hunt and screen for. Our production was based on the number of recruits that finally showed up.

My most stark and fondest memory is what Sunrise did when she was having a great day. She would announce to the troops, "Hey, Gang, I'm kickin' butt!" She didn't have to explain. That said it all.

This year, 2015, Dawnbreak, (She liked my nickname for her) In my seventy-seventh year on this earth, I'm having a great time – yeah! I'm kicking butt!"

Life became very serious, but also very fulfilling, for Josh and Sunrise. They adopted her brother's daughter when the girl turned five. They became devoted parents immediately. Shortly before the last time I saw Sunrise, she went to work for the post office due to high scores on her civil service exam. The job doubled her income and she was thankful. Work by Josh was never mentioned but now he was a parent giving home care to their children.

Going in as a beginner, it was her job to haul the mail bags from one location to another. Her back gave her a bad time and she soon became concerned; not about getting hurt, instead she feared whether she would be able to do the job and do it quickly enough. To complicate further, one of the last things Sunrise shared with me was additional pressures she got from her family. "They're already spending the extra money. Josh is talking new car and my mother wants to get lawn service even for the huge back yard I've tried to do something with forever."

She had never referred to the lump on her back as scoliosis. I'm the one that uses that term. She never stated a time in her health history when she became aware of the lump and the pain. I'm quite sure she never ever claimed herself as handicapped in any way, but still, due to the loss of her father and faulting herself for it, she and he must have been aware of it while he was still in her life.

It is very sad and I worry for her, but I have no way to reach her, so as to alleviate my lingering concern for her. I say a prayer for Sunrise and her family. In writing about her, I was tempted to write a letter to the Tigard post office to inquire about her, but employers are very protective of their personnel and should be; that is, if she survived the hauling of heavy mail bags.

Part 3.

Interview projects weren't always as serious as the Microsoft and Intel ones. Nia, Sunrise, and I worked six days, every six to eight months per year, on the Sunsweet Prune Juice market survey. We had fun with it. Given pages of phone books in major cities such as New York, Chicago, Baltimore and St. Louis, the three of us used a system that worked beautifully to find responders to our survey. We selected first names which were almost guaranteed to be loyal and frequent users of prune juice. Their first names were often: Gertrude, Adelaide, Maude, Gladys, Agatha, Agnes, Helga, Helen, Elsie, Eloise, Matilda, Louise, Prudence, Thelma. Old time names. As interviewers on the project, we all met our quotas by reaching the "sweet old ladies" who willingly shared their enthusiasm for the designated prune juice.

Nia and I became fast friends, even though we were almost twenty-five years apart. Slight of build and very pretty, with brown hair and green eyes, she looked continental. Her father was Danish, an economics professor. There was a quiet, soft spoken manner about her which required a softer, respectful approach to her by others. In her spare time Nia read books in several European languages and wanted to become a librarian. She inquired at University of Washington regarding their program, since there was no graduate program at the time in Portland. Her mother, from Germany, was a librarian. Since I talked about my gardening, Nia invited me to meet her mother and see her mother's garden.

With Nia, on a Sunday after work because we quit at five that day, I drove from Barbur Boulevard, turned off at Terwillinger, which transits the low hills with views of Mt Hood from South Burlingame, to Taylors Ferry Road. All downhill, with the very old and prestigious graveyard on our right, camouflaged by heavy foliage, to take Macadam that runs along the west side of the Willamette River, to cross the Sellwood Bridge to the East side of Portland, turning north through Sellwood, then to West Moreland (on the west side of 99E) on the bluff above the river, and finally East on Bybee Boulevard to the lovely East Moreland (on the east side of 99E), where Reed College is located and the Rhododendron Gardens sit at one end of the golf course.

We passed by the public park with huge wading and casting pools that attract wild ducks and geese. The annual Milk Box Derby for kids and miniature sailboat races are held there. Sckavone baseball field beyond it is named after the pharmacist whose drug store was on 41st and Division in my old neighborhood. Bybee Blvd passes over McLoughlin Boulevard, 99E, and enters an area planned in the 1930s, a combination of family-size traditional and contemporary homes and landscaped yards guarded by huge, healthy trees, on wide slightly winding avenues. Romantic. Stately. Wreaks establishment. Power. Maybe not as great as that of Dunthorpe?! Although, in 2016, being in the city, decidedly increases property values.

It was midsummer so seasonal treats included vivid red trumpet vines spilling over fences, persistent roses, short shrubs to high climbers in dense blooms of reds, oranges, yellow, pinks, apricot, even purple. The clumps of four-foot Shasta Daisies that multiply so readily and crowd its space demanded to be noticed. The spent daffodils and tulips had been planted over by the usual annuals. Tall lilies and gladiolas added a treat. The green lawns all trimmed. A showy hanging basket here and there. It was too late for local peony blooms, nevertheless an Asian Peony tree at the end of a yard was coming on strong with giant exotic blooms in a deep yellow variegated with pink and orange that looked more like a rose.

I had described the lovely Nia to my friend Gart, who had advertised with me when I was in advertising. About that time Gart turned forty. Feeling comfortable financially as Vice President and Finance Officer for his father's bedspread (available in major catalogues) and import fabrics business, Gart wanted to marry and have a family. He wanted to meet Nia.

Driving to meet her mother, Nia told how she wasn't real crazy "about sex." A fellow she knew (that's how she put it), a student at the college, had talked her into trying it. "I didn't like it – like animals – did nothing for me."

"What were your feelings for that guy?"

"I liked him before – didn't like him afterwards. I like a human touch – holding hands, hugging, cuddling…but fornication, forget it. How is your friend, Gart, about sex?" she asked. Nia never minced words, but instead of voicing her point of view emphatically she maintained a quiet, controlled, softness in her voice which required close consideration for some reason.

"I have no idea," I admitted. "We never discussed it. It's not a subject I usually discuss especially with men friends; mostly because they might get the wrong idea about me if I brought it up, if you can appreciate. In fact it isn't a usual subject of mine for discussion." Saying this I thought of the advertiser of motor homes, still only married for a short time, who told me about his wedding night and how he "couldn't get it in." But I didn't share that one.

Instead I said, "I don't pursue the subject with friends. After all, I have a bad marriage and don't discuss it with anyone. One friend, as a Canadian nurse who married an American GI in France in the sixties, told me, 'Kurt just goes ahead and pokes me, no fore play.' With that I didn't probe, let it float away. They had four outstanding children, their girl, a friend of my son's, played short stop on his ball team."

I kept talking, naturally, which is a habit of mine I rarely vacate, "When Tari Hillkline said, 'What's the big deal about sex? Makes me think of Peggy Lee's song, Is that all there is?' I didn't share with Tari either. Tari had two children. Her girl, at eighteen, with her boyfriend in the car, drove off the road and ended up paralyzed from the waist down. Fortunately, Tari, an athlete, officiates at high school volleyball games, gave her daughter intensive physical therapy workouts for several years. She married that boyfriend, worked as a receptionist and brought forth two kids. Maybe sex and love are not necessarily the same thing, after all."

"An outstanding man, looks-wise and intelligence, wanted me to go to bed with him. I turned him down. I was still trying to get my husband to love me. I lucked out. He got around big time. Got himself and a campus secretary in trouble. The poor girl. Sad. He ended up raising another son. But you know he always wanted another son but usually went after women "his equal" according to him. I figure he didn't marry her because he didn't consider her his equal. In addition, with his reputation, it was a one night stand, which he earned a reputation for. He actually avoided relationships, friendships. He was awkward with women. I don't know why, although he went to an all men's college." I was thinking out loud, I realized.

Nia admitted her awkwardness with Jewish families. Her older sister, in pursuit of a PhD, finally married her long time boyfriend in a huge Jewish wedding in New York City. As her Maid of Honor, Nia described how uncomfortable she was with the extra energy and "hulla-baloo" of the families.

"My sister was outgoing and demonstrative – even theatrical – just the opposite of me. Hanna has paid a high price to realize her ambitions, too high for me – she even had an abortion. This stylish haircut of mine, my sister insisted on it, for the wedding."

Other than a flick of a gesture to her hairdo she remained still, motionless, quiet; self-contained, maybe non-demonstrative, showing so little emotion. Maybe she had disciplined herself not to overreact. On stage, so motionless, Nia would be a statue, merely a prop, one though that you would not pass over, nevertheless, a prop – so still, sitting to the right of me in the front seat. She made me think of one of my favorite songs, Once, twice, three times a lady. On the phone, she was lively, engaged, absorbed, responsive and creative. She loved her job, since she was comfortable and interactive with those she was interviewing.

"I love it. It fits you...no other like it. I get tired of long, flowing, heavy hair – hides the eyes, even their faces, and they're always fooling with it."

"It's expensive to maintain but my mother loves it."

"If I had that cut, it would be impossible for me. My hair has a mind of its own."

Nia warmed up. "I describe it as extra-long short hair," she said. "Just have to wash it every day and it falls into place. Don't need to blow dry. But not just any hairdresser can do it. It's like a mop, isn't it?' She actually giggled.

"I even had a beehive," I recalled.

"How fun. They are aptly named. Out of the sixties. How? Where?"

"Pan Am days. In Tokyo the crew told me about the hairdresser on the Ginza who supposedly created the beehive. He did it for me. It didn't last long. It was against company regulations. The uniform hat couldn't stay on top of it. Human Resources called me in. I knew what for. So I worked hard to get out all the back brushed tangles, washed it out and curled my hair before my appointment. The beehive wasn't even discussed. But I had a few hours of people gawking at me."

"In considering your dissatisfaction with intercourse, some women feel the same way. Some find satisfaction in the mysteries found in the clitoris. It's alluded to by Scott Fitzgerald in one of his novels, don't know which one."

"So I find myself avoiding men lately."

"In defense of Gart, he's a very special best friend. He has had a struggle with his Jewish background. Like his mother, he's a Soko Gakkai Buddhist. A very popular student body president at the oldest high school in town. The city's elite bound for college gravitate towards it rather than go private. Pressure to excel among its graduates is enormous. Then he had a regretful experience at college. He felt because he looks Jewish. (I could see Gart in my mind, a Goya painting of a Sephardic Jew depicting the Spanish inquisition, so tragic.) His father, a devout Jew, recently died. Four hundred friends showed up at the man's funeral at Beth Israel. That event made Gart's inner conflict even greater. He and I consider ourselves universalist; that is, value many of the world's religions which have in common, 'Love thy neighbor as thyself.'"

"Yeah, if the neighbor believes like you do."

"So right. But it's something good to hope for with a friend. It helps us avoid mere cynicism. He and I celebrated the Three Gorges dam being built in China. I find people make friendships based on mutual hatreds rather than mutual ideals. That's not Gart or me."

Her mother's garden put my free form, maybe not more than twelve-hours-per-weekend one, to shame. Her labor intensive back yard in a rented house close to the college included graveled, chiseled paths between rows and rows of worked and heaped, fed earth piled high with trenches for deep ground watering. The spoiled, beyond belief, glorious perennials were allowed to realize their magnificence, yes, even though ever so short-lived. I felt humbled by her work of art and expertise. To be welcomed into her home and garden was indeed a privilege. I was somewhat short of words other than, "Ooh-Aah!" "Gorgeous!" "Amazing – what would you call that color?" "I love trumpets of any kind, but I don't have any in my garden, yet. They do need staking, don't they?"

Shortly Nia moved out of her folks' home and into a basement apartment in a house in northwest Portland, a popular area at that time for young professionals and brave new people in search. But she remained close to her family. That was in 1998, when my job ended. At a later time, I attempted to reconnect with her and her family. They had all left town. No forwarding address. At the same time Gart also disappeared and it hurt. Strangely, their building on NW Lovejoy had sold and the only address listing for their company was on North Lombard which did not exist. Gart had considered moving the company to Tennessee who had approached him with a deal. To complicate, he was having problems with a major salesman in New Jersey. Gart had asked me if the one hundred thousand base for that salesmen was reasonable because that fellow was pushing for much more. I searched for them to no avail.

Given his struggle within and his sensitivity – after all he was a devout Buddhist - - I have often considered that Gart is no longer on this earth, by choice, when on a downer. So, for sure, he's in heaven. He was so good to me. He helped me select a Vogue couturier pattern and suggested fabric for my Mother of the Groom costume for my son's wedding in the '80s. He loved my chicken wings, baked in Maude Ward's Prune Sauce I made out of Italian prunes and whole cloves, at my New Years Eve parties which ended in the '90s, when liabilities became so apparent. In his search he had traveled to Israel and connected with rare family in New York City.

Nia and Gart would have enjoyed each other immensely. He would have been delighted with her reserve, and at the same time, directness.

Jack Roberts and Barbara Rovang met each other at one of our parties and lived happily ever after. But I'll never again do the so-called match-maker bit. Nia's reservations and my failure to promote my dearest friend, my failure to convince her of his marvelous character, is probably a greater failure in my life than any other I have experienced. His person was my soul mate. He didn't know how beautiful he was. Nia, also of goodness, didn't know her worth yet, either. But I believe she is in search, like I am. She tries to learn from other human beings, like I do. Another extra special person in my life, loaded with amazing people.

Did I fail my responsibilities to them as a mere human being? One has to deliver big time on so few chances or else pay the price of regret. Am I a fool to feel at times that I failed a fellow man? Especially ones I hold so tight to my heart. They gave me great joy and of course, challenge.

Part Three

A Piece of Someone Else's Life

Kalli and Lindsay

At 11:15 AM, on a Sunday in May 2015, I was on the Internet with Amazon to order a toner for my Samsung printer. It just went out and I needed it to print out articles from *The Columbian* newspaper, manuscripts by fellow writers in my writing class at Mt Hood Community College, and chapters for this book. I used the password for my KDP account. It didn't take so I pressed CALL ME to set a new password. I thought my phone was in my right jacket pocket. My phone started ringing. It was upstairs in my bedroom in another pocket.

I ran upstairs. I didn't make it on time, but there was a voice mail. It was a friend of mine, Kalli O'Keefe. She said:

'Hey, Clancy--Kalli. I'm in serious trouble. There are people trying to—a network, a network of people--trying to take over my home, murder me and take over my home. I'm having an open house today, between noon and three, and if you can bring your big tough guy and, ah, kind of hang around it would be really nice. Okay, and I'll give you details later but I can't talk now, I have to call every friend I know and let them come in to my house. It's being held open and because guys in this network will probably show up. So take care. And I love you darling. Bye.'

After I listened to Kalli's voice mail and returned to my PC in the den downstairs, Sandy with Amazon did call. How fortunate. Up to then I was afraid I missed her call. Sandy was great. I got a new password. I explained how the phone was upstairs.

"I panicked because I thought it was Amazon, relieved that it was a girl friend, although in panic mode," I said. "Despite college degrees, they weren't in math, I don't remember nonsense symbols which passwords require. I have to write them down. Thanks for the trouble you're going to."

Sandy was great and laughed with me, such empathy. Naturally, Amazon asked me to rate their customer service person. I went overboard for Sandy: so patient, so with it!

Kalli said bring "your big tough guy."

I'm sure she was referring to my renter, Jed. She had met him two years ago at Carol's, a friend of mine, who had a barbecue at her daughter's new house out in Fairview. Jed had been the chef.

How to get to Kalli's was my first logistical consideration. Taking the bus is problematic. Kalli's place is ten long blocks from a bus stop, plus that particular bus doesn't run very often, and at my age that is a strenuous hike. Plus, she requested a hunk of a man which made me think of Lindsay Mohlere, a fellow writer, and his wife who have offered to take me shopping on a Sunday in bad weather.

In April, of this year his book, The Grow, was published, a mystery of bad guys versus good guys. He loved my review, which was published on Amazon. and said, "It blew my socks off." He exaggerates...sometimes writers do, or put the em-PHA-sis on the wrong sy-LLA-ble, Jim Ward's favorite statement.

I called and left a message on his voice mail. "A friend of mine is in trouble. Are you available between twelve and two today?" Then I sent an email in an attempt to give him more information.

"I have a friend – just gave me panic call. She's not a panic type – very intelligent – very independent. I left you a voice mail on phone at 11:42 AM. She needs me and a tough man to arrive at her house between 12 and 2 today. It's not a hoax. She always knows what she's talking about. Not an air head – has had some strange people get involved in her life recently, including a vet who is bi-polar she now is afraid of – but it's more complicated than that. Are you available? Can you help me out? 11:46 AM 5/17/2015."

I didn't explain to him that Kalli was the same person whom I asked his wife for contact information on just two weeks ago. I had forgotten about it. Kalli had asked me for the phone number of two persons I met at Lindsay and his wife's home when they hosted his book signing. The two women have a business; matching persons for shared housing. Kalli was looking for someone to share housing expenses with her. Lindsay's wife emailed their business name to me and phone number, I quickly passed it on to Kalli. That's the last time I talked with her.

Lindsay called shortly after I talked to Amazon's Sandy. He needed more information, complicated more so because he was on deadline for an article slated for a magazine he was contracted for. I told him I had known Kalli since 2006. She had modeled in New York in her youth. She was in real estate in California with her husband. After they moved to Oregon he divorced her, not too many years ago, to marry another woman. He and his wife lived on the same street as Kalli's home but sold it approximately a year ago and did pay Kalli moneys he owed her before they moved away. She's always been organized and congenial. I met her sister from California. Kalli and her sister went to a monthly Rose Association meeting with me at Oaks Park. I took her to a casual meeting of young local Three Omega's I was invited to meet and sold a copy of my book to one of them. They liked her immensely. She asked good questions that were appropriate and definitely well-informed on her part about majors and career paths.

He remained silent so I asked, "So you can't go?"

"I'll be there in about twenty minutes," Lindsay said.

"That'll give me time to put on my face. Oh, Thank you!"

After Lindsay picked me up, I took him directly to her home even though I had only been there once before. On the way he pointed out a kid he was coaching currently who was running north on 122nd Avenue, "working out." He honked at the kid as he drove by. We parked outside a cement bench propped up on huge boulders which blocked the driveway that sloped down to the basement. We took stone steps to the front door facing east, through a gorgeous May garden of climbing roses on open board white fences, and past a small, charming tree.

The real estate lady met us at the door, so I asked, "Is Kalli here?" She let us in and Kalli appeared at the edge of the living room. She hugged me. "So glad you made it." I didn't think to introduce Lindsay.

Kalli led us through a living room with a low ceiling, and dark, in spite of the sunny day at 70 degrees and thirty minutes past noon.. The paned windows on the east as well as the west walls, dressed up with antique crocheted lace curtains, did not bring in the light of the day. Oddly, lights from lamps were absent. The room, in dark patterned carpets and dark wood furnishings, generated an eerie feeling, or like rooms out of the 19th century. Luckily, Kalli took us out the back to her favorite garden room. It looked out on another lush garden. Lindsay introduced himself and shook her hand.

"Thank you for coming. I'm afraid these people from the group will show up so I need trusted ones to be here."

I was shocked by Kalli O'Keefe's appearance. She looked thin and frail and in, unfashionable for her, ill fitting black knit pants, an old t-shirt and a worn matching black sweater. Her hair was tied up and covered by an unattractive knitted pill box on two-thirds of her head. What hair showed was gray, whereas she always had gorgeous white hair done up in a chignon or French twist. This is the first time for me to realize that the premature white hair of hers was a dye job.

There were quite a few people milling around to consider the house for purchase. One group entered the garden room and made notice of the brick floor and the cream floor-to-ceiling drapes between the wall to wall windows. Translucent drapes, held by attractive plastic rings the same color as the fabric, let the light in. "I bought those at dollar store for about twenty dollars," Kalli happily related. She added, "I wanted to be an interior decorator."

After that family made their way out into the garden, Kalli handed me a three-page single-spaced, typed explanation. "This will tell you what I've been through," she said.

I handed it to Lindsay. "I'll let him read it first before I read it. He's the criminologist and researcher."

"Are you the writer? She asked. "Clancy invited me to your book signing. You and I should collaborate?"

Lindsay asked, "What do you know about these guys?"

"Very little. Roger was homeless, but a friend of Darren's. He's in jail now – getting treatment for heroin addiction."

Lindsay returned to the manuscript but listened to Kalli tell how, after a meal, she couldn't breathe that night in bed and had to go to emergency. "I think I was subjected to something in the food or the wine."

"Roger's the one with the food stamps who cooked for you and did odd jobs. You trusted him, I thought."

"Yes, he cooked for me, that's for sure. Another fellow, friend of Roger, smelled bad and messed up everything I had just cleaned."

"Where will you go when it's sold?" I asked.

"Far away. Don't know where? Away from these guys. They're out to destroy me. I have a note in safekeeping that starts out, 'After I murder her!' I made copies and have them hidden all over the house."

"Do you still keep your journal?" I asked.

"Yes – but all my personal things get messed with. My auto registration is missing, among other things. They did things in an effort to drive me crazy. Dirty my kitchen. Make a mess. Last night, after I vacuumed for the open house, the one that smelled so bad scattered some kind of brown dust all over my rugs and floors. I had to clean again. I finally kicked him out...too late. I realize he's part of them." She shuddered.

Her demeanor of strong, capable, outgoing, able to haul wood beams or a hod load of bricks, and a sense of humor to boot, was not there. In her place was a defeated, wasted old woman, trying to explain the basis for her fears. Poisoned by arsenic and a garden chemical I didn't recognize, starting with p-e-r. "They left just a little in their containers so I'd be sure to discover and suspect." She mentioned several trips to the hospital. Her blood tests indicated liver damage.

A neighbor woman arrived with a tall fellow, a friend of Kalli's as well. Lindsay knew the guy. They shook hands. He is a county parole officer. Lindsay handed the typed papers to him. I never read them. Later, I asked him what they said. He said, "Same thing she told us."

Kalli continued, "I think they wired under my house because they seem to know my whereabouts at all times. One of them shows up when I'm ready to leave the house. I don't dare leave it unattended."

"Have you changed the locks?" Lindsay asked.

"I do extra. Make police reports in person."

Kalli did not answer his question. Possibly she doesn't have the money, seventy-five dollars minimum for one lock now. If a person is happy with merely a person sharing his food stamps and doing odd jobs, she must be really broke.

She led us outside to the basement door which she proceeded to unlock. Both Lindsay and the officer noted the slight opening in the window next to the door. Lindsay touched the curtains hanging over it to show her, "Are you aware of this, Kalli?"

She said, "Oh, that," and didn't explain further. Odd! Again we entered a clean, cleverly furnished, finished room. She said she painted the north wall yesterday. It was white. She wanted to show the men the ease of access to under the house. She said the mat on the floor had been rolled up the last time she checked it. "Someone would have done that. Something is missing or messed with every day."

Once back outside, Lindsay was ready to go. She said, "Darren's girl friend is currently in prison so he needs the money this place would give him."

That was the first time she revealed that Darren, her one and only lover, had other ties – interests other than her. Is it just a woman scorned?

On our way home, Lindsay said, "She has used bad judgment."

"You mean trusting questionable no counts, leaches, nasty slobs? No one is welcome in my home if they don't pay the rent. One thing I do know, criminal minds first and foremost go after your essential documents. But when did she find out they were criminals?"

"BAD JUDGEMENT" IS THAT ALL? Dear Lindsay: I am grateful to you for taking precious time off to take me to support a friend in trouble. When someone suffers loss – even a lost dream, or their home, of all things it can cause a total breakdown, paranoid, etcetera.

I have now taken time to dredge up the phone calls over the past two years. Let me know if this additional information sheds any further light on the situation.

Approximately two years ago Kalli excitedly told me she had met a handsome, perfect Vet, younger than her. "I've never had such good, wonderful sex in my life." He lived with her for awhile but his alcoholism began to plague her. He drank from awake to asleep so she sent him away. 'If you're ever sober we can get together again,' she related. He returned to Fir Bend.

She visited his home in Fir Bend and cared for his mother, terminally ill, and kept house for two weeks. Again on the phone she told me she made a bid to buy the hotel in that town contingent on the sale of her home. "I will organize sewing and knitting classes, bingo, yoga, other exercise for women in the town. I already have curtains, et al, to gussy the place up. It's a huge lot including parking – "a first rate investment." Eventually someone else got the bid.

A little later she revealed he was bi-polar, a complete nut case, and placed a restraining order on him. In retaliation he bought an orange sofa and had it delivered. She refused it at her doorstep. "It was awkward, infuriating, confusing," she shared.

About nine months ago, Kalli made another offer on an undeveloped property – "an excellent prospect for subdivision for homes in Sweet Home, Oregon," in exchange for her house in Portland. I merely warned, "Sweet Home is a bedrock of conservatism, watch out – city folks get uncomfortable."

"Good. I'm a strict conservative and a devout Christian, to boot."

At the same time she spoke of "Roger, homeless, on food stamps, real handy around the house and yard, buys the food and cooks for both of us. I'm eating great."

Right prior to that time, she said her sister had given her a thousand dollars to finance her class and books to get a real estate license. At that time she said she was spending most of her time studying.

Six or seven months ago she said she bought a Fifth Wheel and a new truck to haul it. "It's parked in my driveway. I will live in it and put my home in foreclosure."

Her home is an ongoing work of art, but she keeps trying to get rid of it as she hunts for investments that will give her a job to do and, hopefully, income. These men knew how to get to her, make fun of her without raping her – just mess with her home and the massive amount of labor she puts into it. Her realization that these men knew each other has caused her to conclude a conspiracy.

That "network" idea turned you off, Lindsay. You surmised, "I don't normally buy into conspiracy theories."

It is possible for them to put a homing device in her car. I thought she had a pick up but she referred to a car. She said they know where she is at all times and show up there.

There are private blood test outfits too. One across from Safeway on about 120th does work for the police and also private parties. You have to tell them what element to look for when they test for you. Apparently she discovered the missing arsenic and Peren (I didn't recognize it) after her blood test and diagnosis on her liver.

Hospitals assume the one being tested is on something, so they look for common drugs like amphetamines and heroine. They don't automatically look for poisons or odd garden fertilizers. And they don't have to tell you what they discover or locate. The examining doctor has the option to keep that information to himself. It's feasible she was exposed to amphetamines. That's what she looks like to me, wasted. And she was so high (over the phone) for so long. The physician could have "assumed" she did it to herself. That would cause "liver damage" real quick, especially at her age, over 62.

In a sense, in looking back she was sort of, but inadvertently, not entirely honest with me. That's okay. But most of all, she's not honest with herself. Now afraid and paranoid and probably angry at herself, and rampant misinterpretations rule her roost. She's bordering on the psychotic – that is, out of touch with reality. But I assure you, if she were wealthy she could engage in legal support that would enable her to raise the kind of hell she feels entitled to.

About one month ago she called to let me know that she would write a letter to me for my now book describing her political differences to mine and why. We thought banter back and forth on today's controversial issues might be a fun excerpt. We were just aiming for one chapter worth. She's a Republican.

Broke, disheveled, and disarmed. No one, especially the police will take her seriously. Cest la vie. Although these days real estate scamming, especially of the elderly is common, but the police retain a distant posture, regardless.

So she has been all over the map with her goals, survival efforts, in and out of love (foolish and probably desperate), disintegrations and humiliations and now loss of her home. At this juncture I will turn to prayer. Is there anything I can do? Or should do? Her phone I'm sure is off limits. I won't try to call.

There was one indication Sunday which gave me a ray of hope. The neighbor who was with the officer asked me who I was, how I knew Kalli, and where I lived? I told her I met her in 2006 at East Portland Community Center when I was a Meals on Wheels volunteer. "She would bring her aging mother to lunch for an outing. (In fact I wonder if her mother decorated that house) I live in a condo in Felony Flats area – close to Les Schwab. I have 29 rose bushes. In fact Les Schwab just gave me gray river rock left over from their landscaping, delivered and distributed it on my garden. I am 77 years old."

She wouldn't have asked me to define myself unless someone in the know is concerned. When one gives information to the police, they don't ever provide you with feedback regarding the results of their follow up. I gave a report of about thirty-five different license plates and descriptions of several persons who visited a condo in the area over a two week period. (Typed it and mailed it) I told them I had observed at random. I was not rear windowing it – only home two afternoons and evenings per week. The traffic soon quit – for more than two years. Now it seems to be starting up again – same girl and a new boyfriend.

Her father pays for the condo. He is a friend of mine and when in town always asks me to cut a rose for him. He's tried everything – but is a Vice President of a construction company based right now in Florida. They were in Oregon. He actually replaced wall heaters in my place and drilled a hole through my den wall above the door to better string the cable for my internet starting in the living room, and so I can close the door to the den in order to heat it efficiently. He's a good man and put laminate floor-ing on the first floor of his daughter's condo at the same time. His wife is defensive about their daughter. She told a condo officer her daughter shouldn't have to pick up the poop her boyfriend's pit bull leaves on the lawns. "It's the law, lady." When the girl was first told to put the dog on a leash, she did so but would not take hold of the leash. For a while, she continued to insist he was "on a leash." Deliver me.

Now once a week I take items Fred Meyers donates to Gresham Meals on Wheels. Quickly she informed me that her family prefers "sweet things." Her father is concerned about her health.

I started out to write to merely thank you for your assistance, mostly to me, this last Sunday. I intend to publish this – but need your position and editing and approval of name changes, including yours, if need be. I hesitated to call your amazing wife by her name.

And always, Clancy Rohring, alias.

An afterthought: Persons and organizations can do things to keep a home from not selling – even to a point where someone who wants it real bad can ultimately get it for a song. A realtor did it to me. He said after I signed that he was not available on weekends, had to attend church be-cause he had his young daughter at that time. Divorced. A member of his church wanted my house but had to sell their trailer house in Wilsonville. He didn't inform me of that. She did so the day she moved in. He only advertised it on internet when in 1999 the Oregonian still dominated real estate searches. He never held an open house. He falsely advertised it as an "Executive find," that I didn't find out about for a long time. He had introduced himself as the son of the former superintendent of Park Rose school district. He was with Century 21. Darren may have subjected Kalli to a stream of power suggestions which motivated her into these outrageous deals.

She did the landscaping for the last half of her property, which was unfinished. Put in stone wall at the end of the driveway and additional brick paths, planted a dogwood and lots of lilies and other bulbs. For years she made extra income by building and antiquing furniture from scraps, which sold well. She's been resourceful and independent up to now.

The last time I talked to Kalli, before this last panic call, she said, "I've decided to keep my home. God doesn't want me to sell it. I accept what he has in store for me."

And always, Clancy R.

KALLI'S STORY, June 14, 2015

Dear Clancy, Here's my rough, it's not my best effort given what's going on in my life. My house sold in three days. Five offers, so I've been trying to dispose of fifteen years of accumulation and ward off the evil forces.

I appreciate so much your support showing up at my open house, I've never been more frightened in my life. Right now I can't leave my house because of more attacks, so things have been very difficult.

My sister is arriving next week so I'll have some backup, I've got to be out of here by July 7th and my hands are tied, can't leave because they hit the house. If I go anywhere they can steal my car and sell it.

Well, I'll stop whining. I'm still alive and well and kicking and have a new cell phone number. I don't text, or get messages, or do call waiting, yet. Too many other things on my mind to master those things. If you want to talk to me it must be live. My new number is (503) 429-6677 temporarily. I'll probably change it again soon. Thanks for being my friend. Kalli PS – Happy Birthday

KALLI'S MANUSCRIPT: Following is her unaltered story she has written for me to share with readers of my book. It can challenge the keenest analyst. In a large sense it is a prototype of persons approaching a time when it is necessary to shift gears or lead themselves to believe they should. Her effort is one of the most complete descriptions of criminal minds operating among unwary persons so I feel obligated as a nonfiction writer to give her this much space for her outpouring. These pages lend themselves to extensive and conflicting discussions. Or maybe the final question will be: Is the unfolding drama merely of people playing games; not engaged in things vital to life? Again, my first resource for information and learning has been decisions made by my fellow human beings. They help me update practical information such as what not to do!

A COUGAR'S TALE 3/4/15 – 7/4/15

My contented resolve of celibacy lasted thirteen years. It was shattered when a fifty-year-old, tall, Texan meandered into my garage sale, returning repeatedly to open my world to a long-distance, bi-polar, alcohol, medicated disease, and an introduction to ruthless greed, burnout, manipulation, and lost American dreams. A walk on the wild side, that ended sadly with a court order, and Darren yelling a hundred and fifty feet away, "FUCK YOU, KALLI!!!"

Alcohol induced seizures, three brain surgeries, and acidosis slowly worked on Darren's early anticipated demise...leaving him reckless and questionably impaired. In this diminished capacity, with little challenge to his mind and body, he sought stimulation from the internet and camaraderie with other redundant, self-medicating men he welcomed into the safe haven of what a New Orleans aristocrat once called "an old world, walled sanctuary," my back yard.

Darren's only qualifications were that the men be further down life's road of despair, so he could feel superior and in control. His disability allotment, and his parent's good graces, provided what he called his "man cave" in Southern Oregon; only he preferred Portland's police tolerance for waywardness, easy access to liquor stores, and what he called my "candy-ass world," but, his heart belonged to Texas.

Born September 1961, he was brilliantly gifted, and a little off center, and an exceedingly entertaining distraction from the boredom of retirement, and the empty world my cat's death had left a few months before. My transient malaise brought a harsh reality of the evilness of the world and my unsuspecting vulnerability with the slow realization of the precariousness of risk, possibly even to my life. It ended in repeated efforts to secure my safety and the illegal, unintended transfer of my finances and assets.

Life had been kind to me. No wonder fifty-year-olds hit on me. I owned a home free and clear, beautifully furnished with antiques, silver, crystal and fine linens. I had a car, an income, no children and no close living relatives nearby. Freed of all these hard living stresses, along with simple rules to live by: regular hours, regular meals, exercise, a good night's sleep, surrounded by beauty, and joyful thankfulness to God for these blessings. All values and principles adamantly shunted by these reckless, homeless men.

Suddenly, my tranquility was dramatically altered with the arrival of the sweet-talking Texan. There were no more peaceful hours in my garden accompanied by hummingbirds, butterflies, and John Buddy circling my legs. It was dreams of bigger and better, unrealistic fears of accomplishments in music that spiced up his fantasy world, and this beautiful, fascinating man had my undivided attention.

At seventy, my San Francisco's image consultants produced an image that "looked rich" producing superficial readings of wealth, that Darren called "class," and the troubled state of my present affairs. That, and a too trusting tender heart, generous nature, and a champion of underdogs; but more so, I was bored, lonely, and timelessly out of my element, and maybe, just maybe, had a subconscious desire to try to fix broken...

I was the perfect mark!!!

Darren's two-year relationship with me gave him a superior edge. He could show off his classy benefactor's place, play "Lord of the Manor" he justified by some obscure Irish aristocracy pedigree in his mother's image. His father, half Cherokee, narrowly escaped Kentucky hillbillyism by joining the military to travel the world, retired as middle class in small town USA, fixating Darren's attitude of arrogance and superiority that reinforced his reign over his guests in my safe haven sanctuary.

All Democrats from middle class families with feelings of entitlements, they squandered resources--food, water, time, money, energy - completely contrary to my philosophy of thrift, productive use of time, abhorrence of waste, and hard gained polished veneer, working as a maid for "old money" in college, and rough edges taken off by a San Francisco modeling agency. This mixed with my impoverished blue collar roots (never forgotten) lent deep abiding empathy for the struggles these men had (I'd never known), and were having. They sensed my tolerance as weakness and vulnerability, and attempted to capitalize upon my generosity of heart.

Darren's slender, six-one, broad-shouldered perfection and part-time sunny disposition made it easy to succumb to his charms. His creative obsessions in construction and design corresponded beautifully with my artistic interior design and real estate background, further enhanced by our heritage recognition, Darren called "family."

Our strange relationship followed a predictable pattern. Weeks of uninterrupted togetherness, disagreeable partings, weeks of separation, and then a sort of wondering what went wrong, remembering the good times, then missing, then forgiving, and then a reunion. He would return and do projects, play heroic designer, build something for me, and then he would fall into his excessive, erratic drinking…frustrated that what he was building was not for himself, but for others. Exhausted, invariably sleep deprived, we would become disagreeable, part, then the cycle began again.

The first such homeless person, Lenny C. (born March 1961), whose new career, panhandling Oregon's I-205 southern corridor, took an abrupt turn when he intervened in an altercation between Darren and me (I thought equitably resolved), when I dumped Darren at the first rest stop heading south, after Darren, in bad boy mode, threatened to "snap your neck, murder you, steal your car." So I decided a two-hundred-mile-closed-capsule vehicle might be too dangerous for my life. Lenny rescued and played "Good Samaritan" among disgruntled parties: Darren, his family, and myself. As reluctant participant in what might have resulted in a serious siege of conscience, I felt an obligatory indebtedness to Lenny for rescuing Darren from my mean deed. I didn't want to hurt Darren, just protect myself against physical violence. As gratitude for his help, I offered a little reprieve (from the confines of Lenny's home, his car) in my sanctuary.

Lenny appeared like an angel. His consoling, Midwestern drawl for twenty-four hours, appeasing all our concerns, surprisingly matched the clean cut man who stepped out of a silver Camry, could easily have been FBI, or boy next door. Because of this, Lenny became an occasional road weary visitor whose insights opened avenues into Darren I didn't want to believe. Darren liked edgy women, blatantly advertising their sexual attributes, none of which I attempted to market. I aspired to understated elegance. Possibly the reason Lenny felt I was fair game. That ended our friendship abruptly, one such snowbound visit. It produced unwelcome advances that altered my perception of the Good Samaritan I found unacceptable. Despite Darren's affinities for lascivious young things, I remained loyal.

The second such person was a shorter, younger version of Lenny, Darren found at "Day Labor." He said, "George D. knows all the scams." Darren's grudging endorsement or approval of George's survival skills implied Darren knew a few himself. George, a chef of superior talent, finding a well-stocked kitchen, lovingly prepared delicacies long denied our pallets. My Fortune 500 interviewing skills from years past rose to the fore with curiosity about how these homeless men became homeless. These probes into their lives raised Darren's ire, either threatened or up-staged by my interest in George's story, or George's welcomed appreciation of my interest, caused Darren to resort to abusive denigration of my character; a strange reaction of illogical reasoning which increased George's protective defenses toward me and alienated Darren, certainly not the desired result he sought.

Darren's one night at what George called home, an abandoned potter's shack on OHSU property he could only access after dark, found this overgrowth of berry vines and rat infestation too primitive for Darren's elevated lineage. Regardless how well George cooked, the relationship was short lived.

The third, Gary Miller (born July 1948), Darren found, July 3, 2014, at Gary's estate sale. He came home excitedly insisting I go look at the free stuff. Reluctantly I complied. Gary's toothless, large, smelly, tobacco-stained, liquor-saturated body lay passed out on his bed in a disheveled tangle of despair, as his two cats watched cautiously from a perch above. His dirty feet and long toenails displayed a shocking dejection along with the rubble strewn about. My revulsion, as prospective beneficiary of his sad defeat, decreased my interest in the few nice pieces that Gary, when routed, said, "Take it all, I don't care!" We parted with several items, hopefully enough to squelch Darren's new obsession for acquisitions of stuff.

My position regarding stuff was, "It's the season to sell, not acquire." My home was filled with treasures, a testament to great acquisitions at incredible prices…often, free stuff. When Darren turned up hours later with the scruffy, Santa Claus-looking man, I was ready to eject, but a look into his sorrowful eyes did not lend muster to this thought. Abandoned by his wife, in the last stages of an eviction, the disabled steel worker had no place to go. I reasoned a diversion from Darren's undivided attentions might not be a bad thing. After a thorough cleansing and pruning, he was allowed to occupy one of my three bedrooms.

July 4th became August in a rapid succession of events. I got more free stuff and a diversion from Darren's attention, who was exhibiting strange obsessive-compulsive behavior. Acquisitiveness became compulsive stealing. His attitude toward Gary repeated the same scenario as George, with a different spin. Darren insisted Gary was "eating my food, drinking my liquor, ogling my lady,"…must leave. Gary and his two cats left. Darren went to jail for going berserk over my selling his recently acquired stuff in a garage sale. Gary and his cats returned. Darren got out of jail and returned with a better attitude towards Gary, who I interviewed during Darren's alcohol-induced catnaps, not classified as sleep, and faded away when Darren had others around.

The fourth, Roger Hobbs Richards (born February 1963), was discovered on August 4, 2014, during a walk to restock Darren's liquor. We stopped for lunch at an outdoor table and Darren spotted what he recognized as a man down on his luck, to whom he offered half his sandwich. He left me interviewing, while he continued on his way. Roger, a somewhat diminished, diminutive version of Darren, was surprisingly well kept for a man who had all his worldly possessions strapped on his bike. We shared honest, painful details of our lives, what one does with strangers one never expects to see again. He said he hadn't taken a shower in weeks, managed to sponge off at McDonald's, but it was hard to get really clean. By the time Darren returned, my generosity had overridden good judgment. I had the solution. He could shower at my place.

Now, there were three men among the hummingbirds, butterflies and two cats circling our legs. All amazingly domesticated; Gary shopped, Darren cooked, and Roger cleaned in between long bouts of what I came to recognize as an artificially induced oblivion in his sleeping bag on the living room floor. Gary contentedly snored in the guest room and Darren and I rotated in our usual fashion; like musical chairs through the two remaining bedrooms, trying to catch sleep in between his cycles of induced comas. He didn't consider sleep. He drank, napped, woke and began again – illogically insisting he never slept. And if the "Lord of the Manor" didn't sleep, nobody else should. I frequently sought the solace of the basement apartment for peace, tranquility and hopeful sleep.

Roger, so pleased to be off the street, could sleep through a war, and Gary's loud snores seemed to endorse this precept. My light sleeping patterns were exacerbated by all the activities above and fear of interruption by the "Lord of the Manor," so I couldn't relax to get to sleep, and depravation interfered with good humor, good judgment and yet, another desire for good riddance of Darren.

The men had much in common: all alpha males, all managers in their field, all talented builders accustomed to following plans and designs of other people's dreams. They were bright, physical, and energetic. My sanctuary reeked of excesses of testosterone and tale-topping laughter of their exploits, so entertaining it was almost delightful. With my real estate and interior design background, I felt like one of the guys, but Darren, on some level, didn't accept that role for me. So their complex, vying male interactions were acutely uncomfortable. I was ostracized from their inner circle of camaraderie.

At first Roger was like a chameleon. He slept unbelievable long hours with the most fascinating expression of enjoyment on his face, intermittently joining in the continuous recapture of life's building adventures at the round table outside my kitchen, where an unspoken seating position evolved. Gary's plump carcass stretched out on the chaise lounge close to the house, with a cat on his lap. I was across the table from Darren, and Roger, offset slightly behind Darren, who had a good view of me and side views of the others.

Darren smoked, drank and dominated the conversation. Gary drank and strained snuff through his beard and on to his belly, nodding appropriately and laughing agreeably. Roger was watchful. His strange, gray, wolf-like eyes took it all in, but mainly he seemed to be studying me. I redirected the conversation occasionally, trying to avoid being a target of interest, and rarely joined in. Darren probably read it differently and somehow perceived me as a threat to his alpha male manliness as top dog, creating an undercurrent of challenge. He wasn't having any part of what he knew was NOT passiveness, and continuously directed pot shots at me testing my ire...narrowly escaping caustic rebuttals.

Darren's greater class gave him grudging top dog status, however his inebriation and disparagement towards me failed to earn their respect which lent an awkward, questionable deference of power. When I did join in, Darren's efforts to show authority lobbed insults at me which made him look small in everybody's eyes. I was pleased to be freed of his single focus and my fulltime babysitting job, and stole away to my basement retreat for time alone and blessed sleep.

Darren's possessive obnoxiousness as "Lord of the Manor" increased daily. His world travel, sophistication, education, intelligence and more affluent circumstances, made him clearly feel above these commoners he found almost intolerable. The men's attentiveness to the real power at the sanctuary brought a repeated pattern of attacks on the object causing, what Darren believed, the dissension. He knew his efforts to keep the "lady" alpha female in her place would never have been allowed privately. But with an audience and to keep the peace, I acquiesced. His acrimonious, abusive verbal behavior rooted in what I believed some primal need for dominance, or....his hillbilly image.

Darren's visit began in late June under the guise of leaving for Texas on July's pay day, but he wanted me to accompany him as babysitter a la supreme, which I refused, so July came and went. My refusal extended his visit another month; reservations were finally made out of August pay day for September. Realizing the only way I was getting him out of my life was to take him to Texas, I promised to stay ten days, get him settled, and return home.

Darren's escalating fervor of emotions were reeling out of control, resulting in exchanges of unbelievable verbal assaults. At the outdoor table between us in our usual positions Darren, needing further affirmation of his alpha male role bragged he was doing his job, he was "fucking me." A final insulting "gloat" that rendered an acid tongue retaliatory remark I didn't believe capable of delivering, I harangued, "You were the worst lay I ever had!" Darren later confessed, was very, very hurtful.

After brooding a couple days, he delivered his rebuttal - a side-winding attack that found me alone, lounging vulnerably in Gary's place. Pummeled with vicious blows, I managed a kick that threw him backward. I followed with self-defensive efforts that left ripped clothes, cuts, bruises, and screams that brought men running. Yes, I fought back. He did not walk away unscathed, even though I feared any blow, with his history, might be fatal. A day later, another eruption with hurling furniture I threw in his path, to slow his pursuit, and another manly intervention. This progression of anger was not getting better, which procured Roger's comments, "You don't have to make the call, I will. When do you want to pull the plug?"

Later, while Darren sat in his usual position in an alcoholic haze, brooding, seemingly spoiling for another confrontation, I assessed the bruises on my body and knew...the time had come. Roger made the call. Two years ended badly. Darren, shuffling along in shackled pink pajamas, saying to the judge, "It was all in fun." Sadly my heart hurt for the unhappiness I caused everyone. Having never experienced this depth of depravity, it took gallons of wine, hummingbirds, butterflies and two loving cats, to soothe my injured soul, the abyss of my despair putting this poor, proud, angry, delusional, lost soul out of my life.

Immediately, a new dynamic developed. Gary cast adoring, soulful eyes. Roger sent propositional notes, and another arrived I could not decipher from whom...nor could I handle further confusion to my anguished heart. Roger peacefully slumbered, Gary bought more food, snored louder, and I wandered from room to room trying to erase reminders of Darren that might trigger forgiving memories I didn't want to experience. The little plaque Darren had given with much ado was hidden out of sight where I might find it someday and perhaps feel differently than my present, painful, raw, aching heart:

"I like being "us"
And I like being "we"
I like all the things
That we share…you and me
I like how you think
And I like what you do…
I don't like anyone,
More'n I like you!

September rolled into October and six weeks after the dust had settled on Darren and Gary's departure, the nightly interviews with Roger turned into a too soon, too intimate, too vulnerable, drunken haze of guilt ridden confusion, the likes I'd certainly never planned for my waning years. Days became months of Roger's unveiling story, and my confusing quest for direction and purpose In lIfe. Red flags sprinkled the new landscape… minor slips painted an entirely different picture of the Boy Scout he was attempting to sell. Roger, a big time jewel thief, was on parole for Felony Theft and heroin addiction and was in an out-patient rehab program; an explosive combination of possibilities and complications along with evidence I was reluctant to acknowledge, and if it were conclusive, knew not what to do.

His skills, in total defiance of my loudly proclaimed complaint of Darren's (maybe he heard), he was doing his damnedest to refute any such complaint on his part. Other skills evidenced themselves and might have been an equalizing redeemer, of emerging material facts. His finish carpentry skills argued with my unrelenting concerns about his demons. My blue collar, practical, Libra fairness tried to balance right and wrong against my appreciation of his multitude of talents. While the motives inspiring the mutually beneficial relationship continued, an undercurrent of grating mistrust thwarted any possibilities of anything more. Insurmountable obstacles – his undisciplined penchant for heroin, his continued street connections and bad boy inclinations, values, education, class--were too great to ignore. Early on he confessed, "I'm not accustomed to being around good people like you."

He resisted all pearls of wisdom and therapeutic efforts to adjustments that might help overcome his demons. His Out-patient Rehab status was doing nothing to change the direction of his life. His preferences centered on his pursuit of euphoric escapism and heightened pleasures that were not realistic. He made senseless, wrong choices, rebelling against all principles of healthy living, and seemed to relish his strong affinity to a NETWORK that victimized elderly citizens, which concerned me.

Energies drained from betrayal of my warring conscience and instincts, sensing all was not right – invariably diverted from prolonged consideration of logical deductions by Roger's manufactured crisis. A multitude of missing items running concurrent with his arrival were becoming too prevalent to ignore. When questioned he blamed Darren, who to my knowledge had never stolen anything from me, and excused with bland face denial all other possibilities, placing responsibility everywhere, except where evidence was leading.

Exhausted from my efforts, I gave up trying to have any semblance of influence on his life or a shared relationship. I looked honestly at what was occurring, and started taking measures of survival for my existence. The realization that the chaotic, diversionary tactics were manipulations, and I needed to hone my chess playing skills; he, was, several moves ahead of me. His motives were evil, but his heroin-altered state camouflaged an honest read of what he was really communicating. He was narrowly tolerating me; lying, cheating, stealing and plotting my demise – and estate take over – the reason the relationship lasted so long.

I was actually not an easy mark. I stopped leaving him alone at the house. I stopped giving him my schedule or telling him when I would return, frequently surprising him, and laid traps he sprung and angrily discovered. I only left when I knew he would be away. I concluded the direction of this crisis-driven relationship had a sinister goal that was getting scary.

As winter turned to spring, the widening gap of disparage became evident. He exhibited defiance to all aspects of healthy living. On the one hand, his "street" connections beckoned him in an empowerment of grandiosity – he laughingly related and thrived on their fetes. He said he liked being around them, it made him feel superior. A somewhat anarchist evil presence permeated all his motives.

The NETWORK of connections had been introduced casually over the months as he told stories about his territory and his mafia affiliations and pointed out locations and places of elderly citizens being victimized by this NETWORK of criminals. He developed thinly disguised menacing tolerance toward me. Anger bubbled just below the surface. I moved him into the RV – the first step to getting him completely out of my life. On the one hand his Boy Scout "sell" distracted my focus – he knew all the cons I refused to process until the glaring connection of dots made unadulterated sense.

He'd say one thing but he did another, his duplicity predictable. If he said he hadn't been snooping in my drawers, he had! If he said he had an opportunity to steal business records and create havoc, but didn't, he had! If asked to do something contrary to his wishes, he made sure he sabotaged in unsuspecting ways. He liked to leave subtle clues of evidence an unsuspecting person would overlook. You had to understand his criminal mind to follow the nuance of his reasoning. Thankfully, a college course in Criminology, married to a locksmith who followed along behind criminals, and a thirty year friendship with a steely-eyed San Francisco detective, made me less trusting when I finally understood his game.

With prideful candor he bragged about his successful ploys. He said, "Always repeat the same story then you don't screw it up. Never give too much detail." Plausible denial was his favorite. He said, "It has to be believable." Declarative elaborate explanations was another, obviously rehearsed, but rang of Shakespeare observations. "Thou protest too much," confirmed guilt. Towards the end, he could hardly contain his anger. He slammed banged kitchen utensils and slopped food in destructive ways with such intensity it was obvious he was having a hard time constraining his true feelings.

When the gloves came off and it hit, the intensity of Roger's attack was on all fronts. The internet, the phone lines, every detail of my life had been tampered with; my business and personal files, my estate plans, the order of my life turned into a shambled array of chaos. His religious and spiritual touts were almost demonic. While he touted faith and goodness his behavior spoke volumes to the contrary. The only time he attended his Adventist faith was at my insistence. Hardly in the door, like a devil, he swore in the vestibules in an unusual manner, looking to create trouble for an exit strategy. He obviously was not a believer. He only gave lip service to such. The seven deadly sins were his mantra's to live by, a joyous relishing of evilness. In a moment of truth he declared the demons were fallen angels with a glow in his eyes that smote of evil reality. The message I thought he conveyed, "You finally figured it out. Didn't you?"

When I refused to take his advice regarding the sale of my home, "Take the money and run," he advised, I explained, it was my money to win or lose this market, not his, and considering where his money management had gotten him I didn't think his advice was sound. His diversionary tactics suddenly became brazenly fast and furious, narrowly contained menacing when conclusive evidence screamed for attention to the contrary. He made statements, "I want things, I just go about getting them the wrong way," "You should be careful who you allow in your home," And "You know more about me than anybody, you know too much," a seeming veiled threat. More perversion, the one thing he said he disliked most about me, "I DIDN'T TRUST HIM."

No fires were put out, only new ones burning. My denial, so long put off, brought about brazen efforts to attract my attention to challenge his activities, I duly noted. I was overwhelmed and unsuspecting far too long. Too much had occurred. I didn't know where to begin. He was empowered with electronic surveillance. I knew my phones were tapped. He'd added all kinds of devices. He knew details he shouldn't have and made counter moves accordingly. Since he knew all my password and security codes, I was overwhelmed with the onslaught of attacks and interference. His vulture NETWORK waiting in the wings for me to topple, when he thought I was ready to go down. The situation was out of control seemingly begging for confrontation. When the facts could no longer be denied (he over played his hand when he tampered with my guns), I blindsided him with an unanticipated restraining order – ousted, shut down, shut out. Then the real trouble began. It was open warfare.

Outraged, thwarted, that his mark was proving so difficult, his reentry efforts were blatant and perverse. Knowing my penchant for privacy, reclusiveness, and lack of communications with neighbors and the outside world, Roger could pop a lock quicker than my locksmith ex-husband. One of his NETWORK connections was a locksmith, so he could access at will against my predictable schedule and lifestyle. Almost anytime I left he entered and left tale-tell evidence of his presence, which continued. His anger and glaring effrontery of destruction is beyond belief; an anarchist totally bent on my death and destruction, probably because I'm a registered Republican.

The police do nothing. His parole officer, a woman says, "Keep self-advocating." My friends and relatives are too busy with their own lives to worry about mine, so I'm pretty much on my own. I'm armed and uncertain what I will do if the choice is between my survival and his. I've never experienced a greater force of evil. I'm surprised God lets him live. I daily await his next attack and hope and pray I survive the nightmare. God only knows. Regrettably, Roger Hobbs Richards is obsessed with my take down...unfortunately it is real and no one believes me...and I know he's not finished yet.

August 11, 2015 Dear Clancy, So much has happened. Thirty days from closing on one house to closing on another--Portland 6/30/15, Sierra Mountains 7/30/15--I'm living in hillbilly hell. My neighbors are all clinging to their guns and their religion. Makes me kind of long for Portland left wing activists.

The owl hoots, crickets chirp, frogs croak, dogs bark, something else screeches and the roosters crow at 4:30. in the morning...makes me long for MAX running through my bedroom all day long.

My very successful nephew who owns several self-storage businesses in Bakersfield, Fresno, Visalia, and Porterville lives a couple miles down the road...his mailbox has a rifle over it that says, "We don't call 911."

I bought a house directly across the street from his twenty-five-year-old son, and my lot backs up to a river and a very steep mountain at the end of a cul-de-sac...no one comes down these country roads that shouldn't ought to. I feel very safe with my arson of guns in this neighborhood...hopefully the "super predators" can't find me...or find it...not worth their time.

Well, my present crisis is sandwitching 1650 square feet of stuff into 640 square feet, which is virtually undoable, but what do we really need. More...only gets us in trouble, as well knows the "Reluctant Landlord."

I would be interested in reading your re-write of your first book, The Grounding of Rosey Colored Glasses...some seemingly paranoia terror scenes in that I couldn't relate to then, but I can now. Preying on the elderly in transition is "big business" and I believe even the protective agencies are in on it. I noticed this marginally when I was a Notary Public, but this recent experience is shocking...how much more damage could they do to someone less competent?

You were the only one who understood. You expressed your understanding at my open house. You "got it." They want to make you think you're a crazy, menopausal, old lady when you're actually a victim of the system. You'll never know what your understanding meant to me at that moment in my life. Thank you!

It's all so strange living in cowpoke country. There's a restaurant less than a mile from me called the "Cowpuncher." Can you believe that? I can't! This lifestyle transition is overwhelmingly challenging. I'm not sure I can make the cut, hiding out in some deadwood town in the Sierra's. Don't count me out! Kalli O'Keefe PS When you respond please type. I can't read your handwriting.

August 18, 2015, Dear Kalli:Your letter was wonderful – describing another world, so remote from anything I have ever known. I couldn't tolerate it. I would crash. Your effort to escape from seekers and takers of tiny lifetime nest eggs – a house, a piece of stock, wheels, or a has-to-be-vague influence with a power magnet – can trigger extremists to destroy our comfort zone and more.

For me, my son and grandchildren have insisted that I do not escape. That I submit to the required treatments for crazy old ladies, quit the battle, cease and desist my effort to explain it to others, water my roses every day, accept the city's handouts at lunch time and celebrate TriMet.

But I have fooled them. In this world I have made peace with, I have found gorgeous, fun, stimulating persons like yourself. They keep me strident and filled with optimism for not only me but the human race, in spite of the republican, and some democrats as well, sell outs in congress.

Even today Kalli, so many emotions like j'accuse or fear or suspicions are not acceptable. But they are caused, triggered by others' actions. They don't just happen out of the blue. As children, even with the boogie man in the dark of our going to bed were told, "foolishness, no such thing" when the sophisticated electronics can send sublimated messages – voices into our space and images of lighted shadows and ghosts into our dense dark. A Filipino priest with the Oregon Archdiocese recently placed a camera into the women's bathroom of his parish church in a small town. Weirdoes have access to the most advanced equipment that intrude and disturb, including remote controlled Drones. Of course, law enforcement pooh poohs. "Why would we be chosen? You and I are nothings! Where's the motive?" Whereas the criminal mind can't resist even the smallest of caches and what appears to be an easy rip-off.

I am encouraged by the bits of progress I see. A stupid doctor insisted to me, "Never let your son sleep in your bed with you." I resentfully obeyed him. My son and his wife have placed no such restrictions on their three. They're growing up very happy. Their fears have been believed. They have been trusted. Their perceptions are not sheer nonsense. Maybe their courage to express innermost thoughts will enable them to brave the storms as you continue to do. After all, particles travel faster than light.

You have been honest in divulging dishonesty. I have attempted to do so myself in examining some of my past in this book, owning up to successes but examining failures as well. Having been there seems to empower me to recognize the best of all possible worlds, which has been gifted to me these last days of my time on earth. I learn the hard way. In spite of practice in the scientific method, trial and error seems to produce results.

I have changed your name to Kalli – give me a last name to use – because I don't think you want me to use your real name – although another fellow who I also have permission to tell about wants me to use his real name. What name do you want me to use for you?

And always, Clancy Rohring – see enclosed new card. 60th high school reunion in September so I had these made to give out to my fellow alums to promote my books.

This is my first impulsive response to your beautifully put and yet, succinct efforts – I want to get it back to you quickly so will not dwell further. Tell me your birthday and give me your initial interpretation of our impossible horoscopes – that was fun and a totally inaccurate prediction. Thanks for ignoring it or at least overriding It. August 24, 2015, 4:41 AM – yes, I'm a morning person but not usually this early – I slept all day Sunday – haven't done that for months – but all slept out about 2 AM this morning – took a shower and hit the PC – feel great. Clancy.

September 3, 2015 Dear Kalli, The fifth or sixth time through your treatise something began to stand out so I will share it with you because I am puzzled by it.

You have said that these crooks, these evil men, picked on you because you were a republican and they were democrats. And you describe yourself as blue collar, from humble beginnings, but now with independent income – due to hard work--an above average education, with building, designer and financial skills, law abiding, relies on her God, generous and honest. (In your house I did admire the bookcases, tables and dressers you built out of scraps. Yes, I can see how you got sucked in by a talented finish carpenter. It is a shock to see talent go to waste.)

I know lots of democrats like you! Were you destined by those factors to be a Republican? If not, why do you choose to be republican? Did the slob of a steelworker say he is a democrat? Did the lying and thieving heroin addict terrorizing you, say he was a democrat? Most Texas and Texas lovers these days are republican. Did your bi-polar veteran with the, as you describe it, superiority complex, say he was a democrat? The reason I ask, I'm a democrat and I'm more like you, a republican, I think, than them!

If they didn't believe in God maybe, did that make them democrats? Or maybe, if they were not Christians like you are, does that make them democrat? Or the fact that they were not law abiding? Or they believe in taking from the rich or that democrats are the homeless and freeloaders and republicans employed and responsible?! Is that it?

Am I to conclude from your report that democrats are evil and republicans are good? That there is a natural war between the two kinds? My final question, since you are these wonderful traits which you feel made you exploitable, Are all republicans like you? Are all republicans then at the mercy of criminals and evil democrats? Is this the only difference between them? Do republicans never get addicted to drugs and become thieves?

In all your interviewing, what do you recall in their childhood or education that made them fall out of grace, turn bad? By your offer of a hot shower and a roof over their head, should these derelicts have turned you down? If they had been republicans would they have said, "No, thanks." Or maybe republicans are never derelict!

In your defense, unwary, intelligent counselors have fallen madly in love with convicted killers serving life sentences. A female prison guard in New York recently got sucked in by two convicted killers who used her to escape.

I stayed in a marriage with a man who didn't love me because my mother who I loved and honored didn't believe in divorce. In addition, I'm sure she had no confidence in me to be on my own. Little did she know my sixty-five hours per week kept the wheels turning. I never told her I didn't even sleep with him for more than ten years. He was a rabid republican and a freeloader.

You have paid a high price for your extension of generosity towards the down and out. You have admitted your motive, boredom and curiosity. (I see it as intellectual curiosity – that always sacrifices one's good health.) I was relieved that you joined your sister. She loves you and is good to you. You need more good friends like her and me.

My new acquaintance, Mary, 69, recently unemployed as a nursing instructor, read your explanation. She said you are very intelligent and a masterful writer. She reads murder mysteries – three last weekend – loved the battle of wit and emotion (the power struggle) between yourself and the bi-polar Texas lover.

If you were in Portland I'd insist you do three things. Since you belong to Kaiser, join a Silver Sneakers at a health and athletic club for the social events – to meet people.

Attend E.P.I.C. at East Precinct police department one Wednesday night per month for criminal data and presentations of police projects sponsored by the commander there on SE 108th.

And start writing your heart out. Use the houses and streets you've lived in – use SFO as a backdrop. You've done a great close-up quick study of a criminal mind. Make it pay dividends for you. Self-publish. If it's good enough agents will seek you out.

You also qualify age wise for Meals on Wheels. Look them up and volunteer. Look for a book club or a writing group where you can get feedback. Anyone spins in the same rut without places to go, people to see, and objectives like a book to write.

Chalk this harrowing ordeal up to mere experience. Is it actually any different than when Somerset Maugham went to India, or Hemingway ran with the bulls, or the author of Moby Dick struggled with a whale? The struggles of good versus evil are classics, never ending, totally human. Your story and our honesty with each other is a priceless addition to *Clancy's Romp, Wrangle, & Warble* which emphasizes my two years, seventy-six to seventy-eight, but describes special experiences and friendships throughout my life, including ours.

Thanks again for reading The Grounding of Rosey Colored Glasses. I don't think I will ever publish it. It's too sad. I prefer to share mostly the happy times, or at the least the ironic, not the frustration of a doomed relationship as described in Hemingway's The Sun Also Rises. Yours ends happy but does put you into another setting definitely ripe for a story. You're foot loose and fancy free once again. Hallelujah! Praise the Lord and pass the ammunition.

You need people – good people. Everybody does, whether they admit it or not. They're out there – to bounce your ideas off of, exchange, to cry with, to hope with and for. You were so wonderful and encouraging with the young Tri-O college graduates.

Lindsay, because he is an author, wants me to use his real name in my book. Do you want me to use your real name – already, I have changed the names of all the men, including the vet – I call him Darren. In the meantime I'm calling you Kalli O'Keefe, to retain the Irish of it. Let me know.

I have three pages re my sister. She told me to call her Matilda. She's blond and blue-eyed. Her oldest daughter's $95,000 per year career ended with the excruciating pain of MS. Her son, a graduate nurse with wife and two sons, had sudden death at 35. Her youngest was born with scoliosis but swam competitively. Tilly blamed herself for many years (she had her at 39) until she found out it was genetic when a cousin moved into town with that same affliction in the family. In college this third child worked as a courier. A bike was her first vehicle for that job until she could afford a car. At her wedding at the big town's country club, she wore a strapless gown with a huge V scrolled on her humped shoulder for "Victory." They have two children. She now has a responsible position at a hospital.

Matilda continues on so strong, maybe because her husband, Tony – technically advanced, an under par golfer, sought after socially, always with a fun anecdote for joy or laughter, (he shares how he flubbed the dub and can laugh at his faux pas)--loves her out of an undying passion. I have envied his devotion to her from its very beginning, in their teens. He chose her as the one and only and never once doubted his selection. She knew he would always take care of her and their loved ones. Her closing advice to each of us at departure time is, "Take care." And always, Clancy PS Strangely enough, we're still debating democrat versus republican – the constant battle I guess can't be avoided. Each person's interpretation of it is the essence, our why?! Actually, change is probably the only Constant we can count on, and of course, our God.

I hang in there for you because you're a fighter, in search for goodness and reasons for your existence. Also, you believe in man's interdependence, "No man stands alone." People need each other. For me, "Each man's joy is joy to me, each man's grief is my own" – some men more than others.

I regretted somewhat the logic I toughed out to Kalli in my letter of September 3rd and hoped she wouldn't just be offended by it. Her letter of September 12, 2015 below indicated that indeed she bounced back and up to undertaking her future with vigor and energy. Included in the manila envelope were three chapters already describing a match made in heaven. She's aiming for the romance market, it appears.

And one page is about a small figurine, an angel that keeps falling off her shelf and breaks. Its beautiful head falls off. She keeps gluing it back together, so attached to it she has become. A tragic and forlorn allegory

I see. She does not interpret – making it even more poignant, just describes actions. In any event, her letter is upbeat and supportive.

Dear Clancy: Kalli O'Keefe sounds just fine. Got to get a touch of the Irish into the mix, to understand the powerful heritage recognition impact on this story, which created trust, empathy and understanding that wouldn't have happened with other American mongrels.

Darren was brilliant, the most gifted, talented, creative, handsome piece of perfected humanity I've ever met. A great sense of humor, he loved music and he loved people. Exceptionally coordinated and graceful, with natural rhythm and artistic ability, needless to say he was good with his hands.

He was sweet, sensitive, poetic and romantic and loved togetherness. He was everything I could have ever wanted in a man and I'm not certain he was a part of this network of crooks. I'm working on finding out with a psychic…a whole other chapter in this book of Kalli O'Keefe.

I'm enclosing the first couple of chapters for you to munch on and hopefully share the significance of his impact on my life…hopefully, not just hustling some lil' ol' lady. Darren came into my life August 2012, Gary came July 4, 2014, and Roger arrived one month later. Darren is very trusting and loves people, and opens himself up for opportunities to be taken advantage of. Because of this, these other two, well that is another story completely.

Roger, the heroin addict, is a total and utter anarchist who thrives on destruction and overthrowing order in people's lives. I'm not certain how Gary fits into this plot, but he was in it up to his eyebrows. I kicked him out when this became apparent. Hopefully, this was not all Darren's masterminding such a scenario…but, I will soon have answers. Now that I am safe and tucked away in hillbilly heaven, I can fight and write from afar.

I will be in Portland in October to finalize some business and will track you down for a POW WOW. I now have a cell phone (568) 421-5863, but must talk to me in person. Don't know how to retrieve messages or text, yet. I'm traveling by train.

You amaze me. You are such an original thinker. It is such a pleasure to be around people who think outside the box. Too bad you've labeled yourself a "DEMOCRAT." I think you're a REPUBLICAN in sheep's clothing. Your friend, Kalli O'Keefe Enclosures

Part Four

The Extra Large Portion

AMAZING PEOPLE IN MY LIFE are forever here. Although some loved ones are deceased, our relationships remain active, still in transition. From my point of view it grows and improves.

My mother and I got off to a bad start. Upon my arrival, my grandfather, the honorable Herbert D. Rolph, the Speaker of the House of the Montana legislature (for ten years at that time), walked me when I continually bawled as if I was in pain. I was. Born at home, the veterinarian who delivered me, a supposed friend of my father's, sutured my tongue to the bottom of my mouth, inviting great pain. Sucking was an excruciating undertaking. It had been a long and painful labor for my mother, an otherwise healthy, five foot four, one hundred and ten pound private duty registered nurse for a member of a highly respected family, twenty-four years old. In her eighties I persisted in describing my mom as strong, sturdy and stalwart. I weighed in at eleven pounds, eleven ounces at birth, in early summer of 1937.

Critics have asked me why the veterinarian did it? I can speculate but, after all, this is nonfiction. It's for real. It happened. The why is in history along with lots of real events. It happened without an explanation, the cause to remain forever a perplexing mystery. Remember I retain odd statements and strange behaviors which don't provide explanations until further information might expose or provide missing pieces to solve the puzzle and satisfy questions; sometimes to the degree that I can finally report the cause of the incidents, even to the degree that might explain my own erratic and "unstable" reactions at the time.

With my secret condition, uttering only guttural sounds for nineteen months, a doctor finally found the cause of my handicap, clipped my tongue loose from its prison and I rolled out sentences with a slight clip.

Later on I justified my twang by suggesting it was probably an accent superimposed by my great-grandmother, Mary Clancy Gau, an immigrant from Ireland, a lifetime maid at the Armour estate in south side Chicago, where she met the postman, a Prussian Jew, who gave her six children, all of whom went on to college. Her second child, Jesse Gau, my mother's mother, taught high school and coached a Michigan State championship girls' basketball team in 1908 in Hancock in the north woods. She homesteaded Montana with my grandfather in 1909. Her brother, an attorney, employed at Glacier county court, welcomed their arrival. After bringing forth eight children, she served as postmaster for Glacier County.

My mother was ecstatic when I came out of my room to greet friends who were visiting on a Friday night for a card game, exercising my newfound freedom, "Daddy, I don't believe I've met these folks."

Before I was given freedom from my affliction, I failed to follow instructions, stood in my highchair and tried to extract myself from its confines, twisted around and crashed backwards into a glass plate of bacon. I not only shattered the dish but split the back of my skull open, which required stitches.

To avoid the veterinarian and the trauma associated with her first born, my mother traveled to Chester, where her uncle George Gau was a Clerk of the Court, to give birth to my brother and sister. The day after my first birthday, in June, my brother was born. The following year after our back to back June birthdays, our little sister was born in July. Growing up together so close in age was a heck of a lot of fun. We still talk with each other almost every week ongoing.

My father, manager of the local state liquor store, built a chain link fence around our huge, mostly level yard, but located on a hillside, to keep us kids safe. At the top of the hill was the airport and weather station. For years, our town, Cut Bank, often registered as one of the coldest spots in the nation. But honestly, I don't recall ever being cold. At the bottom of our street was the main highway leading to town, twenty miles west of Shelby, a Shell Oil refinery town. The football field, with lights and a grandstand, served as an ice rink in the winter time, sat just across the highway. Across our street at the bottom of the hill sat the large home of the local attorney.

My dad had trouble keeping me inside the fence. I have no idea what prompted me to want to explore beyond that fence. I crawled under the gate to the front walk and headed down the hill before I uttered a sound. So he lowered the gate. Then I crawled over the gate. Always learning the hard way, I got as far as the trailer house on the attorney's property. A bull dog scurried away from me and ducked under the trailer. I remember stooping to see him. She had little puppies. I scooted on my stomach to get closer to them.

I woke up on the kitchen counter. I hurt. My mother was patching me up. The bull dog had bitten my butt and I must have passed out.

My dad built a playhouse for us, out the kitchen door, and a table to match the three chairs he had purchased, which he painted red. At ten years my blonde, blue-eyed sister would still set her dolls on those three red chairs at the table and play mother. She would make up stories for them.

Matilda became a fastidious employee and housekeeper, a devoted mother and a first rate, very honest financial manager, serving as Treasurer for several community organizations. A natural leader, so reliable, she was elected president in high school not only for the leading service club, Kle Koe, but later for the popular social club, HiKiKi. My mother loved the role of parent advisor to each of them. My sister wisely shared her school life and romances with my mother. Oddly enough I didn't relate my life's adventures to anyone. I admit it didn't dawn on me to do so. I was a sounding board and keen observer of much human effort but kept what I saw and heard mostly within.

The republicans came to power in Montana in 1940, an overreaction to the New Deal, and grandfather in favor of public power and cooperative organizations, out of office, hired on as Vice President for the innovative National Farmers Union and went on the road. Shortly my dad was replaced by the state liquor commission with a republican. A WWI veteran and fifteen years older than my mother he struggled to find work and became very ill as a security guard outdoors in subzero temperatures. They asked the attorney to be responsible for selling their property. Dad sold his Ford and in 1943 they packed up and moved to Portland for work in the shipyards. The shipyards didn't check the health history of their workers at the time so Dad and Mom, both able, got on at Albina. Human Resource Manager Brownstein became friends of our family.

On Dad's days off he introduced us kids to card games and board games. He took me to tap dance lessons and bought a board for me to practice on so as not to scratch the flooring in our defense house on NW Quimby, between 21st and 22nd avenues. We didn't have a radio so he whistled songs for me to practice with. His favorite song for my mother was "Red Roses for a Blue Lady."

When my brother and sister were in nursery school, he would take me with him wherever he went – shopping at Fred Meyers on 20th & Burnside where I saw my first donut deep fried, Wimpy's bar on 21st and Overton with a long dark mahogany layout and huge mirror, pinball machines, friendly customers and bartender. Dad would order one shot, buy a cigar to take with him (I never saw him smoke) and a horehound candy for me, maybe a Coke, I don't recall. We weren't there long. For Easter he took me downtown to Olds & King's to purchase a gold cross on a chain for me.

As a family, on Sundays, we walked up Vista to the Zoo and Rose Gardens. In his last days, Dad took the trolley from Burnside up the hill; walking, we would meet him at the top. During the war we attended the Montana State picnics at huge Pier Park in North Portland. I recall other states gathering at the same time and place: North and South Dakota, Arkansas, Minnesota, Colorado, Idaho, Oklahoma, and surely some more southern states. My folks found people they knew or had mutual acquaintances.

My dad was social. He liked people and made friends easily. He signed up with the Minnesota Division when he was fifteen. In France he was hit by German gas at the border so spent time in a medical tent with others diagnosed with supposed pneumonia. Associates considered him "worldly." He had worked most of his life as an oil dresser in the oil fields; first in his native Indiana, then followed the action from Houston, Texas, to Calgary, Canada. His library included Poetry by Tennyson, Wordsworth, a worn Shakespeare, Emerson, the complete works of George Eliot, A Bartender's Cocktails, Hoyle's Rules for Card Games and several How-To-Build books. My mom kept the Savings Bonds he had invested. She cashed them to pay tuition for my first year of college.

At the V.A. hospital he looked emaciated, so awful it was too painful for me to see him again following my first time at his bed side. That last visit, I stayed in the car to avoid my pain when mom went to see him. I didn't know he was going to die. Mom said he was disappointed I did not come. Associated as a Mason, he was baptized and given the last rites by a Catholic chaplain before he died. "Walt said I'll become Catholic because of my good wife, Mary," Mom said. That was March 30, 1945.

I was seven but turned eight at the beginning of that summer. When alone, I cried a lot and felt sorry for myself. I missed him. My father left me with good feelings for him and for myself. I searched for more of him in his books and found him in Harvard Classics Volume 5: Essays and English Traits by Emerson c1909, he had penciled:

In the chapter Self Reliance, on page 64, "Great works of art...teach us to abide by our spontaneous impression with good-humored inflexibility..." And on page 84, "Insist on yourself; never imitate." In Compensation, page 100, "Always pay; for first or last you must pay your entire debt..." On page 105, "The soul refuses all limits. It affirms in many always an Optimism, never a Pessimism. His life is a progress, not a station." On page 201 in Character, "Nature never rhymes her children, nor makes two men alike."

No wonder my father and mother loved each other so much. They were soul mates.

Shortly on a Sunday, Mom took us on the Greyhound bus to Kalama, Washington, to visit dad's older brother, Ray, a farmer with five children older than us, and view property on the very top of a hill; most of his days were spent as a longshoreman on the Columbia River docks. On the first trip I got suddenly sick to my stomach, probably motion sickness. Mom was unprepared. I slid the window open and sent my vomit into the wind. It blew back against the windows of the passengers behind. My mother was "fit to be tied." I use a favorite expression of hers to describe her mortification.

A huge man of few words with red hair and blustery complexion, Uncle Ray invited me to the barnyard to watch him behead a chicken for dinner. It flitted blood and itself wildly between the fence rails. I didn't squeal. He let me know he approved of my lack of theatrics. I recall how happy Uncle Ray was for me at my wedding. One of his daughters, June, just graduated from high school, stayed with us a few days to find a job in the city. Hired at First Interstate Bank, June eventually became a vice president and married a longshoreman.

His wife, Aunt Maude, lived a long life. She was burdened with enormous breasts but retained an erect posture and carried them and herself proudly. Into her old age aided by excellent foundations, she would stride forth firmly, shoulders back and squared without a cane or walker – eyes lively and attentive – responsive to the current actions of others.

On one occasion, at Uncle Ray's, we got to meet my father's father, John, of full wit at ninety-five. A German immigrant who farmed in Indiana his entire life, John spoke fluent English without an accent. His third wife was with him and had given him a fifth child. He had children by three wives. My father's mother, Anne Fox, an English school teacher, died at his birth. Grandpa was good looking like my father: firm jaw, wide brow, lively blue eyes, smiled wide and readily, exchanging with enthusiasm. He was with it and delighted with his son's widow and children. This trip to the northwest was important for all of us, including him, because he died before he turned ninety-six.

That same year, still just eight years old, two redheaded twin neighbor boys in their early teens from Mississippi asked me if I wanted to do what Rita Watson was doing with them in a hole under the cut timber pile in the vacant lot on 22nd Avenue next to the Tucker coffee plant. One of them put his index finger to the end of his thumb to form a hole and then poked his third finger from his other hand through the hole. Strangely enough I figured what was going on and said "No!" and ran home and told my mother. She was befuddled, said the family was "white trash" and "rednecks." Thereon Rita grew a very huge belly and I knew how she got that way.

We had some wonderful neighbors, like the Farrells from Ft. Collins, Colorado, who went back there when the war ended. Their son went to Benson; he intended to become an engineer. They had an electric refrigerator instead of an ice box and would give me ice cubes on hot summer days. The Kuhns from Moses Lake –their son Buddy was a friend of mine. (We played army in the vacant lot in the middle of the four-unit defense houses with other neighbor kids our age). His mom, Zelda, always acted like my mom was trying to take her husband away from her. I went to her funeral thirty years later with my mom and bawled when they sang, "Going Home," a wretchedly magnificent song, but mostly because that lady hurt my mom terribly. I never told my mom why I cried.

Sometimes my mother complained that she was not comfortable socially. "Being the oldest, I worked," she said, "no time for play." She scrubbed floors to put herself through nursing school at Sacred Heart in Havre. She scored at 100% in Medicine on the Montana State Board nursing exam. She wanted her kids to have time for fun and friends. Her beloved brother, a year younger, died at twelve as the result of a plow accident. The horse got spooked, causing the plow to gouge the entire length of his leg. Mom kept his obituary in a valuable leather-bound edition of Imitation of Christ, which she gave me before she died. I gave the book to my son's wife, a devout Catholic who was close to my mother, after she brought forth my first grandchild, an amazing girl.

We learned to swim, ice skate and team sports. My brother, in the third grade, was in a boxing smoker organized by Joe Kahut, a former professional heavyweight. CYO team sports gave us all an early start. Soon we all belonged to the Knot Hole Gang and saw the Beavers free from Center Field on Friday evenings.

My mother was thankful for the organized boxing event, because three months prior, Luke had laid into a kid at 5:00 AM on Sunday morning when Mom went with him to roll the *Oregonian* newspapers my seven-year-old brother had to pack on his back, walking. The kid had said, "What's wrong with your old man? Too lazy, so your old lady has to do it?" My brother was resentful without his dad. Mom pulled the two boys apart. They didn't dare swing again. For sure, the punches would have landed on Luke's mother.

Mom did run track in high school. When Mom's father, Grandpa Rolph, came to town they would go to a Beaver ball game. They usually sat behind third base. At one game, in the heat of the summer, the dry wood in front of them smoldered and caught fire. He quickly doused it with a beer. Wintertime they rooted for the hockey team, Portland Eagles; Jim Ward, Sr., a Stanley Cup player, moved to Portland from Montreal.

It was a celebration when Grandpa Rolph visited us. In the old days, in Montana winters, he had operated a short order restaurant in their town Joplin, a Great Northern rail stop. He did all the cooking. For our breakfast he made sour dough pancakes with lots of butter and hot, homemade maple-flavored syrup. For supper he brought Russian Rye, Liverwurst, Limburger cheese, sauerkraut and dill pickles, horseradish and mustard, and Schlitz beer. He grew up in Oshkosh, Wisconsin, but worked summers in the paper mill at Oregon City in his teens to send money home to his family, his aunt. His favorite project in Oregon was his oyster stew. For that one, us kids turned our nose up.

From a Catholic family, as a little guy, he tap danced in fund raisers for the Salvation Army. He would demonstrate his tap dancing when he had the time. What fun! After high school he got a diploma from Oshkosh Business School. Shortly after the war, Grandpa took us to Montana in his road-wise Chrysler to celebrate Christmas with two brothers and three sisters, still in Montana, and cousins our age.

In my fourth grade, for Valentine's Day, Mom paid for all fourteen in my class to ice skate on a Saturday at the arena on 20th and Marshall then come to our house for homemade cookies and punch. I remind myself here that Mom cooked and baked in Portland on a coal stove until I was twelve, with first class results. In Montana she had a gas range, electric refrigerator, and a radio. Handsome and happy Delbert Pedro, from Mexico just that year, wrote "I love you" on his valentine card to me. The teacher went down the aisles to look at each student's cards we had received. I was happy but embarrassed and afraid what she would think when she saw what Delbert wrote in pencil, so I quickly erased it. After she checked mine I regretted what I had done and wished I could have it back to show my mom.

On Mom's vacation that summer, Grandpa took us to visit my mom's youngest sister at their wheat ranch just south of the Canadian border. Aunt Dolly was married to a fifth generation, Scandinavian, a semolina, hard wheat farmer. I rode their pinto pony. Dolly warned he was ornery. In the corral he consistently tried to rub me off against the fence boards, so I swung that leg onto his mane. That didn't work, so he went hell bent for election back to his stable, a low roofed lean-to. I had to lay down flat on my back to avoid getting knocked off backwards. I was afraid to get off. He would crush me with his belly against the wall. Finally I squirmed and squiggled off his back in one piece. Wow! I don't intentionally look for thrill rides.

Delighted by the beautiful soft yellow color of the baby chicks, I jumped across some clapboards to catch one. I fell and couldn't pull my left hand back up from the board to stand up. To break my fall I had pushed my hand onto a nail in the wood. Finally pulling loose, I rushed back to the farm house to find my mom, the nurse. She fretted at the rust color that topped the hole in the palm of my hand, but the farm girl in her, always pragmatic that is, do with what you've got, poured a bottle of peroxide, a little at a time, onto the hole. It fizzed up. I was awestruck by my first exposure to that remedy. It failed to develop complications. Someone watched over us.

A professional woman, she constantly updated her skills with periodicals such as *Hospital Management*. Well read in current affairs, she read a daily newspaper and subscribed to a news magazine, also a

McCall's and humanitarian Catholic publications. She bought and read all the books by a popular Catholic author, Thomas Merton, especially *The Seventh Story Mountain*. Her favorite books though were ones that involved medical personnel. She was a democrat, registered voter and up to date. Men liked to talk with her. At that time their favorite subjects--politics and sports--were also her favorite. She encouraged the athletic interests of my brother and rarely missed a game of his when she was not working. Very aware of human failings and foibles, nevertheless she was never cynical, always optimistic about the future of mankind. She believed that man could solve problems created by man. This part of her in later life I identified with, and in her later years, although she made my sister the executor of her will, she called me her best friend. Our outlook for humanity we shared, celebrated, and at the same time, shed tears for.

After the War

In the fall of 1946, the Quimby property where we lived was sold to the local trucking outfit, Consolidated Freightways, for their truck manufacturing division, Freightliner. CF operated on Saviour, across from our school's playground. They dutifully replaced volleyballs and basketballs truck drivers inadvertently destroyed. Mom felt fortunate to get a larger unit with three bedrooms on NW 20th, between Upshur & Vaughn, still within walking distance of the church, school, shopping, and bus service. She could still get to her job at St. Vincent's Hospital in Kings Heights – only a twenty-six block walk uphill.

I should explain. The streets in Northwest Portland are alphabetical, from Ankeny to Yeon. I don't recall the Z street but there might be one as well. The hospital sat on the hill above Couch and Davis streets, on 27th, so Mom feasibly could have taken the trolley or bus from Thurman to Couch on 23rd Avenue, then walked from 23rd to 27th to get to work. When I went to meet mom for lunch at work in the summertime, I walked that distance to look at the houses and their gardens.

At this new location there were more units with kids our age but no vacant lots. We played touch football in the street and ditch-'em after dark. We built bonfires in the street to roast potatoes and marshmallows. Bev, my same age, a neighbor in the four-unit defense house behind ours, and I would play Canasta. I cheated one time (it was so easy with the loads of rummy-like combinations spread all over her bed and the floor in her room) when she went to the bathroom, but felt so guilty I quickly told her about it when she returned.

Two families, the Duggans, from a deep south state, and the Franks, were in upper grades at St. Patricks. Their sons later graduated from Portland State. Mr. Duggan, in a wheelchair, was an accountant at ESCO, now a fortune 500 industrial company that wields major clout regarding developments in NW Portland. The company succeeded in keeping Costco out of their area. It is a mining equipment manufacturer for the international market. Their foundry sat behind the ballpark at 24th and Vaughn. It now occupies that space as well. They are a major employer in Portland, Oregon.

The Duggan's hefty daughter, Pat, a year ahead of me, when at bat, swung and hit the back of my head. I was playing catcher as a sixth grader. I saw stars but stayed in the game. Long before that, she used to complain to me about being so big and overweight. At fourth and fifth grade we were both in the same piano recital. At fifth & sixth we were in the same play. Pat had the lead.

Dr. Becic, a widow and practicing physician, an immigrant from Croatia, lived in a house across from the ball park. My brother always liked her daughter, in his class. Her two handsome sons, older than me, graduated from University of Portland.

The shoe repairman on the corner of 22nd and Thurman was from Yugoslavia. It was a salt-box like building. The family lived upstairs above his shop. His beautiful daughters, one blonde, one brunette, took the bus every day to St. Mary's Academy downtown. Or street car. I don't remember when buses replaced the streetcars. I do recall the increase of automobile traffic, which resented the street car tracks. Streetcars did dominate during the war to save gasoline.

Mom shopped at Uglesitch's on the corner of 23rd & Thurman. We usually had rump roast or Swiss steak on Sundays, ham on special occasions with pineapple rings and brown sugar. Now, Homer Medico, operates a store at that location, married Joyce McClellan of Irish immigrants. Their sons graduated from Ivy League schools and will become the heirs of adjacent blocks of property Homer has acquired. His father, an immigrant from Eastern Europe, operated a grocery store on 22nd and Thurman, one block east of Uglesitch's. For years, Homer's mother could be found behind the counter at her husband's store and, until a few years ago, at Homer's store; always a fit and sharp lady.

On March 17 St. Patrick's Day, Rocky Benevento from Italy, the ground-skeeper at the Beaver ball park, was chef for the annual spaghetti feed, a fundraiser for the school. His son Richard was in my brother's class. Exhibit booths for baked goods and home-sewn kitchen and bed linens were available. A wheel of fortune and the Cake Walk were favorites for the kids. One year the raffle included a giant refrigerator an appliance company donated, so big, Mom said, "It would blow our fuses." She didn't buy a raffle ticket.

In my eighth grade, the third baseman for the Boston Red Sox, Johnny Pesky came to visit his mother, a widow, and his two brothers, the Peskalavitch's, and spoke to our class. He encouraged us that our hard work would pay off. St. Patrick's had a tradition of immigrants in the area. The Irish established the church, after them the Poles came, then the Germans, and finally, the Slavs. In recent years St. Patrick's has been a mission for the Hispanics.

In 1946 my mother's youngest brother, Bud, just out of the Navy, stayed with us for several months. He worked in the woods felling timber, until he got into an apprenticeship and found a room. There was a housing shortage at the end of the war. He stayed in the third bedroom where Mom kept the washing machine, strung clothes lines for rainy days, the ironing board set up ready to go, a heavy duty portable Singer sewing machine she brought from Montana that I learned to sew on, a cot for an extra bed, and general storage, mostly books. He smoked Lucky Strikes and my sister, Tilly, six not more than seven, tried to light one up in our bathroom without success.

Uncle Bud had a radio and let us kids use it. On Friday night, we listened and shuddered when What Evil Lurks in the Hearts of Men, The Shadow Knows. Saturday morning, Let's Pretend and Grimm's Fairy Tales started at 8:30 AM. I remember Luke and I, at some time in there, heard some of Hitler's speeches. I remember how those speeches made such an impression on my brother. Luke, who did not speak German, said, "He sounds so wound up...like a wild man. I don't know what he's saying but I listen to every word. His voice makes me think it's something important. You gotta listen to it."

Soon Uncle Bud married a little Italian beauty, who lived with her Uncle and Aunt in southeast Portland. Her husband was lost in action in WWII and left her with a little girl, Kathy. Ava worked as an accountant in a construction company where Bud met her on a contract job. Courtships were short in those days. They quickly married and went to Las Vegas on their honeymoon. Upon their return she told the story of losing her wedding ring in the hotel swimming pool. Uncle Bud was quite a gambler. The suspicion that he hocked the ring to keep gambling was one that persisted throughout his entire life. Later, on his twenty acres Grandpa bought in Boring, he raised Greyhounds for racing.

Uncle Bud became my dearest uncle my entire life. He had a car, and in 1948 took us to Blue Lake on Memorial Day for a picnic, where we heard of the break in the dikes at Vanport. It destroyed federal housing for many low income people like my family, who had moved here for work in the shipyards. He also introduced us to pizza for the first time at Pietro's in Milwaukie, just across the city of Portland's southeast boundary, and my first steak out at Saylor's Country Kitchen. He gave me a ride home after my eighth grade graduation party and picked me up after my pre-graduation party from University of Oregon in Eugene. First he tried to become a baker but ended up a cement finisher and put in our aggregate concrete walks and patio in my new house in 1970.

That first Christmas without my dad, my mom put our Christmas presents on the little front porch on Quimby to lead us to believe that Santa delivered them. It included a highchair my sister so wanted for her dolls. When on NW 20th we walked on Vaughn Street towards the ball park on 24th, to Christmas tree lots to select a tree. I always insisted on the biggest, tallest, fullest. Us kids had conflicting opinions. Mom stayed practical because she carried it home and decorated most of it. I remember she carefully placed a yellow porcelain pear that had been on their first Christmas tree in Cut Bank.

On payday we celebrated on Friday night with hamburgers and pie ala mode at Quality Pie on 23rd across from Good Sam hospital, then a movie at the Esquire down the street. We three would complicate the walk home by arguing about whatever. Mom would get disgusted with our straggling and doddling behind her, and say, "I look like an Indian squaw herding her papooses. Please quit meandering so. Let's get on home."

She made special trips to Nob Hill Pharmacy, on 21st and Everett for Jewell pineapple crush ice cream and to Luthe's bakery on 24th and Thurman for a chocolate cake for my brother and a white one with lemon filling for me on our birthdays, in June, back to back days.

Traffic on NW 19th automatically swung into Vaughn Street. It was a thoroughfare leading to Highway 30 along the Columbia that goes to Guilds Lake, the St. Johns Bridge, Linnton, St. Helens, Scappoose, Rainier and their bridge over that river to Longview, Washington. Of course, it was heavily travelled. Due to transport, port, and industrial activity in the area, accidents did occur. On a Friday right after Mom got home from work, she was out in the front yard, which faced 20th and looked out on Vaughn as well, planting nasturtiums. She heard the loud screech and crash of auto and truck.

She heard a woman's high-pitched screams, "Help, someone help!" Mom anticipated what had to be done. She grabbed scraps of fabric from her third bedroom and rushed to the scene. The woman's husband's arm was gushing blood. He had been behind the wheel. His arm had been gashed by the window broken when the truck that crossed over the yellow line in the then two-lane street and smashed into their car. Mom tied a tourniquet on the man's upper arm. The blood flow quickly stopped.

Not too long after, it became controversial regarding Good Samaritan gestures such as hers and the necessity for laws protecting their liability. I heard my mother discuss the ramifications of these acts with several acquaintances. It was an issue that perplexed her as a professional nurse.

My mother was a devout Catholic. Somehow that became a barrier for her and me. At twelve I began to question the religion I was brought up in, and authority in general. Confirmation lessons were directed by Father Thielen, who became director of Education for the Archdiocese.

In sixth grade I had my first dance and first kiss with Dick Satalich at his older twin brothers', Adolph and Rudolph, party in their folk's basement. In college at the time at University of Portland, the twins eventually became Longshoremen on the Portland docks. It was wonderful. So I challenged Father on sexual matters, "Father, I do not believe that sex is only for procreation." Since then I have reasoned that the loving God who made us and gave us a sex drive wouldn't make it so damned difficult on human beings. I have seen the results of unwanted babies brought forth. In his beginning, a child deserves to be wanted.

"You are an iconoclast. How blasphemous! What have you been up to? I'll have to discuss this with your mother."

I knew what blasphemy meant, but I had to look up the word iconoclast. Could I actually be that off base? It made me feel odd, a total nonconformist, too different, must keep my "revolutionary" ideas to myself. I often judged ideas and others actions by how it made me feel. That dance and kiss made me feel good. Now he was going to expose my crazy ideas to my mother. I felt threatened.

I have put off telling you about an incident that dominated my life throughout grade school, and probably for many years thereafter. It rears its complex head quite often. Years later a fellow employee and great friend, Rad Czarec, a graduate of Loyola University of Los Angeles, told me, "Catholics, those practicing and ones withdrawn alike, suffer one thing in common their entire lives."

"What's that, Rad?"

"A guilt complex. They punish themselves over and over for their transgressions, so-called sins of the past."

"You're so right, Rad. I have one I can't ever get rid of," I concluded. But I did not explain further. In fact I've never told this one before to any living soul.

Rad didn't expect me to. He had a MS in History. His thesis was U.S. Foreign Policy in Nicaragua. Of Polish parents, he spoke Polish, English and Spanish. Pushing fifty, his wife was much younger and in school. They had two boys, a Yelty he loved, rented a house off NE 60th near Normandale Park. He specialized in peppers in his garden. He smoked and drank close to a bottle of whiskey each night. I never knew why, never delved into it for cause. He was my Inside Salesman and an outstanding one. He opened up resorts, the coast, and sold my double truck specials for subjects like Travel and Spring Projects. He had worked for the Police Gazette for years before I hired him. He let me know he loved to work with me. We were both newspaper lovers scratching out an existence.

Here we go. In the third grade, after my dad died, I had come along in piano lessons so quickly with the nuns that I was allowed to play the organ to accompany the seventh and eighth grade choir at Benediction on Sunday nights at the church. But access to the organ stopped abruptly that year due to an incident with Nancy Hargen's mother and the nuns. Her mother's Victorian house was trashy and uninviting. She was a mean, ugly lady. Just once Nancy and I played in her play house in the backyard by a tree infested with caterpillars.

In that hut, Nancy and I took a large kitchen towel, pressed it in three or four folds then rolled it tightly into a flat firm ball. We laid on top of each other on the short cot for seating (we weren't very big) and put the rolled knot between us against our pelvic areas and pressed our bodies together. The pressure down there felt real good. Not for long. We quit and looked for something else to do. What led us to do so, I have no idea. Who got the idea to begin with, is beyond me.

The next week Nancy invited herself to come to my house to play my piano. We walked the three blocks together from school to my home. Once we were inside Nancy said, "I shouldn't be here. My mother told me not to play with you. Cross your heart and hope to die, promise you won't ever tell that I came to your house today. I have to go now."

"I promise," I said.

"Cross your heart."

"Okay. There," I made the sign of a cross across my chest.

Later that afternoon Sister telephoned. "Was Nancy at your house, today?"

"No, Sister."

"Are you sure?"

"She wasn't at my house."

I lied because I promised Nancy I would not tell on her. Whether it was my horrible guilt feeling from that day on – I felt everybody was concerned about me because I lied. They think maybe Clancy is a sociopath – or just plain untrustworthy. I came to believe that some in authority indeed thought I had a serious problem. They seemed to look at and treat me different. My mother asked me about the phone call the next day. I held to my oath. I wish now I had at least shared the truth with my mother, of all people. I swore then to never lie again – but possibly it was too late for that. In my defense, the sister should have told me WHY she was asking me that question.

Nancy was never at school again. No one acknowledged or explained her disappearance. I felt responsible. Possibly she had told her mother the truth – that she had been to my house – and then I made her out a liar. Nancy was afraid of her mother, I was afraid of her mother for Nancy's sake. I never got to play the organ again. I couldn't reach the floor base pedals anyway.

I didn't give another thought to our actions in that hut until all of this happened. Reviewing the events, such as Nancy telling me her mother forbid her to play with me, triggered me to think that I did something wrong and that towel business must be it. After the phone call, the guilt set in twofold. I guess Nancy and I weren't supposed to play that way. That's for sure. Now it all fell into place. I moved from ignorant and innocent to realizing my behavior was a no-no. That's the real reason I continued to hide it from my mother. How awful I am. I don't want my mother to know how really bad I've been.

And it was feasible that Nancy told her mother of our "play" and the mother told the nuns, etcetera; so I ended up a sex maniac or an awful Lesbian. Pope Francis has recently spoken out to his church leaders for some consideration for the homosexual condemned-to-hell sinners. In our defense, we didn't take our clothes off or touch each other, you awful woman!

◆ ◆ ◆

At ten I attended Farmers Union camp when school was out. The first one was on the Molalla River in Clackamas County, like an outdoor school, with mostly farm kids. We had classes in the morning on co-operative organization, farm issues such as the adequate worldwide distribution of their harvests, and the importance of saving the family farm emphasized by NFU versus The Farm Bureau, which at that time promoted large corporate farming. The benefits of Bonneville and the Tennessee Valley Administration and other government supported pro-grams, and the poverty and evils of share-cropping, were explored. We swam, hiked in the woods and had song fests, "We shall not, we shall not be moved" and the state's song, "What did Ida-ho, boys, What did Ida-ho?"

"She hoe-d a Mary-Land, boys, She hoe-d a Mary-Land.

"What did Io-Wa, boys, what did Io-wa?

"She weighed a Washing-ton, boys, she weighed a Washing-ton.

"How did Flora-die, boys? Too much Missis-sip....

"What made Miss-ery, boys? Too much Mini-sodas...

"How did Wiscon-sin, boys? He stole the New-Brass-Key...

"Where has Ore-gone, boys? He's seeing Okla-home...

"What did Dela-ware, boys? She wore a New Jersey...

"What did Tenne-see, boys? She saw what Arkan-saw...

I listed so many because they were so clever, especially to a ten-year-old.

After supper, a first-rate square-dance caller put the music on and we ho-downed. Great food. (Well, not as good as my mom's cooking. Her cooking and baking for the holidays plus everyday can't be duplicated.) The kids KP'd the dishes and the garbage. Most of the campers were older than me.

Mom's cooking reminds me of the time we three kids tried to reach the upper shelves of Fibber McGee's closet where Mom hid the fresh-baked cookies she put in our lunches. We ended up pulling down her electric toaster, a Toastmaster, breaking off one of the handles. It still worked, but she wasn't too happy about it.

When us kids fought, sometimes the one most hurt would call Mom at work and say, "Luke said"...etcetera. In a fight I locked him out of the house. After pushing in the stiff metal screen, he tried to crawl back in a bedroom window. I pushed the screen against him as he came through the open window and hit him square on the nose. That time Mom came home from work in the middle of the day and took him to emergency. I broke my brother's nose. After that, we never fought again.

The broken nose became indented in family history. I was probably sent to camp to broaden my horizons and become more acclimated... socially. Years later my mother said I was kind of a "bull in a china shop" when I was a kid. "I never knew what's next?" she said.

I walked pigeon-toed until a fellow student called my attention to it in the fourth grade. I'm glad somebody did. Right then, I conscientiously worked very hard to point my flat feet forward when I took a step. At the same time I learned to do the Charleston by holding onto the back of a kitchen chair. Eventually I could do several of the steps without support. I didn't hesitate to show off my new skill if music came on when my fellow students were gathered.

My dad had flat feet but it didn't keep him out of the army. My brother has flat feet and so do two of my grandchildren. So far they haven't been a handicap, that is, didn't keep us from pursuing our choice of physical activities.

They have caused hurt at times. Mom bought me Buster Brown shoes at Spellman's on SW Broadway, downtown Portland, fitted with custom metal and leather arch-supports. They killed my feet, evidenced by the fact that eventually, especially with the left foot, I walked on the outer sides of the laced brown leather oxfords, as if I was club-footed. My feet without an arch, slid off of the upper curves of the rigid arch supports.

Eventually Mom gave up and allowed me to wear ordinary shoes like flats. In high school I wore saddles and white bucks (laced-up oxford-cut). My extra-long feet for my size made friends call me "Snow Shoes." I loved the name. It was fun. The high heels of adulthood lifted my arches and reduced the pain, but they developed hammer toes, because my feet, jammed into pointed-toed shoes, forced my toes to curl up, like that of a ballet dancer. The tennis shoes of the NOW are a Godsend.

The next year, when I was eleven, Flossie Harris, a former teacher from Denver (NFU headquarters), Education Director for NFU, brought her fourteen-year-old son, Jim, and drove us to a camp on the Washington coast. Remember, she drove all the way from Denver to get here, was an amazing teacher, plus good looking, and well dressed. Jim was good to me and let me sleep on his shoulder all the way back home to Portland. I still have the gorgeous blue and pink glass earrings bound in gold fili-gree Mrs. Harris sent to me for graduation from grade school. I certainly intended to follow in her footsteps.

At school with first generation immigrants at St. Patrick's, mostly from Eastern Europe, conditioned me for a primary interest in history studies of human beings. As early as fourth grade geography, which introduced me to the native tribes of Papua, the Amazon, and Australia, caused me to be most comfortable with the examination of divergent human beings, their beliefs and organizations. Eventually, I found human beings to have a lot in common.

In fourth grade, I also visited my Aunt Helen's fourth grade class at George Elementary in North Portland. The noise and the chaos of the more than 40 students made me appreciate the order of the nuns in small classes at St. Patrick's, even though we had one teacher per two classes in the same room, such as my third and fourth together. A sister of my father and her family of four girls had recently moved to Portland, close to Columbia Park. Their father, Uncle Milt, worked as a janitor for a school district and kept his opinions to himself in "a household of five women."

Her youngest daughter, Marjorie, was my age and we were able to get together sometimes, especially for movies and get-togethers with her friends. She was a top student but very shy so we didn't share much, but I respected her. In the early days we played Old Maid and Authors with her and her big sisters. When I was eighteen and a freshman in col-lege, Marjorie wanted me to be in her wedding. My mother told me to get permission from the pastor. Father Thielen would not give me permission because it was not a Catholic wedding. It was in a Protestant church.

As a result I decided I could never be in anybody's wedding or ask anyone to be in my wedding since I couldn't be in my first cousin's wedding. Even though along the way I was no longer Catholic. If I had done so it would have hurt my cousin immensely. I would have never done that to her. Instead, I bought a wonderful red silk dress with an empire waistline, slim skirt, and short puff sleeves, to serve coffee at her reception. So lucky. Marked way down, for one reason the size was mismarked, or because it wasn't exactly in style, kind of experimental, at Meier & Frank's, now Macy's.

My best friend was Betty Byer. Her father and mother were from Germany. He worked at an ice house close to school. In fact I never heard him speak a sentence in English but off work he swung his powerful arms around his daughter and kissed the top of her naturally curly brown hair. We would go to the ice house after school, wait for him to get off work and ride with him to their farm of perfectly maintained animals, fences, gardens demonstrating a great exertion of expertise and labor. It was on the south side of the Bonny Slope area, out Lovejoy and Cornell Road. Mr. Byer continued to buy and develop adjoining properties and ultimately his children became property owners in the now elite Bethany area.

Betty's older sister, a natural leader, a blond beauty, sang in the seventh/eighth grade choir, and a brother in the grade behind us was outstanding in football. They all went to college and Betty married a graduate from OSU in pharmacy. I met him when I was nineteen. He trimmed Mom's trees away from the power lines on her street facing the house we moved to when I was thirteen, for PGE in the summer time to pay for his schooling. We reminisced about St. Pat's and Betty. Handsome and hardy, of Nordic descent, he was a wonderful young man. Until ten years ago he had his own pharmacy in a major city in northern California. They had six children.

In the spring of fifth grade, Betty wore a lovely, Swiss cotton, slightly gathered, powder blue skirt with a lace edge her mother bought her for

Easter. Betty was distraught as she showed me the three inch dark blue pen mark in the middle of her new skirt. "My mother will be very unhappy. What should I do?" she moaned.

We were in the bathroom. A bottle of Clorox sat at the sink. I took a paper towel, doused it with the bottle to soak it, and applied it to the ink mark. It immediately removed the ink but left a clear space in the blue. It took out the color and left a blank spot. We rushed to Sister. Sister reprimanded me, "Why Clorox, Clancy? That's bleach for white stuff. You should know better." Betty said her mother tried to dye the entire skirt but the white blotch didn't take. Her mother remained angry about it. I never made a trip again to the wonderful farm house with Betty, my dear friend. Naturally, I got a chemistry lesson, hands on. It left an indelible mark on my brain, but mostly on my heart.

This reminds me of my other chemistry lesson. When I was nine, horse chestnuts looked a lot like Ohio State University's Buckeyes. Recent Chinese immigrants I know relish their roasted chestnuts. In any event, our street was loaded with giant chestnut trees. I removed their spiny vivid green covers, peeled off the chestnut-colored skin to expose the round nut, put them in a pan for the oven, added milk and sugar and baked them. I don't remember how long but I tested the milk for heat level and gave it to my six-year-old sister, Tilly, for lunch. She ate quite a lot, got sick right away and vomited. When Mom got home from work at 4 PM, she assured us that they are poisonous. She said so more than once. To this day I avoid mushrooms and chestnuts.

In the summer of 1947, Grandpa Rolph took us three grandchildren to Salem on a business trip. He told us to bring our swimsuits because the grass seed farmer he had an appointment with had an outdoor swim pool. Mr. Jones' colonial home was on 99E, just north of town. We had our first barbecued hamburgers and changed clothes in a four-unit bath house. It was amazing.

Years later I found out that Grandpa had helped Oregon and Washington grass seed farmers establish a cooperative for marketing and export, which became the greatest farm product income for Oregon until 2008, according to the Capitol Press, out of Salem. He was also an Agricultural Advisor to President Truman and went to southern Italy to estimate that area's needs for farm implements for the Marshall Plan.

By sixth grade, I debated on behalf of Harry Truman for President for re-election in 1948 against Patrick Tabor who supported Thomas Dewey. Patrick's mother was an accountant, single and used a cane to walk. She let us have parties for our class at her house on 24th north of Thurman, just around the corner from the movie theatre, where we saw Zorro, Roy Rogers and Looney Tunes on Saturdays, when we were younger. We played post office, spin-the-bottle and musical chairs.

At that same time my sister and I went by bus to the Weatherly building across the Morrison Bridge to Dr. Gersinger, $5.00 a visit for our braces. She had sucked her thumb. I had an underbite, so the orthodontist put pressure behind my upper teeth to give me a normal bite and smile.

When Couch pool, an indoor one at the school by the same name, on Couch Street and NW 21st, where we learned to swim, was closed, I went on the bus to Sellwood Park or Columbia pools to swim in the summer. That same year the nuns gave me tickets to the Junior Symphony on Saturday mornings led by Dr. Ashlanomov. The Third Avenue bus took me all the way to the auditorium downtown. As an adult in the sixties I sang in his All City Choir to perform Mozart's Requiem. They also gave me passes to the Portland Playhouse. I saw Sunday matinees of *The Glass Menagerie* and *Streetcar named Desire* by Tennessee Williams all by myself. A special treat was their ticket for me to the delightful play, *Arsenic and Old Lace*, at Central Catholic High School. With no girls in the school, all parts in the play, the aunts and their pretty niece Elaine, were acted by the men in the student body. It was amazing to me.

When I was ten, Mom met a man while providing morphine to his grandmother, a terminal cancer patient in his folks' home in King's Heights. A Catholic and a veteran, Ken Mitchell was attempting to manufacture items made out of war surplus, had a shop in a Quonset on Swan Island, and was building a house he had designed on 114th off of SE Division. He had an eight-year-old son and just divorced from his wife who lived on SW 3rd avenue (in the then predominately Italian St. Lawrence parish, view property, later demolished by Portland Development Commission urban renewal funds. Continued construction replaced the homes by upscale tall rise apartments and business buildings between downtown and the hills of Lair Park).

More than one time Ken parked, with us kids in the car, in front of his wife's house so he could give her his support money for the month. She was a gorgeous, white-skinned, redhead, and over-endowed. She always answered the door oozing out of a lingerie-like robe or just outgrowing or overcoming some kind of a see-through thing. He took us often to Blue Lake and once to fish at Battleground Lake.

Of medium height, weight and build, as well as complexion with a full head of sandy hair, his fair face was always clean shaven. Not muscular, but with no tattoos, Ken did not drink or smoke but sported a somewhat serious, slim line across his forehead, almost like a scar, a worry crease. Even though a serious businessman, his lips were slightly turned up on the ends when someone spoke to him because he did consider himself to be a good guy, and he was. The heavy duty pants, similar to today's Carhartts, were always a neutral color, never dark, like jeans, topped by a nondescript sweatshirt. Ken wasn't in for much color. To spray paint in his shop, he wore a plastic, full sleeved, cover-all to remain spotless. But some of his shoes had paint on them. We never saw him in a suit, whereas our dad wore a suit quite often. We kids liked Ken but we didn't love him.

For one of his projects: Ken took a huge round of obsolete, unbleached ticker tape, approximately one-half-inch thick, with a wider circumference than a family pizza. It had hard cardboard hole in the center. He placed it on his potter's wheel, guided it up by hand into the shape of a flower pot, and sealed it with industrial glue. Eventually he spray painted it, then set it again on a metal storage rack to dry before packing it with other pots to deliver to florists and retail nurseries he seemed to have orders for.

Needless to say the flower pots were precarious; oversensitive to water and affected by fertilizers. He worked overtime to perfect his invention since he had a roomful to the ceiling of ticker tape rolls. Even I, at the age of ten, could see the futility of Ken's project. I had no opinion of Mom's relationship at the time, but at the same time I felt kind of sorry for the guy. He was smarter than that – just stuck or obsessed with a bad idea. When I see eight-inch or ten-inch paper pots today they remind me of the "dreamer" Ken Mitchell, which is how my mother later referred to him, just one time, years later. For every successful innovation that works there are hundreds of people, like Ken, who struggle with a losing effort. Aren't writers somehow included in that category?

Mom and Ken applied to the church to get dispensation to marry. The authorities chastised my mother for dating a divorced man. She withdrew from the relationship. Ken got a real job with Consolidated Freightways and moved to Montana to be a terminal manager. My mother never dated anyone ever again. My sister asked Mom about that relationship so has all the details. I never probed. I rarely ask. I wait for people to offer information.

The next few years – my teen years – are going to be a doozie for my mom, who I loved very much. I probably cared too much for what she thought of me. I continued to hope for her to be proud of me, or at least not to disappoint or hurt her. But I continue to talk to my mom up in heaven and thank my Lord for her. The tales I have to tell made me appear wild to her, but I never considered me to be so. There were some crazy circumstances, at the wrong place at the right time.

Our Dream Home

In 1950 when I turned thirteen, my mother bought a house built in 1915 for $4500.00, a two-story Craftsman with three bedrooms, one bath, in southeast Portland, just four blocks from the grade school. For us kids the extra space was unbelievable – a huge upstairs bedroom for my sister and me. My brother had the smaller room all to himself. We didn't have to share the backyard. An enclosed back porch provided storage for Mom's lawnmower and garden tools. The covered front porch facing east was huge. The extra large windows gave lots of light. There was ample space in the kitchen for an electric range and refrigerator.

She reestablished her Fibber McGee's closet on the first floor next to the bathroom. A pantry in the landing to the basement was a Godsend for her to store canned goods and canning jars. In the basement, mom set up her manual washing machine, with two wash tubs and a window above them for extra light and strung lines to dry the clothes. Mom quickly used the breakfast nook, facing north and west, for her many, beloved Christmas cactus. They did very well there.

A really important thing that my Mom did in our new house was to provide adequate lighting. There were no lights in the ceiling in the large living room, so she invested in floor and table lamps mostly for anyone anywhere to read or, more so, study by. She did so for every room in the house. It was of primary importance to her. All of us have followed her example in our homes. That was not the case in many homes I have visited during my lifetime.

Mom purchased second hand furniture to fill the enormous space including an oak round table, my daughter-in-law has had restored, and chairs. Leaves for the table extended to seat eight. They came in handy, along with her use of card tables and fold-out chairs she kept in Fibber

McGee's closet. At Christmas time her folks, brothers and sisters would gather for Mom's great cookin', beer, Norwegian Wist, and lots of chiding and laughter. Uncle Jim, from Pendleton, would pour beer into a small Kraft cheese glass for us kids as we took turns as a fourth at the two card tables for the game.

I loved my mother's family, not only grandpa and grandma. My favorites were Aunt Rita, wife of Mom's very quiet but handsome brother, Mike. She was chubby and cheery, laughed with a lilt, and always hugged me hello. She made her living as a small restaurant manager so very comfortable with people, especially on a one on one basis. In my adulthood, when on the road with McGraw-Hill, I stopped for coffee at her shop in The Dalles in the Columbia gorge. I found her to be very well read, especially in current events. They had moved there when Uncle Mike retired as a ranch hand in the Maupin area. Regular basketball fans at the local high school, the students at the games organized a special night of appreciation for them before they left town. That was an unforgettable night for gentle, unassuming Uncle Mike, who was further distinguished by his prematurely white hair, which he kept short-cropped, and blue eyes. All of Mom's and Dad's people were exceptionally good looking and had a clean cut aura about them. Not a slob among them. Definitely people us kids could emulate, be proud of being related to.

Our house was in the Richmond neighborhood, which in 2014, sixty-four years later, Sunset magazine recommended, "ideal to buy into." I think one reason for its draw is the wide range of incomes the mixed housing accommodates.

My mother was curious as to why she was so lucky in getting such a good buy. The house was on a 100'x150' corner lot of 45th and Sherman. The neighbor behind her at 44th and Sherman turned out to be a Negro man, who kept very much to himself so she suspected the real estate had kept that fact "quiet." The big house across the street on the north had been divided into apartments for renters. That also disappointed her. It didn't matter to my mom except she hoped to have some friendly exchange with her neighbors. In fact, it took a long time for her to gain the trust of the lady next door on 45th. Mrs. Hilsenkopf, whose main social outlet was Job's Daughters, finally sat on Mom's front porch with her and shared concerns for her only daughter, years later in hot summer days when Mom's work day was done. This gave satisfaction to my mom.

One reason she bought it is because she was led to believe it was in St. Ignatius parish, operated by the Jesuits. After moving in, she found that she was in St. Stephens parish and school where my brother and sister would attend. I wanted to finish at St. Patrick's so for my eighth grade I opted to take two buses to get there.

Some of the same persons rode the bus to and from. Usually standing in the morning, I often talked with an attorney on his way downtown. He talked shop, was kindly and treated me like I had a brain in my head. I recall wearing lipstick on the trip in an effort to look like all the other women on the bus, most of them on their way to work. On the way home I'll never forget an older fellow who got on at 12th and Division. Disheveled and dirty, he stunk like rotten chicken and always sat in the back of the bus. People opened windows or even moved to the front of the bus in an effort to escape his odor, which permeated the entire space. I tried hard not to breathe in to avoid the overwhelming stench. The poor man, or maybe he was indeed fortunate, because he seemed immune to his own odor.

Sister Dorina disapproved of my makeup. Lipstick was not allowed in the eighth grade classroom. But she did two huge favors for me. One, she showed me the collection in the library of the Greek classics which included the efforts for democracy and the rights of man. Sister advised me to read them over the summer break Second, when the media scourged Ingrid Bergman due to her affair with the Italian movie producer when she was a married woman, Sister Dorina warned us to be wary of mass media, not only for their so-called factual reporting but their public opinion-making drives and pervasive power.

Years later I read Ingrid Bergman's autobiography. Her attachment to her lover and choice of him was based on an outstanding, philosophical film she loved, which she mistakenly thought her lover had made. She later found out that another filmmaker, with the same name, had made that film. It took years for Ingrid to discover the mistaken identity. It was a slow and painful uncovering, finally verified when the real filmmaker was revealed to her.

She had given love and trust to a man she had believed shared her same values and intuition, who did not do so. It was another man's creation she had fallen in love with. They both had the Italian name, Rossini. So very tragic, a mistaken identity that should go down in history. In a way, it's like the very private and remote man I thought I loved when I actually came to love and trust all of his beautiful, open, vital, warm friends, so of course, my man had to be like them. Taken down the primrose path, delusions eventually own up and hurt bad.

In 1950 since mom took the *Oregonian* which my brother delivered I was exposed to full coverage of the Rose Festival court selection. Each day in late spring the newspaper gave a comprehensive profile of each princess selected. Thea Collins was selected by her Lincoln high school students. She was about the same size as me, wore her hair short and slightly curled, with green eyes. She was from Czechoslovakia. I hoped I was kind of like her. That year Lipman Wolfe's downtown, across from Meier & Frank, had large photographs of each princess in their windows. At that age Rose Festival Court was a big deal with me. I looked up to their activities and interests and definitely tried to emulate them but Thea's appearance is what I tried to copy.

About the same time, I had a radio beside my bed and when I woke late at night I would turn it on. At Christmas time the Lewis & Clark college choir sang a song I had never heard before and it became my favorite, *The Little Drummer Boy*. I also listened to the speeches of each princess at the Queen's coronations on Friday nights and picked my favorite, on the basis of their speech.

In our old home, in northwest Portland, when I was eleven, in summer there was opportunity for harvest buses to take us to Hillsboro to pick strawberries, and Sauvies Island for cucumbers, green beans, blackberries and boysenberries. I jumped on the chance. We sang songs on the bus: Ninety-nine bottles of beer on the Wall, *John Jacob don Hammerschmidt,* dots my name too.

Stew Holbrook, seven feet tall, who became one of the first phenomenally tall basketball centers at Lincoln High and Oregon State University, was in our crew. He was quite a sight in the strawberry fields. He straddled the rows, bent over in half and picked vigorously. He was very poor and needed the money.

My mother let me keep every dime I ever earned, which eventually was $10.00 a day per season in the fields. Once we moved I caught a bus at 5:30 AM at Richmond School, organized by a local lady, and headed to Bub Nelson's berry farm in Gresham. Return after lunch, take a bath and head for Creston Park to swim. My brother resumed his paper route on the east side of Portland but needed to invest in a bike. He found a blue-green Columbia for $50.00 we would share. Since I had more money at the time, I paid $35.00 towards it. He paid $15.00.

I rarely rode it. The bike was his business. It was a boy's bike. My brother was hardworking and enterprising. Ultimately he became very successful, career wise, and has always been generous to me. My seventy percent investment has been paid back many times over, not only in fiduciary kind but in essential emotional support. His contributions to me cannot be measured. It's a long list. All thirteen of the students in my eighth grade at St. Patrick's, including me graduated that year, 1951.

The first summer in my new neighborhood was a fun one. After berry picking in the morning, I walked to Creston Park on SE Powell to swim. In the late afternoon the lifeguard refereed a water polo match, which included fellows who became lifetime friends of mine. Dave Smith, Gary Spears, Ron Lusted, and two deaf fellows in a special program at Hosford School, just north of southeast 28th and Division provided by Portland Public Schools. The lifeguard invited other park water polo teams to compete with us. It was great fun.

The lifeguard took me under her wing. I did a great Jackknife off the three foot board but could never master the odd posture of the Swan. On Mondays when the pool was closed she took me to St. Helens outdoor pool, where she taught school, and coached me at diving off their ten-foot platform, especially to teach me the pike and roll formations. If lucky, my attempts ended in cannon balls, but most of them were splats on my back or worse, face forward, to learn one and one-half pikes.

I admit I wasn't too committed. I was void in sheer bravery essential to the sport. The Jackknife remained my only achievement. She also entered me in a regional Australian crawl swim meet for my age at Jantzen Beach. I barely came in at fourth place. All I remember is the blinding glare of the blue water with the sun hitting the huge Olympic size pool, and the water, so heavy. I felt especially sluggish in my attempt to kick and stroke. What a struggle. I remained unmotivated by the promise of competition. I guess I prefer team efforts. I continued to play water polo until I was seventeen when I found a steady summer job.

Along with Sharon MacDougall and Dotty Gould, Gary, Dave, Ron and I would end the day at Sckavone's drug store at southeast 41st and Division for a coke. Mary Kelly was always at the long lunch counter. She was friendly and happy to see us. She talked of her children: a son at Central Catholic High School and a very beautiful daughter, Angie, at St. Mary's Academy in Biology who got a scholarship at Oregon State College and eventually married a farmer from Eastern Oregon. Mary lived in the neighborhood within walking distance of her job. Looking back, of course, she allowed our gang to loiter.

Our gang loved to look at the advertisements in the back of magazines--Mr. Atlas, bra and lingerie ads--and used them as a basis for silly, giddy comments. Unsophisticated as we were at thirteen and fourteen. Dave Smith had a ukulele so we would head across the street over to the Richmond school grounds to take advantage of its large open spaces to sing at the top of our lungs, *Down* By *the Riverside*. That's the only song Dave knew but he was trying to learn another one for us. I forget what it was. A few other kids, our same age, joined us once in a while, Ron Kinsfather, Jim Erickson, and Jim Smith but they weren't part of our water polo team.

At about that time Dave and I once kissed and kissed in my backyard until my mother called me in for supper. I liked kissing Dave but had a crush for some reason on Gary Spears that lasted for several years. In other words, no other took his place in my romantic illusions. I remained faithful to Gary. In my sophomore and junior years, when I didn't go right to sleep I would get up and write a love letter directed towards Gary. I never gave them to him. That first summer I attempted to call Gary at his house, one time. His mother answered and told me never to call there again.

His folks were old friends with a girl's parents Gary grew up with. Gary watched out for her like a brother and eventually married her. Carol C. was her name. Just one time Gary and I double dated with Warren Williams and Carol in the back seat. Warren treated Carol badly and Gary stopped the car several times and reprimanded Warren for his behavior.

I had a great chat with Gary and Carol in 1986, at Bev and Cy Green's open house in Lake Oswego. Bev was one of my Aunt Helen's daughters, married to Cy, who became President of Fred Meyers. Cy had started with Fred Meyer in North Portland as a box boy. Gary and Carol lived next door to the Greens in Milwaukie. Gary and I both ended up in the newspaper business, he with the *Oregonian*, so we had lots to talk about.

The summer of 1951, Ron had a party. Gary took me to it. Sitting next to him on the sofa he leaned forward and put the end of his nose onto the end of my nose. Quickly he went through the motion of rubbing noses. "Eskimos rub noses to have a little snot," Gary said. Naturally, I laughed. Gary was always joking, never serious. He made me laugh. Not knowing much else about Gary, a persistent unknown factor, so a challenge, was probably the attraction. I was never kissed or even hugged by Gary. In my book he was a totally honorable fellow.

We had all this energy. It was Friday night. Dave, Gary, Ron, Sharon MacDougal, her brother, Don and I had walked to Hawthorne. We stopped at the record store at Ott's Audio shop and Don, Sharon and Ron crowded into one booth to listen to a new recording by Johnny Ray, a Franklin graduate, recently famous for two reasons. He was partially deaf and had two hit records, *Cry* and *The Little Cloud that Cried*. We didn't buy anything.

We all had supper at home before we met at the school. The usual routines found us with very little money on hand. We were not the lucrative market that merchants since the eighties have found among teenagers. I related that Dick Satalich and his friends, after playing basketball at the Jewish Community Center in southwest Portland on weekends, saw movies by sneaking into the Blue Mouse or United Artists. I could visualize Dick climbing the fire escape at that theatre so high up on the second story.

We put in our quarters, dimes and nickles and gave it to Ron, five-foot-six, to buy a ticket to the Baghdad theatre. Although underfed and wiry, he was capable of executing the most amazing feats. Always confident, he had a reputation for success at whatever he attempted.

So as not to look so obvious we split up into two and three and headed down the block. Two of us crossed the street and strolled down SE 37th looking at the row houses with mostly flowering bushes like hydrangeas and weigelia. All of us kept one eye peeled on the back exit door. When it finally opened and held ajar by a piece of leather, one of us would peel off, enter in a crouched position. Once in the door, crawl on our knees to the edge of the heavy velvet curtains covering the exit alcove. The sudden blackness was always a problem. Peek for attendants out the edge of the curtain, then dash and sneak into an aisle between the seats and stop, catch our breath, look up. Thank goodness for the light from the screen. Crawl to the center aisle, stand up and quickly walk up the aisle to go to the bathroom, than head for the balcony where we said we would all meet.

This time Sharon didn't make it. She had rheumatic fever when she was eight and still got short of breath, with a cough, when there was too much excitement. This was Sharon's first attempt. It was mine too, for that matter. Her cough and sneeze in the alcove, at a quiet time in the movie, was just her luck, gave it away to the attendants. They rushed down to walk her up the aisle and out the front door and secure the exit door once more.

Four of us had already made it in. Seeing a free movie was our objective rather than seeing a movie. We didn't want Sharon to walk home alone and knew she couldn't loiter outside the movie house. We left one at a time by different exits and caught up with Sharon in front of Ott's. Naturally, the Baghdad increased security. The adventure of a free movie soon wore off.

Movies were no big deal at the time. Lots of musicals. The best seemed to be Xavier Cugat and Carmen Miranda. One of my favorites, was the Esther Williams stories although they left no reasons to remember the plots. They were lightweight. Even then I liked Newsreel, rodeo, boxing and college football stories. Loved the show about Jim Thorpe, American Indian Olympic runner, the stories about Lou Gehrig and Jackie Robinson.

At the end of the summer before I was to attend Immaculata Academy in North Portland, Gary and Dave invited me to Franklin High School's jamboree, to start off Portland Interscholastic Football League season, at the Multnomah stadium. We went on the bus. I was Gary's date. Dave's date was a girl from Gary's grade school, Creston. A western singer, who was already a paid performer and being featured on the radio, she stood out in any crowd. She was tall, about five foot nine. Fortunately Dave was six foot four. Her very golden hair, lots of it, was long and dressed, that is, it flowed and had a shine to it. I'd never seen hair like that, including the color, not even in the movies.

Her eyes were big with eyelashes extra long and curled back, eye brows dominant. It was almost embarrassing to look at her – almost unreal. She talked about country outfits she performed at and named her favorite songs, all Greek to me. I didn't know about the guys. She was comfortable and gestured with her hands, long nails polished red, when she talked whereas, at that time I recall not ever being quite at ease as she was, that day, and at our age. She performed, accustomed to taking center stage.

She was overwhelming. I tried to avoid the center of attention. I remember enjoying conversations with one person at a time. Got stage fright if there seemed to be an audience; that is, more than one person giving attention to my utterances. I recall re-evaluating my person as a result of this encounter and decided for some reason I could never go her route. I had no reason to. On the other hand, I realized she had a reason to get gussied up that way.

I had again learned the hard way. Early that summer, Dotty Gould and I found something silly to do, like silly girls do. We decided to try peroxide on just a few strands of hair. I tried it on a left clump of my bangs and it took. But it wouldn't grow out. Maybe the chlorine water and the sun kept bleaching the spot. It made me feel conspicuous, like I was trying to get attention. It seemed that the color was permanent, growing even at the roots, rather than growing out. I panicked, so I cut the clump out to the roots. It left a bald spot on the left corner of my head. I didn't care. It would grow back, I hoped, and maybe, prayed. Since then, I have avoided permanents, dyes, rinses, anything that is even semi-temporary. I hesitate to subject myself to experiments.

Something happened too which caused me not to want to be like Dotty Gould. She didn't say much about her folks and I never saw them. She lived in a huge three-story house at a T on 42nd Ave, with a huge yard west of it. I was never invited inside but two times I saw several guys in the neighborhood coming out of there early afternoon when I was taking a different route to the park.

"Dave, I saw guys, our age, in our neighborhood. I'm sure you know them….come out of Dotty's house?" I suspected but it was still far-fetched as far as I was concerned.

"Yeah, I know them," Dave said, kind of disgusted.

"Are they friends of hers?"

"Sort of," Dave said. "Stay away from there." He shrugged his shoulders like he was uncomfortable with the subject.

"Thanks, Dave, you're a good friend."

Just once, I made Dave unhappy. When making a wet silhouette on dry pavement, my flat feet had five points because there's no arch. Dave had the most beautiful, perfect feet, amazing, each toe stretched out its entire length, and since Dave was extra tall – he eventually played center on Varsity when Franklin took the state championship in basketball – they were narrow but very long. On the other hand my toes were all curled up. I tried to point out the difference in our feet. "You have gorgeous, perfect feet, Dave!" I expounded. For some reason Dave was self-conscious about his feet, did not want attention called to them. A hurt look came over his face. Without a word he slumped his shoulders, turned sideways away from the pool and walked away. I never mentioned feet to him again.

When I attended our ten year reunion Dave asked me to dance. We talked of old times. "Why didn't the guys ever date me, Dave? I usually spent New Years Eve in the bathtub."

"Clancy, you were extra special," Dave said. That shut me up. Dave dated Pearl who was dark, had a bump in her pointed nose, was extra short, and had big boobs. She never smiled and seemed to have Dave on a yo-yo string. Friends couldn't understand their relationship ever. Dave's brother, just out of the service and his girl friend who lived with him, fall term my freshman year at Portland State, drove Dave and I to school each morning in his auto.

Mid-year, Dave dropped out, completed an apprenticeship as a construction plumber and sent his money home to Pearl, who he had married, when he worked overseas, including Viet Nam during the war. In the meantime Pearl found another guy, spent Dave's earnings and broke his heart. Nobody knows what happened to Dave after that. By the twentieth reunion no one had been able to locate him. He was a handsome fellow with a big and good heart. He avoided confrontation for sure. Gentle and peace loving, he wouldn't do to another what was done to him. I was so lucky he kissed me in my youth as a best friend. He always made me feel special.

Some of my best friends continue to be men. Same goes for my son. Some of his best friends have been women in school, college, the work place, and some of his wife's five sisters.

My first high school jamboree was thrilling. Right away I identified with the band music and the rally girls – bouncy, athletic, fun routines, happy, smiling with mostly practical hairdos and built average like me. Their makeup, if they had some, retained a natural look for them, no long, painted nails as far as I could tell.

Nothing was really revealed about football at the gathering of all eight Portland public high schools: Roosevelt, Jefferson, Grant, Washington, Lincoln, Franklin, Cleveland and Benson (an all men's mostly technical school at the time). There was an all girls Polytechnic but with no football team. There were four games for two schools each - playing only one-quarter, so it didn't give any school an opportunity to show their stuff. The bands in all their regalia were a best part of it. But colors and mascots and maybe, new uniforms could make it worthwhile. It had become a traditional social event, not much else. Sometime in the 1950s was the last time it was held.

Parochial

For my freshman year my mother insisted I attend Immaculata Academy instead of Franklin High School. Fortunately the 39th Avenue bus took me all the way to N. Williams Avenue where the school was located. Something was definitely missing at the school. There were no men.

I excelled in my academic classes enough to make the Honor Roll at the end of first term. We wore uniforms: a dark skirt, white blouse and a sweater. Our freshman class voted to choose class colors, green and white, St. Patrick's Irish colors. We all wore our class colors in a Dehen heavy duty letterman sweater, which worked well in the change of seasons regardless of the temperature.

My mother had found fabric, for the required white blouses, she was delighted with. On her Singer sewing machine she brought from Montana, she made two blouses of white, no-iron fabric with Peter Pan collars and button-down front. With an attachment, she succeeded in finishing all of the many button holes. Her favorite creation was the third blouse out of dotted Swiss, somewhat sheer and very comfortable in the fall weather of September, which warmed up every afternoon.

The principal called me into her office. Remember, not particularly comfortable with authority, I entered her office already full of fear and dread. Sister invited me to sit down at a small round table across from her but got right to the point. "As you know, we have strict rules regarding our uniform. The blouse you have on does not meet our regulations."

I was wearing my mother's pride and joy, the dotted Swiss. Sister kept talking and I began to cry – not because I was hurt. Rather, I was angry and defensive – but couldn't get my words out to explain. My mother spent hours making them. You don't understand. This one was a labor of love. What does it matter, Lady? I always wear a sweater over it except on the bus on the way home when it gets too warm.

"It has a pattern. We require plain white on white. Plus, one can see through it," she continued. My tears continued to flow. So frustrated, I couldn't get a word out.

I can't tell Mom I'm not suppose to wear it. It will hurt her terribly. She shouldn't have to be told this. How do I just wear two? My mom will think I don't like it. That will hurt her even more.

I couldn't stop crying. As Sister talked, I became more angry and choked. In my fourteen-year-old world and heart this was a major problem, a dilemma. I couldn't cope. I continued to hold that principal responsible and failed to contain my undying resentment toward her.

Fortunately the physical exertion required by the basketball games provided, above all, emotional release. Girls basketball rules in 1952 were for the birds. As a guard I was confined to only half-court play. Teamed with another guard to play against three forwards on the opposing team, we were required to check the efforts of those forwards to score, retrieve the ball and successfully pass it across the center line to one of our team's forwards on the other half of the court.

The rules made for a clumsy, slow moving, cumbersome and awkward contest. In our third game (I had survived the first two), Shirley Sauly, a six foot hefty blond, my fellow guard, and I both jumped up to go for a missed shot coming off the backboard. We came full force against each other. I crashed to the floor and couldn't get up. My left foot immediately grew to twice its size. Two people lifted me up and I limped off the floor with their support.

My mother took me to emergency on the bus and they x-rayed. No bones were broken, just vessels and muscles in shock. Lots of ice packs were recommended. It soured me on girls basketball...I still yearned for the more logical water polo game with that entire swimming pool to maneuver in. The constant exertion of treading water was invigorating. Girls basketball had to be played in too close of quarters. It provided no space to run, or maneuver.

Fortunately, girls were eventually allowed to play boys rules. The result has been one of excellent achievements and the making of real careers. Above all, athletic college scholarships for both men and women. In reality, Women's Foundation Sports points out that approximately 28% of college recruiting money today goes to women, as a result of Title IX, passed in 1972, which initially opened up high school and college sports programs for women "in equity" to that of the men, if those schools receive federal funds. Once into professional contests, regardless of how successful and/or popular the women games are, their financial return is measly compared to any occupation available to women, so requires exorbitant sacrifices by the athletes to continue to compete.

What I missed most at Immaculata was the opposite sex. Girls dancing with each other at the noon hour made me uncomfortable. I didn't give a lot of thought to it but I definitely avoided that activity, even though I love to dance. But it gave me one more good reason to vacate the Academy.

What I didn't realize is I gave up at least three years of an academic and college prep education, but at the time the price for it seemed too high.

I recall that our cultural environment was devoid of really serious issues but I remember how harrowing my trip home alone after basketball practice was from the bus stop at SE 39th and Division to our home on 45th. Taking a short cut through the dimly lit and eerie Richmond school yard, I would hear something, probably my own noise, turn around, see my shadow, fear that it was another person behind me, then start running for home, hell bent for election.

At fourteen I had a lively imagination-- a best friend and a worst enemy. A mere suggestion, that is possible if not feasible, can still shoot up my blood pressure. I don't automatically doubt, rather I'm inclined to consider the possibilities, unless absolutely ludicrous or just plain sinister or cruel or mean-spirited. I attempt to avoid gossipy people, but lived next door to a vicious female, Reva, for thirty years, loaded with venom. God finally delivered me.

A good friend at Immaculata, Sharon Setera, of Hispanic descent, shorter than me, blond and fun, a serious student, rode the bus home with me. We talked shop sometimes but sitting in the back we usually tried to say and do things that would make each other laugh. School was pretty intense daily, we were unwinding. It was hot that spring so I put my bare feet out the window. The bus driver stopped the bus and over the loud speaker told me to put my feet back in the bus.

Sharon's brother, Dennis, attended Catholic Central, had an auto and was good friends with Mike Lawler, a student at Franklin and a good friend of mine from Creston Park. They came by the house with Sharon MacDougall and told me there was a party on 36th off Hawthorne, mostly Washington High School guys. "Ask your mother if you can go. We'll be back by nine." I invited them in and introduced them to Mom. I explained who Dennis Setera and Mike Lawler were – then asked her if I could go. She gave us the go ahead.

We walked up the five or six wooden stairs to the big house just south of Hawthorne. It was mostly guys milling around on the first floor. Dennis and Mike got a beer for each of us but suddenly they seemed to hover over us.

Mike said, "This isn't exactly what it was cracked up to be. My apology. Take a few swigs then let's get out of here. The girl that lives here is upstairs taking them on. I'm sorry," he said.

Right then, the police walked in. Dennis and Mike explained to the police, "We just arrived. We brought these two girls. We didn't know it was this kind of party. They're good girls. Totally innocent."

A police woman took me home. She told me to go into the kitchen "while I have a word with your mother." To this day I don't know what she told Mom. Mom did say later, "Be careful with the kind of activities your friends want to do. Use your own judgment."

But throughout high school she never put restrictions on us kids, Luke, Matilda (she preferred Matilda to Tilly), and me, by my senior year all in high school at the same time. She said, "Come home when the fun is over, when it's time to quit." She would doze halfway in her bed waiting for each of us to tell her about our evening out. "Goodnight. God bless you, thanks for waiting up, Mom," we would all say. After we were all in she would finally turn out her bedside table lamp for the night.

The summer before my sophomore year was the same routine as the year before. Harvesting crops, water polo in the afternoons, some quieter activities for the most part with my gang. My acquaintances expanded through my friends. The Frier sisters, who I met through Sharon MacDougall, lived in the Sunnyside area and were students at Washington High School. Sharon and I had walked the long distance to SE 32nd, north of Hawthorne, from 43rd off Lincoln, where Sharon lived, to visit them, at their invite.

Helga Frier, the older one, was anxious to create something for us to do. Her folks weren't home. She said she could start her folks' 1938 Plymouth, which sat in the driveway outside their rambling two-story house built in the 19th century, typical of that area. "Let's go for a ride," she said. "We can all take turns driving."

We drove up and down the narrow streets of the old Sunnyside area with Helga at the wheel and me in the front seat next to her – her sister and Sharon in the back. In 1952, there were literally no parked cars at the curbs of the relatively short city streets filled with old houses with lots of prolific gardens of trees and shrubs.

We were all loaded with excitement and elated giggles. "Can I drive?" I squealed. Usually the only ride I took was by bus, the public one whose advertising eventually claimed, LEAVE THE DRIVING TO US.

"Sure," Helga said, "but I don't dare stop. It will kill. Just change places with me," she shouted. "Have to keep pressure on the gas pedal."

To this day I don't know how Helga and I were able to change places, but I was behind the wheel with my foot on the gas pedal – again the steering wheel too playful. We came to a "T" in the road so suddenly I had to turn a corner. Everything seemed to be in speed-up motion beyond my capacity to control. I made a wild, wide turn on to the next street and swung back in towards the curb. Yes, as usual, there were no cars on the entire block darkened by lots of heavy foliage and overgrowth, except a late model Lincoln Continental which I scooped the side out of then pulled away.

I landed a direct hit onto the front panel of the passenger's door and dented the Plymouth's left front fender. Our continual girly chatter and laughter chilled. Shock set in. I don't remember if the auto stopped, but I surely did take my foot off the gas pedal, didn't I? Helga replaced me in the driver's seat. Sharon and I rushed the few miles back to our homes in silence. We never talked of it ever again.

My mother was notified of the situation several days later but never tried to discuss it with me or even explain to me how she found out about it or, more so, what she had been told about the incident. Strange. Maybe another odd incident her daughter might have instigated, totally guilty of misbehavior? At the least, devoid of good judgment. To Mom, this was worse than the school's complaint to her my freshman year last spring when I put my bare feet out the back window of the bus, to make my friend, Sharon Setera laugh. Other students from Immaculata, on the bus at the time, must have reported the incident to the sisters.

The only parked car for miles around just waiting for me. Years later, for a very short instant, I considered suicide as an option. I quickly decided then and there, with my luck I would botch the job and be dependent on others for the rest of my life, which I would abhor. The reality of disasters waiting to happen cured me of any serious gambling problem. That included not giving into impulsive so-called romantic opportunities. For sure I'd end up pregnant or worse. Or contact a venereal disease which destroys one's brain. Ugh!

Why? My Friend?

My friendship with Madeleine Brant was the best thing that came out of my freshman year. She was a year ahead of me but we had a lot to share at Immaculata and continued exchanges at Portland State. In her junior year she transferred to University of Oregon to study architecture, a five year program. She joined a sorority too. We shared our dissatisfaction with the seeming pretention and their basis for so-called selection of us. Both of us were putting ourselves through school with serious intent for preparation for a job. So many of our "sisters," were pampered, and/or social climbers, basing their limited information on the economic position of certain others while looking for someone to marry.

As early as my seventh grade, I had become aware of Madeleine's great art talent. Her advanced couture fashion designs featured in Lipman-Wolfe's windows in downtown Portland that year I never forgot. She was the first artist I admired and got to befriend. I invited her for dinner when we were allowed a guest night my senior year, after I returned to Oregon. She loved my room. The antique gold 9x12 foot cotton rug I found at Woolworth's. The cotton curtains for the window and skirts on the sofa bed with a gold corduroy cover, I made. I had painted the dressers ivory, and found prints of four musicians, each playing a different instrument, fit them in 8x12 inch black frames hung above the sofa bed. The multi-colored cotton was a copy of Thai silk plaids, which are hard to come by.

Madeleine graduated a year early for an architect student in my year, 1959, and was one of five Phi Beta Kappas out of my class at University of Oregon, along with Joan Long, my roommate that year. In February, 1960, she sent me a letter two weeks in advance of her trip to San Francisco for an interview with the large firm, Owings, Merrill, & Owings, and hoped she could stay with me. My trips on the Boeing 707 in 1960, as a Stewardess with Pan American World Airways, were never more than seven days, but I didn't get the letter until after her dates to visit. At that time I had three other roommates, all stewardesses. One of them, Nancy Craft, I had gone to high school with, and she seemed to know more about me and my friends than I did. To this day I avoid her. I had trouble maintaining communication with some of my most dear friends. We all accessed the same mail box.

My first Christmas, 1961, after I married and was back in Portland working as Employment Security Interviewer I at the state of Oregon Employment Service, a civil service position, I designed a special card to send to special friends. I drew a circle, an oblong, and a triangle and oil painted each black, gold, white and red to depict three kings. Madeleine wrote back that she didn't see three races.

"I see hundreds of varieties, actually billions. I'm a miscegenist," she said. "Knowing you, I highly doubt that you're a racial purist?"

I wrote back to share my civil rights efforts. The card was an over-simplified effort to be merely artistic. "My real calling is one thrilled by outstanding art, like yours. I wasn't trying to make any kind of a statement – love colors and geometric shapes. I realize it doesn't even qualify for cubism." I hoped to assure her we were on the same wave length.

Some time later, her address disappeared from my file. Typical of me, I tend to blame unfriendly intruders or silent controllers.

Several years later, Nancy Craft offered some real salacious gossip about Madeleine, involving a married man. I had lost touch with her. Nancy seemed to be in touch with her but didn't specify how, didn't tell the source of her information, but so often she insisted first term relations with people who were important to me. She even told me at a high school reunion that my chemistry friend, Charles Vanderhey, had died? At that time I commented, "He always had a cold – maybe, poor health."

Years later a girl, Annette, who lives in his neighborhood, told me Charles was very much alive and very successful! One of the last times I saw Nancy, she informed me that Ridge Wurl had died of a heart attack.

He was a boss of mine, the Operations Manager for a publishing company, 1983 to 1984. How did she ever know I even knew him or worked for him? I had no reason to mention him to anybody. Over the years other statements of hers stood out: "Austria is going Nazi," and "South Korea is nothing but a military-police state."

In 1996 I found out that her mother, father, and Nancy were friends of my gossipy, next door neighbor, Reva. Nancy had never told me of this fact. Reva was a vitriolic, mean woman, one year older than me who, because my husband was old friends with her husband, had full access to my house. Brad told them where the emergency key to the house was stored, in a flower box in the backyard. My grandfather's first edition of Wendell Wilkies' *One World* disappeared, as did original editions of newsletters I had published as Advertising Director at AAR Western Skyways, 1979 to 1982 (all of which would help me get another good job); as did the Vice President Don Fagan's excellent recommendation for me from that company.

1981-82 saw an economic downturn and upswing of the unemployed in Portland due partially to the exit of Georgia Pacific. Don Fagan had written the recommendation for my boss, the CEO, Dennis Nichols, because Dennis was let go shortly before we were all shut down.

We had taken our patented prototype for a modification of cargo doors for the Cessna Conquest to the 1981 Parls Air Show and sold many contracts for them. At the start of the recession Cessna closed their doors (there was also strange interference in our effort to talk with Cessna) so we could not get shipment of the Conquest, a turbo prop, very much in demand by Pacific Island shippers (as an island hopper). Unable to fulfill contracts, AAR Western Skyways, a fixed base operator at Troutdale Airport, staffed by engineers, pilots, and Air & Power Mechanics (a microcosm of Pan Am people for me), founded in the 1930s by Barnstormers, had to go out of business. Dan was Vice President and marketing manager. His forte was the successful remanufactured engines division. He went on to Flightcraft, at Portland International as an executive as well.

The CEO, Dennis Nichols, an Annapolis graduate who flew jets off carriers, was in marketing with Lockheed before becoming a President and CEO with AAR. Married to a beautiful lady, a former Miss Alabama, who cooked turkey dinner for their family of four children every Thursday, was a great boss, astute at marketing also, and taught me a great deal about the more technical factors of aeronautics. It was his idea for the employee newsletter and its name, *The Wind Soc*. I used it to reduce the animosity dividing the employees that Dennis inherited due to the previous union walkout by fifty percent of the personnel which resulted in the acquisition of the proud company by AAR, an international company. Wisely, I exchanged with all on a one-on-one basis and made the monthly newsletter very much theirs. It was the funnest one-tenth of my job.

Shortly after that, the last time I talked with Nancy's mother, who I checked on by phone because she had macular degeneration, said, "Clancy, they're going to have you ride the bus," and hung up. I called back right away.

The reason I did so is because the last time Nancy was in town in the summertime, she and her mother had visited at my home. Vera asked for a beer so I poured the can into a special beer glass that I used for the first time (one of twelve my sister had given to me when she had to pack for a transfer from Portland to Tacoma). She dwelled on "taking the bus as a girl" and "how unpleasant it was." Nancy seemed to get real anxious. This was unlike Nancy because ever since charm school, her junior year in high school, she promoted "Act, don't react," which to her meant, "Pretend, remain poised."

After Nancy's efforts to change the subject, she intruded in her mother's speech, suggesting that Vera was getting senile, "Mother, there you go back in time again, we're at Brad and Clancy Bloch's house."

Her mother said, "Hush, child, I jolly well know where I am. Such nonsense."

Nancy decided they had to be someplace. "I didn't realize how late it is."

"But I haven't even drank any of my beer, yet," Vera protested.

"Mother, you rarely drink beer."

"I drink it when I'm with friends, out having a good time."

I believed Vera. In the past she had expressed her love of the colors I had painted and wallpapered, different in each room, the Japanese wood block prints and Chinese silk screen from Tokyo and Pan Am days, and the twenty-three blue hydrangeas that bloomed all summer around the backyard making it look like an English garden. This visit was the first time she didn't ask to take a scenic tour. She definitely had something on her mind to share with me.

My callback was answered by a woman who merely said, "Mrs. Craft has retired for the night." Click. Within five months, Nancy's mother had died. I went to her funeral. Vera Craft had always been good to me.

There is a sixtieth high school reunion for 1955 coming up in September at a hotel on the Columbia River. In spite of Nancy, I try to attend the reunions. She extracts more than just one thread of paranoid out of my person. Strangely enough, I sold my auto in 2004 and do ride the bus. I use to wonder, "Who is they?" Now I'm happy. There are an abundance of good people in my life. Others give me adequate and reasonable challenge. No one is tossing tidbits of odd information at me. I tend to go overboard to provide my source of information when I offer it, possibly to a fault. So I couldn't care less who "they" are, these days.

Public High School

My first experience at Franklin High was an odd one. At the registration/class scheduling front desk I was informed that my intention to take second year Latin required the Latin teacher's permission to get into her class. It was tricky finding her room in the theatre wing at the southeast end of the school. Her classroom seemed to be an afterthought. After I entered the foyer to the auditorium with the stage for plays and assemblies, I found the stairs to her rooms on the second floor, narrow ones that curved around in a circle to a room at the top of the stairs in a turret-like space. The teacher was a thin, little lady, sort of older, like the room itself.

"I like to keep the class at six, we're already at eight," she said. Already I was getting claustrophobia in this small room with the low ceiling and one high, round window for daylight.

"I don't get paid enough for such large classes, huge changes, extra work," she said.

"I got mostly A's. I need a language for a B.A. in college," I said.

"We will probably go too slow for you, due to where you're from. We don't talk religion in the class. Our library source is the Roman classics. I don't need to remind you, Latin is a dead language. Better to take one that's spoken today."

"But it has improved my vocabulary a lot," I persisted. "All those root words."

"It would be wise for you to look for something else."

With that, I assumed she was shutting the door on me. I left confused. I didn't even consider starting over with another language so ended up with an elective of Journalism. Classes were closed. There was no second-year Algebra, so I got stuck with a study hall, which was a waste of time. It drove me up a wall because there was no homework.

I did exert effort to get A's in Ms. Bruckner's sophomore English class, which was nothing but grammar all year long, very little literature. Can you imagine? I didn't take a book home for three years, but I had a great time.

Years later, in 1967, I played bridge at noon hour with Ms. Bruckner at Cleveland High School when I substituted there one day. She said something odd to me I retained, because I didn't understand what she intended. She said, "You were an overachiever." Did she mean I just worked hard but surely wasn't gifted? Or did she mean I was one of the many Franklin students who were economically disadvantaged, one of the few at that time from a single-parent household, therefore dependent on scholarship and good fortune to go onto college? She never explained her use of an educator's typical jargon, almost as indecipherable as that of psychiatrists.

Next stop for me was John Peery's tryouts for "A" Choir. He played chords on the piano and I did scales with my mouth wide open saying "Ah." He said, "Although you have a wide range, you're definitely a Contralto. My alto section is my largest section."

"I am comfortable at the tenor level," I offered. "Do you need tenors?"

"I do. Karen Richards, a freshman, is also going to join the tenor section. Do you know her?"

"No, sir."

"She's real friendly. Studied piano, like you have."

Making "A" Choir was the best thing that ever happened to me at Franklin High School, not only because of the singer who sat next to me for three years, Karen Richards, but due to the giant-hearted choir director, John Peery. He not only introduced us to great music but shared the triumphs and sorrows of his life with his entire choir. He made us feel like family, or at least trusted co-workers.

Patiently, he helped us master some of his favorites: *Smoke get in your eyes, No Man is an Island,* a poem by John Dunne set to music, *HMS Pinafore, The Hallelujah Chorus, For Unto Us a Child is Born.* In between workouts he would share his life with us. He had a patent, and manufactured convertible risers, which he sold to choir groups, and convertible platform steps, which worked well for band groups and some symphony organizations.

His plant was in a big barn on his property in Milwaukie, overlooking the Willamette River. He invited us kids to his home at least once. His house was a large Dutch Colonial with a huge family kitchen. He barbecued hot dogs and hamburgers for all sixty of us in the choir. Some of the senior fellows, mostly basses, took over the cooking duties for him.

He was very proud of his two daughters, Ann and Esther, who were also students at their local high school. He shared his great joy when Esther was selected to join the junior symphony directed by Jacob Ashlanomov. In addition to conducting, Jacob was also a composer who Mr. Peery greatly admired. He introduced some of his compositions for us to get familiar with; very advanced, very difficult. Years later, I was in Dr. Ashlanomov's All City choir to do Mozart's *Requiem.*

In our senior year, Mr. Peery and his wife adopted a baby boy who immediately had complications that required stomach surgery. This was the first time we saw tears of fear on that giant of a man. Before, we had seen only a few tears of sheer joy. It is only now that I recall, did not remember this when I first thought of him, that Mr. Peery actually had a handicap, which he also shared. I saw him as passionate, forthright, tall and hefty, and open; he could easily have loomed up for me to be as much as six foot five.

One of his forearms, I think his left one – honestly I don't recall for some reason, mostly because his impact on my heart and soul had nothing to do with his lame arm, but according to him everything to do with it-below the elbow was crippled, shriveled, giving his hand only a precarious grip with a thumb and maybe a twisted finger from birth. I now realize that it was probable that Mr. Peery feared his new son would also, as a child, be hampered with limitations. Childhood with a limit is the most painful time for a person.

That year Journalism was a disaster. A new teacher, a very short roly poly fellow who the students, outside of class, referred to as "Meatball," turned out to be rather single-minded, on a one track--the technical aspects of publishing. He stood at the front of the class of fifteen or so, to use the blackboard to emphasize the technical aspects of publishing. He posted the dimensions of various size pages from magazine to tabloid to the size of the dailies published by the *Oregonian* and *The Journal.* Then he divided them into the typical columns that would be most logical, according to him. He followed with the number of letters per line that would be allowed for each and concluded, "The journalist must diligently count each letter and carefully plan what he is going to say according to the space allotted to him."

Meatball talked mathematically day in and day out, whereas I wanted to know how to research and write an article. Plus I yearned for insight to decide what subject or person or issue was newsworthy. I sat in the back of the room, out of earshot to avoid the teacher's humdrum of numbers, which held nothing for me. The sports reporter, Gary Hval, sat at the table next to me.

"He's giving us all kinds of information we'll never retain or ever have a chance of putting to work," Gary said. "I have to shut him out and just stick to what I have to do."

I knew Gary was also on the golf team, had been since he was a freshman. "I've never golfed – oh, garden golf – I'm terrible."

"Putting is the toughest part for me, too. Garden golf does golf an injustice. It is a great physical exertion, bar none. Requires stamina."

Years later Gary Hval was my mother's dentist. When Gary's son took over, he also was my mother's dentist.

When Gary wasn't in class I went bonkers. September afternoons in Oregon turn hot. The windows on the south wall of the classroom were wide open. The bottom sill on the first floor was only two feet from the ground on the outside. Impulsively I crawled out the window, entered the doors to a hallway right next to it, turned the corner of the room, and came back in the only door at the back of the classroom, just to see if Meatball saw me. He was absorbed in his configurations on the blackboard.

Shortly, I decided to go through the same motions once more. I wasn't too creative, at my age, at occupying myself with more innovative activities, I admit. Jeremy Duncan, the fifteen year old main character in one of my favorite comic strips, *ZITS*, doesn't even do dumb things like it. This time when I reentered the classroom, Meatball referred to me directly, "Clancy, you have just earned my dunce cap." He drew a circle on the blackboard. "Come forward and see if you can fit your nose into this circle."

Of course, I was never inclined to disobey a teacher or authority of any kind. Phenomenal, the circle was at a perfect height for my nose.

"Now remain there until the end of class, which is five minutes away," he ordered, then bowed out of the action by fussing with an assortment of papers on his desk.

The class didn't make a sound. There were mostly men in the group, some of whom I recognized, with reputations of "serious" or "good" student. Always up front in the large classroom, they had adhered to every word Meatball uttered. When Meatball quit talking, a silence fell over the class. No one tittered. No one laughed. I was embarrassed, but not ashamed, or even humiliated. But, of course, I never in my lifetime related this ornery naughtiness to another. I guess my antics were my way of letting someone, anyone, know that I was not learning a thing during this entire hour in this damned classroom, because honestly, up to this time, I had always been reached by the teacher to some degree.

In looking back, Meatball never made any attempt to engage me in a chat with him, but strangely enough, he gave me a "C" as a final grade. That's the only response I got from him other than the circle on the board just for me, that proved he was aware of my presence in his classroom. In fact the only time I became aware of him talking to, not with, an individual student is when one of the fellows would raise their hand and ask him a question. To his detriment was the sour fact that his mumbling voice just did not carry, a seemingly essential requirement for a teacher who relies on the lecture mode.

Gradually, though, I did abandon "body language" to express my disappointments or frustrations. I learned to absorb it, keep it inside and bear with it. It took a lifetime to learn to give verbal expression to my feelings.

Tom Colosuano, my biology teacher, was a godsend. His lab experiments -- dissecting a worm, a clam, and then a frog were absolute heaven for me. I had no trouble with the rote memorization of organs and their functions. They made sense to me. Mr. Colosuano was delighted with my participation and achievements. He loved his subject and I did too.

He loved life, was always happy, and engaged on a one-on-one basis with each of us. He made us want to dig in and discover. He also had a sense of humor. When we dissected crustaceans, he knew how to shock us or just leave us squeamish by raising the shell high in the air, opening his mouth wide and tossing a huge, raw clam, whole out of the shell with the juice, and down his throat, swallowing it, not even chew.

I loved biology, especially the lab work, but didn't feel the same about botany. That disappointed him and he wisely discussed my shift in interest with me. He was working towards a PhD, which he eventually completed, and ultimately became Director of the State of Oregon Department of Public Health. He died young. Fortunately, I continued to read newspapers and saw his obituary. Funny how we love some teachers and feel nonplus about so many.

Plants? Foolish of me. I didn't consider them alive, whereas animals were live. That's odd! Years later I became a lover of gardens, live ones. When they die off in a vase, sometimes their artwork stays vital for me as well. Like I stated in my 99-page pictorial with captions of 2005 I did for my fiftieth high school reunion, Flowers in Felony Flats. It is mostly of special people in my life at that time, neighbors, fellow workers, regulars on my bus trips, and flowers in my garden. So maybe I'll finally grant it to them, flowers can also be people. Why not? These days, corporations are, created on paper by laws of the state. It doesn't even have to have employees to be considered people? I have a good friend, Gerard B., a fellow journalist and great bridge buff, who treasures his three cockatoos as necessary companions.

I didn't have the math background for chemistry, just Algebra I at Immaculata, but survived that subject due to my astute reports as a result of hands-on lab experiments. I dropped Physics at the end of the first day. His entire lecture was on gravity and I figured it was so logical,

What was the big deal? We had it in fourth grade. Since then I've spent a lifetime catching up to basic principles of physics.

My favorite subject, bar none, was social science and the history of human behavior, especially achievements. For instance, good history describes the impact of scientific discoveries on human beings, as well as labor, money and political organization. That's what turned me on more than an in depth examination of science itself. I did skip over details of war battles, but I gave attention to the developments of new weaponry.

Two of my history teachers, sophomore year and senior year, gave me opposite experiences. The first one was total frustration through no fault of his. Mr. McKee never discussed politics, economics, or sociology. In the real estate business on the side, his class, QUIZ 'EM, was for the sole purpose of grooming his students for the weekly contest on the radio. Each day we were to answer his questions based on the Journal newspaper, which we were supposed to read.

Dumb me. My mother took the *Oregonian*. I did mention just once to Mom that for this class I needed to read the *Journal*. Mom said, "If it's a good newspaper, the news will be the same." So I read the *Oregonian* from cover to cover, but rarely was I able to answer Mr. McKee's questions. The reason I was able to "float" in this class of fourteen is because practically none of us had the answer to his questions.

The only person who did answer one question after another was Virginia Johnson, a beautiful girl who was Mormon, just recently moved to Portland from Utah. Her family was renting a duplex on Division.

My senior year, Mr. McKee was suppose to coach me as one of the three chosen to speak at Commencement. The subjects were: Political, Economic, Social. He told me my subject was Economic and gave me no further instructions except the time limit for the speech. Turned out the commencement program listed my speech was to be on Social, not Economic. Needless to say, my comments weren't too relevant to the subject I was suppose to speak of. In my forties my Mom and I would have supper at a restaurant where Mr. McKee and his wife would be a few tables away but he avoided acknowledging our presence, neither with eye contact or a mere nod of his head. He never did know I had no access to the *Journal* newspaper. Would he have even cared? Would it have made a difference? Teachers are human first, teacher second, so have likes and dislikes as well.

His message in my yearbook he entered after the commencement reveals his assumptions about me. "Remember that comm speech? Can you ever forget it? Actually, did you ever learn it? Lots of luck. Jim H.C.McKee "Mac," Department Chairman.

Besides Tom Colosuano and John Peery, my other favorite teacher was Mr. Devlin for Economics and Asian Studies. A retired army officer ("a double dipper" as some envious teachers referred to him), what he cared about was down my alley. He led class discussions and encouraged us to do research and exchange in small groups with each other.

He was a tough taskmaster and corralled me. Choir was third period at the far west end of the building, so I had to travel long hallways to get to Mr. Devlin's class at the far east end. In the beginning, I would arrive not quite on time. Devlin put a stop to that. "You say hi and talk to everybody on the way, Clancy. You're going to have to do that on your time, not on mine. Quit the socializing and get to my class on time."

I had to hustle, but I was never late another day. For our research projects, he gave us a time to deliver our findings to the class. I was shocked by the birth practices, the caste system, kitchen deaths, dowries (obsession with gold) and the poverty of "modern" India, despite Mahatma Gandhi's battle with the British over the salt tax. My information predominated for me over and above the claims so many western scholars make regarding India's "superior" transcendental philosophies. It actually "feeds" some people, so they fast.

I didn't give up easily on India. My freshman year in college I studied at the Reed College library in the evenings, which was open to anyone at that time and practiced the honor system. I walked out with a book on Hindu philosophy, an intriguing one, loaded with beautiful and simple solutions for all of humanity. So attached to it, I kept it in my library from

1956 to 1965, nine years, and even took it with me to Texas in 1964 when my husband was transferred to Houston.

When I returned to Portland in 1965, I immediately returned it to the Reed College library. The Houston experience brought my heart and mind Thump! Back to reality. Fortunately, my trip with that book did not take a lifetime. My conclusion: that philosophy is out of touch with us. Besides it made me a thief, big time. It taught me that theft makes a damned fool out of me. Honestly, I felt guilty about it the entire time it was in my possession. My overestimate of its value did not hold water, whether it be a diamond or gold. How about a loaf of bread? Or rainfall?

I excelled in Devlin's economics studies. My early experiences with my grandfather's co-operative marketing for small farmers, public power debates, crop parities, and my early work in the berry fields, with entire families dependent for their continued existence on that work, and budgeting experiences surely assisted. Knowing that my mother had to use her entire nurse's salary for nursery school for my brother and sister, and pay for rent, food, transportation and clothes with social security and the veteran's pension didn't hurt. The federal benefits to my family of low cost housing, HUD, enabled me to respect the positive role of government in my beloved country to my livelihood.

I was aware of mentally retarded fellow students in special education and government efforts for them. I recognized them in the hallways and said hello to them. There definitely existed varied levels of capacity to learn among us, and unique ways by which some things came easy for each of us.

But at that age I wasn't cognizant of all that I had already become aware of, and no teacher other than the ones I mentioned were aware of that about me. Whereas, some students at my age, fifteen and sixteen, were very sure of themselves and their capacity for being in the know. I was still swimming and having a great time learning from others, including some fellow students. By the end of my sophomore year, my grandfather told me that a teacher had told my mother that I was "not responsible," but no teacher or counselor approached me with that information or coached me with a suggested direction, not one.

In fact, Nancy Craft joined me and Jim Todd and a few others that sophomore year as we watched a Junior Varsity basketball game after school. Nancy worked in Miss Bowers' sophomore counseling office as a student secretary. Nancy blurted out the following information but didn't say how she acquired it. "Clancy Rohring and Jim Todd have the highest IQs in our sophomore class." I wasn't shocked particularly by the information, although it was the first and last time I ever heard it. But what riled me was Nancy's possession of such information.

But, as usual, I didn't even take the news home to my mother. Maybe what I loved about Devlin's class was the encouragement to express myself, but not about my person, not ever. I pursued a friendly and hope-you're-as-happy-as-I-am reputation. If I could make someone feel good about themselves or their situation, it was very satisfying for me. Won the Girl of the Month for Personality by vote the following year as a junior.

That year Paul Frozki invited me to the Junior Prom. Nancy Craft's political action group of four or five women, her fans and supporters, were all a twitter about my invitation. I really didn't know Paul or of Paul. I had never been in a class with him, actually never saw him in the halls chatting with others. They considered him a real "catch." "He's going to be a doctor," they said.

Of course, the first thing Paul did was to introduce us to the chaperones at the dance. I introduced Paul to my mother, Mrs. Rohring. Further down the line were his folks. He said, "Clancy, I want you to meet Doctor and Mrs. Forzki."

I extended my right hand to shake theirs and said, "I'm happy to meet you, Mister and Mrs. Forzki."

Right away, Paul uttered, "It's Doctor Forzki."

"Okay, then, you can call my mother Nurse Rohring."

He turned away so I didn't see any expression on his face and said very little the rest of the evening. We must have danced but I don't recall. Did chat with lots of acquaintances. I had a good time though, and when he drove me home, before I opened my door to get out, I leaned over and kissed him on his right cheek, and said, "Thank you." He looked astonished, like he had never experienced the gesture ever before. He touched his cheek, rubbed his index finger against it then, looked at his finger. I guess to check for lip stick color. I immediately opened my door and got out. I doubt if I said another word. I rarely probe following my impulsive actions.

My mother was awake as usual and let me know how much she enjoyed the "Nurse Rohring" retort. She wasn't a frustrated feminist but definitely a democrat and a progressive.

Monday, Nancy Craft's cronies all gathered at lunch hour wanting to hear every detail of the Saturday night time with one of their favorites, Paul Forzki. I told them about the kiss. That seemed to titillate their wildest dreams about the, in their eyes, odd choice on the part of Paul, for a date.

In fact, then or now, he never engaged me in a conversation. This is a fact – because I recall most wonderful conversations with wonderful people. His senior year Paul did seem to be terribly in love with a sophomore, a serious student who had no trouble expressing herself. Amy was very popular. Her single mother operated a beauty shop. She lived in my Richmond neighborhood. Often I saw him walking Amy home after school. For some reason I was concerned for both of them because I sensed that the doctor and his Mrs. probably wouldn't welcome this relationship with open hearts…er, minds, or maybe just pocketbooks. Paul's choice of Amy and his apparent devotion to her, made me take him to my heart forever. From thereon I cared what happened to not only Amy, but Paul too. I hoped they both would come out on top of their worlds.

In fact, one of the Craft women, who was the most aggressive promoter of her loyalty to Nancy, became a devoted friend of Paul's. She visited him in Boston, when they were both in college, and flaunted a photograph of her and him in a boat on a waterway, a mill race. It seemed important to her to be associated with important and successful persons. On our high school Year Book staff she wrote the caption for each person's odd future, which were supposed to be funny. For me she wrote, "Crazy, mixed-up kid."

Eventually, the Craft women pointed out that Paul went to Harvard and practices very advanced, orthopedic surgery with Portland as his base, married, with two children, 'a pillar of Eastmoreland.' When I asked her girls about Amy? "Amy, who?"

I got A's from Mr. Devlin on my two-page comparison, "Communism versus Democracy." Concepts like that were rarely taught in the classes I was allowed to take. Finally, today, some educators want to insert conceptual questionnaires into testing of comprehension, instead of facts and dates. Fortunately for me, concepts have dominated civil service exams for years and, also publications, a compelling industry for me. Those opposed to it say they are too difficult for most students. Some educators consistently underestimate the capacity and potential of their students.

Nine years later I recalled my mind-boggling experiences at Franklin High School as a sophomore. In 1964 at a metro high school outside of Portland, in addition to my five classes, I had to take over a World History class for sophomores, from a teacher who was let go on short notice. It turned out his kids loved him because he only taught bible stories instead of the curriculum. They could relate to his subject and feel comfortable with plots and characters they knew well because they had had it in church ever since they were three or four years old.

The real subject of World History with me scared them. They struggled and grew distant. Because it was a small class, to cope with their fears, after assigning a chapter from the text book and questions to answer relative to their reading, I worked with each one of them to sort out each one's individual comprehension of the subject to encourage verbal exchange.

At fifteen, students relied on the exact sentences in a text that answered my question and repeated it verbatim. The problem with this is they were using someone else's words but not acknowledging the source of them. It was my goal to help them put the answers into their own words, to actually understand what the idea was telling them, rather than to try so hard to memorize answers verbatim. It would help them think about them and relate the event or the conflict or the idea to things they are familiar with in their lives now, or what they see on television or a magazine or, more recently, the internet.

It took them a long time to get comfortable with my routine. Even at that time in history, people weren't comfortable, outside of family, or possibly even at home, to engage in one-on-one exchange with another. It almost seems that they feared their private world might get exposed and maybe be considered unacceptable. At least teenagers now can get it off their chest by texting to trusted friends.

Alesha and Her Daughter

Karen Richards became one of my best friends. A swimmer, too. In the summer when she got her brother, Chad's auto, she would take us to High Rocks, a swimming hole on the Clackamas River, out 82nd Avenue. Before the dam went in upriver, the rocks were perfect height for diving into the snow-melt, fresh water, yet stacked so that one could easily climb back out of the water. A railroad trestle crossed high above the river and some brave fellows would actually dive off of it.

Karen loved to lay in the sun. At Richmond grade school she had been selected as an example of one in perfect health. Her best friend, Marcia, also got that award. She lived around the block from Karen. Marcia was on rally with Karen and me my senior year. We went to Eugene for the state basketball tournament in 1955 so I could root for my brother, the Point Guard on the team that won it all. Karen had a boyfriend on the team, forward Chris Maddox, so spent her time between games with him. I introduced Marcia to one of my cousin, Harriet's twin boys. They hit it off. Marcia, on the phone fifty-five years, later said "I still recall Jason Bruce with warm feelings." We remember times and people who make us feel good, or in some cases, bug the hell out of us, return to us again and again for interpretation or reinterpretation.

Karen's folks were always welcoming. Her father, manager for the Shell Oil operation in Northwest Portland, St. Helens Road, west of the St. Johns Bridge, was transferred to Portland from Longview. He engaged me often regarding political news. From Alabama, he was a strict con-servative and spent many hours gardening. His small, mostly front yard, facing west, was a showcase on Mt. Tabor of roses and annuals when in season. When he did retire, Mr. Richards bought a new house in Lake

Oswego with a huge lot for gardening. He was a smoker of unfiltered cigarettes and ultimately died of lung cancer.

Karen's brother sometimes gave her and me a ride home in his automobile. I recall Chad explaining why he could relate to Tom Wolfe's *You Can't Go Home Again*. Chad, a serious student, won a Bell Labs full scholarship to Stanford University to study Physics. Shortly, he quit automobiles entirely, rode public transportation and relied on a bicycle to get around campus. Upon graduation he refused to go to work for Bell Labs. He opted to stay on campus at Stanford to do research and work towards advanced degrees. Years later, after a short stint as instructor at University of Washington, he moved home, after his father's death, and connected with the local hi-tech industries as an independent consultant.

Karen, a year behind me, joined my sorority at Oregon and entered the Honors College majoring in mathematics. She ran for Miss Eugene. She was five foot six inches, shapely, with long athletic legs. She selected a Rachmaninoff piece for her talent. She was absolutely stunning. Like her father, olive skin with a dark tan, and prominent, rich black brows, and dark eyes (although her father's were a light blue) that gave off sparks of light when she spoke and laughed. Her mother, Alesha, and Karen both had Burmese and Siamese thoroughbreds with papers. The cats displayed obvious loyalty and affection for both women.

Alesha became one of my favorite people to converse with. When Chad entered college she found a part time job as an accounting teacher at a private business college in downtown Portland and worked there for many years. She talked with me in person and over the phone about what was most important to her, her family and her job. She had a great sense of humor. Like my sister's husband, she would relate how she flubbed the dub and get me to laugh with her as she laughed at the situation. I can still hear her infectious joyfulness.

Shortly before my last contact with her, she fell on an icy day at her mailbox out on the street curb and broke her tailbone. After that my address book disappeared and I had no way of contacting her.

I let Karen down as well. Her junior year in college, she was frustrated in calculus and began to rely on a fellow student, boyfriend, for his coaching, like a tutor. Allen Cranston was graduating and slated for an engineering position in Seattle with Boeing. He pressed her to marry him and finish school at U of W. Mr. Richards opposed the marriage so refused to give Karen away. Karen walked down the aisle by herself. Because of Father Thielen's dictum against my cousin's request for me to be a bridesmaid, I couldn't be in Karen's wedding.

In 1969, when my son was four years old, Karen and Allen invited my family for a Sunday visit to water ski at their place in Kirkland on Lake Washington. Her daughter and three- year-old-son skied like naturals. My son couldn't get up after several tries, so it wasn't a great day for him. Karen served barbecued country-style spare ribs and gave me the recipe I used for many years. Mine was a sad marriage and I had had some major setbacks at the time so didn't share them with my dear friend. It appeared she was in fat city.

It turned out that Allen was a hayseed from Pendleton, Oregon, with no bent for the finer things in life such as art, music, philosophy, people, or even sports. He drank and took his foul moods out on my dear friend. She finally divorced him and too quickly married an Olympic swim coach. Alesha said of him, "He wasn't as smart as Karen." Karen was sucked in because her major exercise was lap swim, which she did in excess to control her weight and spend extra energy. High intellects often possess more energy, which Karen had. She also suffered from periodic migraines. Again she became corralled by an expert that obsessively knows one thing and nothing else. Eventually she won medals in Senior Olympics for Australian crawl and breast stroke, over fifty-five.

According to Alesha, Allen died of too much alcohol. His body was found in a motel in Alabama. He did a good turn. After the divorce he gave Karen title to the house in Kirkland on the lake. She taught math in the Seattle school district all her life to pay the taxes on that property and provide for her three children.

Karen and I shared happy times together but couldn't connect in our troubled eras. I guess we didn't trust each other enough. We never did share any real serious, personal concerns. When she was in town one time I visited her at her family's home in Lake Oswego. We related again and laughed again about our trip up west Burnside, as teenagers, to visit my mother at the old St. Vincent's, in Kings Heights.

With earnings from his summer job as a truck driver in eastern Oregon pea fields, my brother, Luke, purchased a 1948 two-door Chevrolet. I got a learner's permit. Karen had her Oregon Driver's license and was willing to go with me, driving his auto.

West Burnside was a very narrow four lanes, still is, and the right side wheels of the car started riding on the curb. I put off veering left, for fear I would run into traffic in the lane next to me. The steering wheel had so much play in it, I didn't trust it. But silly girls that we were, we started laughing uncontrollably at the bizarre situation. Finally we rode off the curb at the end of the block, probably at 18th, so we were back on level ground again.

That isn't all. On the hill the parking lot for visitors was sloped. It scared me. There were only two autos in the entire place. I parked at the far west end, next to the one whose nose was sloped downward. When it was time to return home, having no idea of what it would take to get the car out of the downward slope I pushed hard on the gas and the car leaped hugely out of the slope, swept across the entire parking lot and came in contact with a pickup truck parked on the other side.

Assessing the damage – fortunately there was no harm done to the truck but the chrome strip on the driver's side was wrinkled up and on the asphalt. The holes in the side of the car, that had held the chrome strip, were visible but there wasn't a dent or loss of paint whatsoever, no other damage. We put the crumpled chrome in the back set and cautiously headed home. To this day I can't recall what part of the truck I came in contact with. I realize the situation could have been a total disaster. See, God watches out for me. This was worse than breaking my brother's nose, I did believe. He was so proud of that car and took such good care of it. That minor damage trashed it.

"If I did that to my brother's car he'd never let me drive it again," Karen said. I don't recall ever driving Luke's car again, but wisely I never ever asked for it.

To synchronize the clutch and gas pedal was difficult for me to maneuver. In fact I never did master it. Finally I bought an auto with automatic transmission in 1987. My friend Karen had to contend with a total neophyte and nervous twitch at the wheel, which I don't think she was aware of at the time. After all, we were only fifteen and sixteen year olds in the fifties, not the technically astute teenagers of the twenty-first century. The manual transmission was more complicated to execute than the clever same off and on button on a computer or remote control. I was all thumbs, slightly schizo, but hadn't arrived at the level of a *ZITS* comics character, as yet. I recall my first time on a computer keyboard compared to an electric typewriter, the reflex action was so fast and touch so sensitive, I feared I would never be able to catch up to it.

In my defense, as Production Typist for the attorney, Mr. David Turtledove, in the fall of 1955, my first job to pay for college my freshman year at Portland State, I tested at 90 words per minute on a manual, to type collection letters. Of great historical importance, I was replaced by a huge word processor that barely fit in the width of his tiny office, operated by a Chinese girl who put my stellar production to shame.

Maybe Chad was right. You can't go home again, or rather, you can't reproduce good times and friendships of yesteryear, even though they and you still continue to exist.

Plays and Musicals

In my sophomore year I won the walk-on part of Anna in the play, *I Remember Mama,* directed by the drama teacher, James Shaffer. I was to utter three or four expletives in just two scenes which did get full laughter from the audience, Mr. Shaffer's objective. He knew how to extract it or create it. I was a girlfriend of the teenage girl telling the story about her immigrant mother in Brooklyn adjusting to her new home in America.

He had me walk with extra large steps, leaning forward at a 45 degree angle, and behave completely hyperactive. It was shades of a Carol Burnett character like the janitress well before she captured us on TV – extreme posture, distorted, unique facial expressions and a voice screeching a few choice words from a high register of excitement and "enthuse-usi-asm," (as Diane Schneider, a roommate my sophomore year in college, use to spout) to a low-ground-level swallowing of shock and disbelief.

It was so fun and so well received that the Drama club gave me a trophy for Supporting Actress at the end of the year, even though I wasn't a member of their club. Odd thing about Mr. Shaffer, Nancy Craft's Political Action Club would gossip about him suggesting that he was a womanizer, "fell in love with his leading ladies." Later in life he did divorce his first wife and married another. He never came on to me, no one did. But at our ten year reunion in 1965, I was pregnant with my first. He asked me what year I got married? I said 1961. He said, "Why did it take you so long to get pregnant?"

"We just finally figured out how to?" I touted. Wisely, he didn't attempt to probe that. He seemed satisfied with that response, although a slight sense of dissatisfaction passed over his usual controlled countenance. He directed and interpreted plays, but I don't think he ever wrote one.

The next year, Louise Thomas was my vigorous friend who liked to talk for hours on the phone with me before bedtime. I would sit on the back steps of the enclosed porch out the kitchen door and converse with her on the family phone. Mom would get disgusted at such lengthy calls and suggest "it's time to call it a day."

We had a lot to talk about. Her mother was recently divorced and moved her family back to Portland from Idaho. She was a licensed drug clerk and got a job at the drug store in Lents so rented a house close by off Foster Road. Louise had a younger brother and sister, she took responsibility for, probably from their beginnings. She watched out even more closely for her beautiful blond sister who suffered a scoliosis condition.

Tied down by her family at home for many hours, Louise was an insatiable reader of current literature. She was especially entertained by the controversial new book, *Catcher in the Rye*. One of her favorite passages was about the old duffer with "his thumb right up in there," in his nostril. She related other excerpts other times that amused her.

Ironically, in 1973 as Counselor at Estacada High School, I was asked to evaluate that same book available in the school's library. A religious-based group of people had requested that Catcher in the Rye be removed from our library on the basis that the teenage boy telling his story in the book sets a bad example to our young people. The request was so out of touch with the young people's lives even then that I sarcastically said to the superintendent who requested it: "It can go either way, which conclusion do you prefer?" I admitted to him that his request for my review and recommendation was out of touch with the lives of young people in the 1970s.

In conclusion, I'm not and have never been a book burner but personally avoid gore, the actions of cruel and hateful persons, and destruction of people and the fruits of their labor, in fiction. If it's real, I'll read it, but avoid Ann Rule and Truman Capote because the images they paint never leave me alone, they persist. I prefer to see beauty and goodness in my mind. The domination of murder and crime seem to manufacture constant emotions of fear and negativism. To me, that's unhealthy.

GULICK Service Club went to Mt Hood each year and stayed at the MAZAMA Lodge owned by a skier's club. Louise and I were both members so I begged my mom to let me try skiing. It would be my first time to the mountains. With a hundred dollars I bought pants, boots, a black parka with red piping and a big pocket across the chest with a zipper, gloves and a stocking cap. I could rent skis once up there. I didn't have a sleeping bag and hesitated to ask Mom for additional. I had already spent my money for school clothes for the year. Louise said hers was double so we could share it.

I was exhilarated by the gorgeous vistas and the crisp air. I caught on gradually on a nearby hill, Bumble Bee, developing a massive bruise on my left thigh. That night after supper we skied some more on the shorter hill behind the MAZAMA lodge under lights until it turned too icy. An attractive teacher staying at the lodge spoke with me and gave me hints regarding skiing. That night she sat on one of the benches at a wooden table to read a book. I wanted to be like her.

My love affair with skiing, although I never did get to buy a pair of skis, always rented, made me eligible for the queen's contest to be voted on by all the colleges which organized the first intercollegiate Winter Carnival when I was a freshman at Portland State. It was sort of dominated by Portland State students, since we were in closest proximity to Mt Hood, so I did win. An outstanding fellow student and skier, the congenial Dick Potratz, was crowned King.

My date became jealous when I danced with several fellows at Log Lodge after the ceremony but just said he was ill and would have to turn in for the night. We stayed at my friends, Sid and Joan Pearson's cabin halfway between Sandy and Timberline. He didn't inform me of his still ill health so would not be able to take me to launch the racing events at Timberline until after it was too late to get another ride. Sid and Joan and the others had already left for the festivities.

A cell phone would have helped. I became a no show Queen and serious skiers, some of them future longshoremen, never let me forget it. One of them who I played pinochle with at times called me "Queenie," which wasn't exactly comforting. No one knows the reason, until now. I wasn't sick, my date was. He delivered me to my home in Portland early that day. In my disappointment I still tried to be a good sport about it. My effort at good sportsmanship will continue ad infinitum. Ridiculous. Dick and I got our pictures with our crowns on, featured in the next day's *Oregonian*, with a story on the outcome of the ski races. That made me feel even worse.

That night Louise sweated profusely. It made the sleeping bag, stretched on a top bunk in an unheated sleeping porch, almost suffocating. I was half awake all night. I tried to remain in one place – not move so as not to wake her. I swore then I would never share another's sleeping bag ever.

In Menlo Park, while training with Pan Am, my roommates, who were teachers, made friends with MBA students at Stanford. I told one of the friends of a fellow dating a teacher, about my highly uncomfortable, and only one time, never again, experience, sharing a sleeping bag. He started it, I went along. "We'll do Europe with one sleeping bag between us; back to back, and belly to belly." We both laughed. He was a big, homely Greek galut I never took serious. Years later I wish I would have. He made me laugh. He was a good Joe.

The most fun Louise and I had was in the musical *Finian's Rainbow* our junior year. We were the singing duet for just two scenes, a church scene and the last one for the wedding finale. Encouraged to ham it up big time, we exaggerated and warbled in a high range at times. Louise, a soprano, could hit higher notes than me; sometimes in unison, other times as treble and tenor, a real screech. We had a hard time to keep from laughing, breaking character, due to the audiences har-de-har-har. Supposedly old ladies singing our hearts out with joy, for a wedding of a young couple, and the Lord. Mr. Peery and Mr. Shaffer collaborated. We wore wigs and outlandish Easter Parade-like bonnets and floral dresses with stuffing to emphasize our matron-like stage in life.

Maybe no one in the audience knew who we were – although Louise had a distinguished long face and a firm jaw with a cleft in her chin, giving her an extra large, beautiful smile with perfect teeth, and large brown eyes. Her very creamy complexion colored readily by a natural blushing. She didn't have to wear makeup. My deep voice and pointed beak of a nose possibly would give me away.

In the late spring, shortly after the musical, I had a slumber party. My sister made arrangements to stay that Saturday night with a friend, to let me have our big bedroom for five friends. Mom offered to make her special homemade caramel-pecan-cinnamon rolls for our breakfast the next day. Naturally we stayed up all night, except Louise who crashed out.

About 5 AM we were restless and looking for something to do other than talk. We needed exercise. We pulled the sheets off my double bed. The bottom sheet wasn't fitted either. Tied them together, then tied one end to the metal post (not too big around and was joined to a metal cross bar so the sheet wouldn't slide off the post even if the pressure on the sheet moved the knot up the post) at the head of the bed closest to the window. Each of us climbed out the second story front window over the porch, then ran down 45th to Division and back to the house. Louise slept through it.

Back at the house we realized we were locked out. Had not taken that into account. No way could we trust the sheet rope we made – we had dropped off it to the entry pavement. The sheet rope didn't hang out of the window far enough. That was probably a good thing under the circumstances. We thought about hollering for Louise, try to wake her. That was a bad idea too, because it would probably wake up the neighbors before it woke Louise. She could sleep through anything. We were becoming real problem solvers.

As a last resort, in our pajamas after all, we rang the door bell. My Mom got out of bed that Sunday AM, early, to open the front door. She had a disgusted look on her face. When we were all in and heading for the upstairs sheepish-like, Mom spoke up for all to hear, "I bet you're ready for breakfast. I'll put it in the oven now. It'll be ready in an hour. There's only room in the bathroom for one at a time. Take turns, girls."

After the girls left and the day quieted down, Mom said, "I'm so fortunate because I buy quality sheets for the beds at Penney's. But what if someone got hurt, Clancy?"

One of Louise's best friends was Linda, a serious French student. I should explain here that Lents, at that time, was home to many very low income persons including students at Franklin. Louise befriended many of them including Linda, who was on her own at an early age but survived due to her high IQ and passion for knowledge. No wonder she was swept off her feet by a fellow who passed himself off as just as dedicated to the subject matter as she was. Louise was also friends to a boy and girl who had lived together since they were twelve and were also students at Franklin. He worked part time as carry-out at a grocery store – initially he lied about his age to get the job--and it, by hook or crook, supported them and paid the rent for the studio they lived in, with a bathroom down the hall.

Linda and I double dated my freshman year at Portland State for a trip to Astoria and Fort Stevens. Tom H. was his name, an upper classman, he led me to believe, was a history major and this was his third trip for the purpose of exploring Fort Stevens more closely. Anyway, on that trip, he took advantage of Linda I found out much later from Louise. And shortly after that trip, Linda committed suicide. Years later I found out that Tom H. ended up as a history professor at McGill University in Canada.

At first, Louise thought that maybe I approved of such behavior. I was totally unaware of his and her behavior as we went separate ways touring the Fort, which was a labyrinth of narrow dark passageways. My date was a buddy of mine and a perfect gentleman. If he knew about Tom he never shared it with me.

It turns out this was Linda's first date with a fellow, but Tom had flirted with her in Western Civilization class, where he was a grad assistant.

So Louise mistrusted my date, even more than she did me. And he was a friend of the engineering student who she married her sophomore year in college. Fred H. gave her a good life. Louise got her dream house in Alameda, with a view. She totally remodeled the interior and had three children. But tragedy seemed to stalk her loved ones. Her two daughters, after graduating from college, were both killed in the same auto accident. Her grief along with poor health shortened her life prematurely. She didn't live to see fifty. After he retired from his company as an engineer, a reliable coworker of Fred's told me that her widower was an early developer in Ridgefield, now the fastest growing town in 2015 in Washington.

My Brother and Sister

At St. Stephens School, in seventh and eighth grades, to replace his paper route so he could play sports, Luke was given a janitorial job after classes, and in between football and basketball practice and games. Reliable and thorough but dyslexic, undiagnosed at the time, those persons in decision making positions assumed that the kid, since he struggled with reading although a whiz at math, was slated for grunt and muscle work, not anything that took schooling. Whereas today, those born with dyslexia are recognized as potential, with great capacity for learning and encouraged to spend their time developing facilities in reading and spelling to achieve academic pursuits. Nelson D. Rockefeller, dyslexic, graduated magna cum laude from Dartmouth. My granddaughter, with Luke's dyslexia and my flat feet, is a scholar/athlete.

In summers my brother went to Athena, twenty miles out of Pendleton, for pea harvests. Mom's brother, Uncle Jim, was a mechanic for the pea equipment there and his wife's daughter was going with the son of the Lieuellen's, a large family of local farmers. Jim had dropped out of Carleton College to join the Air Force and was stationed in Pendleton, Oregon, as an airplane mechanic during the war.

For the first two years my brother was too young to qualify for a driver's license, but he did drive trucks loaded with peas down a winding road off the top of a hill, which scared the hell out of him – the brakes were not too trusty. He was advised to just jump out, "bail," if he lost total control, which, for some reason, never happened. It was sun up, sun down labor and he banked his earnings. When of age, he purchased a 1948 two-door Chevrolet, which made school activities, especially practices, easier to manage and still get home for supper.

At Franklin High School my brother became recognized as an athlete and a beautiful human being and a gentleman by his peers-- a playmaker and natural leader in three major sports. As Point Guard and co-captain of the basketball team, he worked with his friend, Bjarne Jensen, the six foot nine inch center and other talent, including Dave Smith and Bob Matthews, forwards, to win the state championship for his high school. As a running back in the Shriner's all star game – city versus the state – he was selected the Outstanding Back at the end of the game. A short stop in baseball, the team again was competitive. My sister's husband was also on that team. Ultimately Luke was selected for City of Portland's Interscholastic League's Hall of Fame. I can see my brother do stretching exercises by jumping in the living room to reach the high ceiling. He finally succeeded in leaving his finger prints on the white paint up there, but he never reached a six foot designation. His stats remained, 5'11", 145 pounds.

I was on rally at the time and got a reputation for demonstrating outstanding spirit for the school's teams. In reality, I was mostly rooting for my brother. I was his greatest fan. He struggled as a student on some classes; the teachers passed him over for Athlete of the Year. Instead the teachers chose a scholar, the son of a doctor, who swam competitively. That was in 1957, his senior year. This decision broke his heart. Possibly he made a commitment to prove the experts totally wrong about him. By God and country and hard work and yes, opportunity, he did.

Luke paid for his two years with savings at University of Oregon and played varsity baseball. The football coach, Casanova, said Luke was "too injury-prone to consider." He had broken a collar bone in high school which healed quickly. He got B's in biology out of over 200 students taking the course, but he needed a sports scholarship to stay in school. After voluntary military duty in the Marines, (He's a straight shooter and honorable, like a marine's reputation), he went to work. Years later he continued his education in Marketing at a California college.

As a Manager at Firestone, a regular customer, a regional manager for Federal Mogul, impressed with Luke's person, offered him a job. He got experience in sales and management with that company's industrial parts, but refused a transfer to the headquarters in Detroit. Instead, he invested his savings to become an independent defense contractor and distributor. Ultimately Luke developed an exclusive contract with a Taiwanese manufacturer whose O'rings have become the most in demand by the space, aeronautic, ship building, and nuclear submarine industries throughout the world.

The fellow who got the Athlete of the Year award eventually became a dentist in Portland and remained a friend of my brother. In 1980, the dentist, Dr. Ron N. said to Luke, "You should have gotten the Athlete of the Year award. I have never ever led myself to believe that I deserved it. What's wrong with teachers?"

A few years ago, looking back, Luke said, "No one ever hugged me." In the fifties in sports and socially he's right...hugging wasn't in style. Luke wasn't the only one that didn't get a hug in those days. Now hugging, high fives, fist bumps, even a buss on the cheek is in order.

Eventually Luke ended up with four children, three boys and a girl. They all went on to college and independent lives.

My sister was always wise. Her field was art and keeping records: scrap books and/or keeping track of her money and her wardrobe. In her sixth and seventh grade, just behind our brother, she modeled for a popular junior store in Moreland on SE Bybee Boulevard for their spring and fall shows. At a size six, she followed instructions to the letter and was invited back, until the owner sold his location to another type of business. Then Lady MacTavish, mom's name for her, got a summer job at an independent ice cream store at 42nd and Hawthorne. In high school she was selected from her class to be the school's representative at Charles F. Berg and continued to work there when she attended the Portland Art Museum after high school.

My brother had a fit when she started smoking cigarettes, lighting up with her friends her junior year at the local coke and hamburger joint at 50th and Powell. He also had a fit one time when she came out of the bathroom in only a bra on top. We were all very modest even while sharing one bathroom. A story we all like to tell on her is how she passed out in Anatomy at the Portland Art Museum art school when a nude male model disrobed. Tilly had never seen a nude man before. Honest! Tilly was on rally her freshman year and swam back stroke on the swim team. But a knee injury requiring surgery put an end to both those activities.

Tilly had a boyfriend her freshman and sophomore year. She started dating Guy M. her senior year and planned to marry him. She saved her money and invested in household and kitchen items towards that event. First she worked at Triple A auto insurance then advanced to S.J. Pounder Realty as his Sales Secretary. When they married, Mr. Pounder's gift for her was a huge rock maple dining table, chairs and hutch from the leader, Brunke's. When Guy, a Terminal Manager, in charge of sales and operations, was transferred to Tacoma with Bend-Portland Trucking, the Josi family operation in Oregon and Washington, she had to leave her job. Eventually they ended up in Bend, Oregon with that firm and became well liked by the business community in town. My sister had three beautiful and bright children, two girls and a boy, all of whom went on to college.

Mom's Injury

The year, 1950, for the new house was a major year in my mom's life for another reason as well. On Two North, a ward for men only, she attempted to keep a drunken patient from falling out of bed. She wrenched her back and suffered a slipped disk which put pressure on her sciatic nerve. That weekend she spent at home in bed with a makeshift traction but returned to work, without fail, at seven AM Monday morning. She never missed a day of work due to her injury and subsequent pain. Ruling out surgery, due to the history of damages that seemed to occur, at that time, to the spinal cord, she resorted to see a chiropractor only twice but learned to avoid them from thereon. They had other treatments in mind to so-called take her mind off the pain.

Ten years later her left leg had shriveled to half its normal size and caused drop foot. To keep going she invested in a custom brace to control her foot, especially to lift it for elevators and stairs. She wisely limited herself to a few aspirin, had a cold beer in July when she ironed on a hot evening. In her later years, at Christmas time, she would buy a bottle of rum for hot toddies, like Tom and Jerry's, one of my dad's holiday favorites.

My mother was exceedingly quiet about this major interference in her life. She did not let it interfere in our lives or in her career at the hospital. That same year she was promoted to Director of Central Services. Due to her research, she introduced scopes, a major invention for the health industry. Surgeons would ask her to make a trip to their operating table in preparing for surgery to install one of them. So new, they hesitated to try to do it themselves.

When the scopes first arrived, the doctors in surgery called her department for Mary to come and "install the blasted device."

She was a working manager, always on her feet. She was especially valuable to Human Resources because she was willing and very able to train her staff. Eventually she ended up with twenty-three employees, mostly minorities. Other department heads would ask her to take an employee they said they "can't do a thing with. You seem to work wonders." Mom seemed never to give up on anybody.

When St. Vincent built their new hospital on Barnes Road in southwest Portland she designed her Central Services to include built-in gas sterilizers. Due to her recommendation to build a separate hallway and elevator for personnel to transit, in an effort to isolate and reduce the transmission of staphylococcus disease, those facilities were added by the architectural team, who consulted with the department managers.

I was overly concerned for my mother due to her pain, which she never gave voice to. Looking back, my concern was three fold. First, she was my mother and I was in need of her. Two, she was the bread winner and we kids readily comprehended where the money came from. And three, her accident, in a sense made her extra fragile and us more diligent in following through on our obligations we must fulfill.

Years later we kids acknowledged that each of us internalized similar reactions I have heretofore expressed. She was an extraordinary, exceptional human being who did not push – yet, we knew what her expectations were for herself and, surely, that's the least we could demand of ourselves. Finally, in our maturity, each of us admit that once in awhile we tell ourselves Mom would be proud of me, us.

In1958, my junior year in college, I returned home and went to night school. I worked full time at Westinghouse Electric Supply from January to September, and returned to Oregon my senior year. To establish credit, I bought my mother a Zenith television, her first, at Meier & Frank and paid for it on time. She got hooked on television. That was before programs became overwhelmed by advertising. With Pan Am I was able to fly her to San Francisco and we did the Fisherman's Wharf and China Town. She loved it. I purchased Noritake china for her and a monkey pod huge bowl for varied nuts in shell she always displayed at Christmas time. It had a second smaller hole beside the big one so that the shells could be easily disposed of by anyone cracking the nuts. Listing these makes me realize how little I did in return for her contribution to me.

The pain was always there. A constant. We kids knew it was there but we never asked, "Does it hurt, Mom?" She never uttered, muttered, cringed or complained. The pain remained a dark cloud in our midst, but it never made a sound. It remained silent, indefinable. No attempt was ever made to register the degrees of or comparisons to. No one-to-ten or one-to-five hundred was ever driven home. When pushed to the limit in her late seventies she resorted to the use of a cane and gradually began to bend ever so reluctantly at the waist to keep on her feet, to achieve the goal she had set for herself at the time.

Finally discovering tennis shoes and giving in to a walker, such a release, she set records for getting there. Her pride, her self-determination, never failed her. We three were so grateful and, yes, humbled by this super human being who chose to bring us into the world and loved us "each to his own needs." She never let us down. She never gave up on us. She never gave in. She is a prime paradigm of August Wilson's statement by the papa, the major character in his play, as a parent reiterating his commitment to his son, "I brought you into the world, so I owe's ya."

Actually, more pragmatic than spiritual, she gave credit to the nuns managing the hospital at the time for recognizing her exceptionalism. They're the ones who promoted her. When she had her major infarct at the age of sixty, after she recovered they put her back to work in her same capacity, enabling her to retire at the proper age, sixty-five. She tried to repay them by leaving one-fourth of her estate to the Sisters of Providence. The other three-fourths went to us, divided equally.

Bored and rested after a year of retirement, she applied at St. Joseph's retirement hospital as a part-time Central Supply director and was hired. Operating a Plymouth to get to work, and selling her house for an economical studio in a retirement home close to Holy Rosary church, with a view of Mt. St. Helens and Mt. Adams to the north, she finally retired for good at seventy-six. Sadly, she found very few people she could identify with. The inhabitants were mostly women who were retired on their husband's labor, not their own, with little interest in politics, economics, or sports, not even bridge, cribbage, or pinochle....Mom's games.

In the summer of 1995, my mother told me the doctor has said she was in "heart failure." That weekend, Mom took the bus to Bend to visit my sister and her family and died in her sleep in Matilda's guest room. Matilda took care of getting her back to Portland. My mother had made complete arrangements for her mortuary and funeral mass at Holy Rosary. She died July fourth which is a tribute to her. She fought for human rights and opportunity and justice for all and believed in democracy.

At the end of the ceremony we all joined in to sing, "Take me out to the ball game." Mom would have approved. She was a sports fan, especially for college football, golf, depending on who was playing – her favorite was Lee Trevino who dominated in the '70s - and major league basketball and baseball. She had watched O.J. Simpson when he played for UCLA, followed the trial and continued to believe in him. She never ceased to be an independent thinker her entire life.

She did have trouble regarding the rules put forth by her church versus her own sense of ethical choices, as many devout Catholics experience, but she hesitated to give voice to her questions. In later years she expressed her view regarding a woman's reasons for abortion. "An unwanted child should not have to be brought into the world," she said. "To make it in this world and beyond, he must be wanted very badly. Who in hell do these politicians think they are? God?"

"Man has the tools now to intrude big time so as to keep us from death, that is, sustain vegetation. Is that the human life my God intended? Tell them to keep their meddling off me."

Ciao, Good Heart

Sunday, September 27, 2015 was a full day. I wrote my opposition to Ted Wheeler's just announced candidacy for Mayor of Portland. He is Secretary of the Treasury for the state of Oregon, claims to be a democrat (the city and the county majority happen to be democrat), but his total power maneuvers include a mean spirited reputation for dealing with underlings at his mercy and criticisms of fellows in other elected positions accusing them of ineptness, unresponsiveness and, above all, wasting money. According to Mr. Wheeler, he is the only one who sees the real problems created by their stupidity and insists he is the only one who can solve them.

I explained two examples of his flaunting misuse of power when he was Chairman of Multnomah County commissioners. Typical of demagogues, as usual they avoid dealing with the real tough problems. Instead they create or at least dwell only on those issues that cause fear for one's own survival, or give false information to rev up the public's insecurities, anger, and outrage. (Two embassies hit in Obama's administration, whereas there were six of them hit in Bush's reign, the President that manufactured the war on Iraq).

So far the opposition to the executive branch elected by the majority offer nothing short of war to satisfy our desire for absolute security, even though we object to anyone listening to our private phone calls to make a date to have sex or buy a stolen automobile. They deny money, food, and help to the unemployed and displaced workers, or the disabled or refugee, because that "just produces more lazy people and dependency." So far homelessness is not on Wheeler's agenda, but it is on that of every serious mayor on the West Coast, at the least. I have no idea how he feels about our need for rain, but that one could put him further on my defeat list.

I sent my four paragraphs of information on his past little known exploits in the mail to the Pamplin papers' starting with The Portland Tribune who is outcirculating and outadvertising the Oregonian (recently purchased by a far right Republican organization out of Orange County, California – same county that went belly up due to investments in derivatives several years ago), the Willamette Week whose investigative reporting is legendary, and the elected representatives who happen to be democrat organizing their conference next month in Sun River, south of Bend, Oregon,, (since Ted Wheeler says he is a democrat).

As a result, I didn't get to Fred Meyers to shop for the week until after 4 PM. The theme for the week was to feature products out of Italy or that we connect with the Italians, like pasta, meatballs, olive oil, and tomatoes. On the back of the employees black t-shirts was printed the words, Ciao. "Ciao" caused me to reproduce one huge memory which, maybe, was a fate changer. I'll never know.

♦ ♦ ♦

The whine of jet engines from the airport down the road filled the silence. The sound grew to a roar as the commercial plane took off, flying low over me as my taxi turned into the San Francisco international airport. I watched it and wished I was on it.

When the plane was just a small point of light in the blue sky already over the Pacific Ocean, my tears began. The full impact of this reality, the 8 AM departure of Flight 444, a Boeing 707 for HNN, then on to HKK, without me, crew member L54688, finally hit me. Every airline employee's worst nightmare finally happened to me. Why me? Why this flight of all flights?

I was going to meet Klars in Hong Kong. Can't call him. Don't know his accommodations. He's in transit from Sydney to Tel Aviv to build another Hilton. He was going to contact me at the Peninsula Hotel on the Bay in Kowloon where the crew always stays. We were going to do two days of the Chinese New Year, especially the fireworks off the ships in the harbor. It's 1961. The Peninsula's huge lobby overlooks the bay. Starting Feburary 15th/it's the year of the Ox. Born in June, 1937, that makes 1961 my year. I'm a Fire Oxen, that's positive, in addition to being a frog.

We've been honorable, damn it, for the sake of long time college Sweethearts: his is, I refer to her as Rhonda Ivy of Boston; mine, Brad, a fellow history major, trying his hand at life insurance in Portland, Oregon. Klars, from Oslo, has a Masters in Physics from Cornell but studied architecture and mathematics at the Berlin Institute.

I met Klars Hoyer at a party in Menlo Park where he was on construction projects for Ampex and Hewlett-Packard. He stood out in the crowd. Extra tall, blond, blue eyes. For roommates Nancy and Dina, and their dates, I made, using Dina's cookbook, real giant meatballs and spaghetti. Cooked the sauce all day. A triumph.

Earlier he had marveled at my swimming but he never got in. He stood by the side of the pool to admire me taking laps, Esther Williams style. We did the Kingston Trio at L'omelette's on El Camino Real in Palo Alto. He took me to a rich, swanky bar in downtown San Francisco. A sophisticated black at a piano bar sang songs like *Smoke Gets in Your Eyes* and June Cristy's *Midnight Sun*. We had one drink.

One Sunday drive, we toured Atherton – surely beautiful homes that reeked of money spent on fru fru nonessentials in order to flaunt an exclusivity they were seeking or achieving. To me big houses always look like extra hours of labor just to manage and maintain. I still suffer my dishonesty that day. When looking at a handsome colonial I said, "That's like my grandfather's house." Actually grandpa and grandma retired in a small cottage beside the forested creek on twenty acres in the Boring lowlands. Uncle Bud and his family of five lived in the big house there with a façade of four silly colonial columns. Inside it had no central heating, just several fire places for wood, although the house did have a swim pool behind it. After his folks passed away Bud tore down both houses and lived in a deluxe trailer on the valuable property.

Klars always hugs me hello; gives reinforcement for my swimming, my attire. It was too good to be true. I'm not accustomed to such warmth and sheer joyfulness. He makes me feel wonderful. But I have behaved with reservations, doubts about me, not him. I don't really qualify for this relationship. I worked my way through college on a dollar and a quarter an hour Production Typist job. The oldest of three beautiful achievers, raised by a widow, an R.N. from the highlands of rural Montana, a long time manager of central services at the largest hospital in a small state of less than three million people.

California had just surpassed New York State with sixteen million inhabitants. An amateur player, even if I am a Frog rather than a Turtle, in a huge, sophisticated arena. I'm still a peon. It's more than that. His father is an executive of Standard Oil of Norway. After the war, my grandfather, a champion of family farmers and sharecroppers, and human rights in general, stated that Standard Oil took advantage of wartime demands for oil and made "exorbitant, excessive profits." Instead he bought stock in Boeing and the Chicago White Sox to reinforce his love of sport in general, baseball in particular. He belonged to United's One-Hundred-thousand-mile club – quite a feat in his day. Trusted and recognized as an executive in his own right, he knew House Speaker Sam Rayburn personally, he did tour the SAC base in Omaha, Nebraska, and recommended farm implements for southern Italy farmers for the Marshall Plan, as an advisor to President Truman.

Thank goodness I got to a phone on the Bay Shore Freeway to call. First, I called Pan Am scheduling so they could call a stand-by, then for Triple A., finally, a Taxi. I never gave up hope I would make it, left home at 4 A.M. to allow for exceptions, intrusions. The last consideration on my part was a simple/complex flat tire. I was tempted to keep driving on it clank clank-clunkity-de-lump, but absolutely no options. Weekday traffic hamstrung the taxi. Why didn't the flat happen in my parking lot?

When I'm with him I feel so beautiful, competent, necessary, and beginning to get up the courage to be totally honest with Klars. Alone again, I come back down to earth, accept my limits. I don't dare to dream. Missing this flight closes the door to a possibility, however impossible. I can't call him. He is in transit. Will send a note to his new contact in

Tel Aviv. It will never get to him. Hochtief is a very old, giant German company. He will think I did this intentionally. He can't help but take it personally. He always takes the lead. He can't help but read it as a final rejection.

Hey, maybe I could catch another 707 to Honolulu for the 10 AM flight tomorrow. No, the Peninsula is booked, always. There's no way I could be registered for him. Arriving February fifteenth – 2 PM HKK time – sixteen hours beyond Pacific Standard Time.

Showers allowed at the Hotel – 3-6 PM due to water shortage, politics in the territories. 4 PM start of New Year celebration – Buffet in the hotel Lobby overlooking the Bay. He was closing out in Sydney on the twelfth. He was on his way to Hong Kong today, but ferrying to Macao for business. Back in Hong Kong on the fifteenth. Hochtief has no office in Hong Kong. They merely set up field offices for projects. He has to be in Tel Aviv on the 18th. I'll try to reach that new office, after the fact. After all, his favorite goodbye was in Italian, "Ciao, good heart", translated, "We'll meet again" or "until next time."

Just one time I was almost late for pre-flight briefing. To make it I parked my 1954 Chevrolet Bel Air in a fifteen minute zone and ran. It was a nine day flight to Manila on the old Stratocruiser, Boeing 337. The one with the lounge in the belly, making it look like the Amphibian, Infamous China Clipper. This was my last piston aircraft assignment. In 1959 passenger traffic doubled internationally prompting the introduction of the 707 tested for five years by the US Army. In January, 1960, I flew the first maiden flight out of SFO, on the Boeing 707 jet to Fairbanks, where the runway had been extended.

Our flight pattern out of Honolulu followed that of Air Force One to Wake Island, which we combed and double checked, stayed there overnight, then on to Guam, where we picked up military officers. In Manila I got to see President Eisenhower eight feet away from me, in the Manila Hotel hallway leading to the banquet room. Our Pan Am crew cards gave us security access. He was headed for the first free nation Economic Conference, held in Tokyo in May of 1960.

Anyway, upon return to San Francisco, I taxied clear to Redwood City to retrieve my auto from towed status. It was worth every penny. Given a choice I would have done it again – that is, parked in a fifteen minute parking space to make a flight. So vital, so viable, so real Klar's unreal. He challenges my energy. I wanted to be, at the least, his friend, forever.

At this point, this is a futile situation. Neither a punt nor a prayer is in order. My future has been decided by one damnable flat tire.

Not long after that I married Brad and the first thing he did was sell my 1954 Chev, all paid for. Shortly the reality of real human struggle set in – married to a poverty of spirit and a façade of real character, only then did I revisit my fated, missed flight. I invited a temptation which wasn't there at the time. At least I should have gambled and revealed to Klars the real me. Then I believed that people differed greatly in what they cared for most of all. I had assumed that Klars could never care for my choices, my loyalty to the teaming masses – their human struggles, my concern for the common good, my attachment to Thomas Jefferson, Abe Lincoln, FDR, Truman and John Maynard Keynes. To this day I believe that human intelligence, skills, talents, creativity, can be discovered in the least of these, every color, origin, and economic level. But I'm not a gambler. I had already chickened out. To avoid ultimate rejection? "A fool and afraid," said Lady Macbeth. In regret I never gave him the chance to choose. What if? My husband didn't even like me. Maybe Klars would have loved me.

Pan Am too was unreal. At the time my intentions for leaving were to build a life. It took me more than thirteen years, including ten years in the teaching profession, and I still didn't match the annual salary and perks plus free travel I enjoyed as a Stew. Most of all, its personnel were by far the most open-minded, informed, energetic, accepting and generous people I have ever worked with, bar none. Eventually it got blown out of the sky. That great company just disappeared in December 1991.

In 1961 a stewardess couldn't be married and be employed with the company. In 1969 they changed their policy and opened the ranks to married women. They notified me of the change in policy and offered me my job back. I had a four-year-old who I couldn't bear to be away from even eight hours at a time. In fact I was teaching at the time and suppose to coach tennis after classes ended for the day. I abandoned the courts to pick up my son from Montessori, and disappointed the one girl who wished to play tennis at that time. I had asked Brad to give Herb to me. My son was always number one in my world. He liked to say, "I was in my mommy's tummy in Houston, Texas." About this time he also asked me to give him a little sister. I could not deliver. I knew when I was pregnant with him there would be no more. That's one reason I wished him to be twins, big time. I gained forty pounds, all out front. I thought he would be twins – my grandfather was a twin. He was so active, never let me forget him. No ultra sound. I knew God would give me a bright and healthy boy. He did.

♦ ♦ ♦

I returned from Fred Meyers at 7 PM and immediately began to water the garden. Racquelle, next door, on her way to her car to go to the store thanked me for Franz's everything bagels I left on her doorstep last Friday,"They're my favorites,"

"My favorite is onion, but can never find them. Not at Freddies who donated these to Meals on Wheels – but, they were Franz, weren't they? Franz, too, delivers their day old bread on Friday at Gresham," I added.

"I want to volunteer for Meals on Wheels. How do I do that?" she asked.

Robin, at East Portland Community Center needs people badly to deliver. She would be happy to hear from you. I can give you her phone number."

"I'll come and get it as soon as I come back from the store."

I finished watering – counted slowly, only to twenty this time for the big pots with roses, to eight for the small pots of geraniums, petunias, et al. I shut the water off, unscrewed the nozzle from the hose, wound it in a circle, came back in the house but left the front door open to welcome Racquelle. I also turned on the porch lights because it was getting dark.

Ciao made me think of the DC-6 in December, 1959 – before the 707 – over Alaskan waters headed for Annette Island. The square-shoul-dered Purser woke me – the cabin was silent. She said the engines had stopped – descending to de-ice – trigger. Emergency procedures are in order. She put her finger to her lips – I didn't say a word. We pulled the giant rafts from the upper storage – ready to inflate. The engines started. We gave the high sign and a grin. I went back to sleep. At breakfast, not a word was said about our harrowing night out there. Conversation was on the news of the day out of Viet Nam. Strange, I didn't take time to consider fear or ultimate ramifications? Merely took it in my stride. Looking back?!

When Racquelle arrived I gave her the number for Robin at Meals on Wheels from my address book. "Tell her I gave the information to you. She is a recent college graduate and speaks Chinese which helps our large group of Chinese and Vietnamese who come for lunch. Does an excellent job. I rode with a friend to help out when she had cataract surgery to help her deliver the meals, but I found the people, mostly in apartments, very depressing. Robin took over my troubleshooting duties with the old timer Asians and Russians so I've just been kp duty – until I got replaced by a couple of mentally retarded trainees. Now I just manage Cherry Blossom Bridge for seniors on Tuesdays there. Go to Gresham otherwise, because just have to take one bus, the number four."

Racquelle explained, "I want to do it two times a week. Did you know our condo will be auctioned off tomorrow? Roy says he's going to try for it. We pay eight hundred and fifty dollars rent. He said if he gets it, noth-ing will change for us. I'm going to the auction – want to find out what's happening right away. Can't wait."

"Roy's a good man, good manager. He drives for Providence Hospital – they're from Costa Rica. Don't you love their dog? I hope it happens for you, Racquelle."

Racquelle does not work. Her husband is an early morning chef at a popular restaurant on Sandy Blvd. She is partially deaf, since three years old. She reads lips mostly. Can only use her sign language with others with sign language.

Part Five

Finale Members – However Temporary

Steamed Clams

Scheduled to play duplicate bridge at a retirement home in the Lloyd center area on a Saturday in June, predicted to reach 100 degrees, I donned black Bermuda shorts topped with a white sheer cotton embroidered blouse with puff sleeves, and black walking sandals, watered the garden deep, counting to forty for the big pots, read The *Columbian* on line and removed all the fund raising requests from the democrats going bonkers on my eMail. They were celebrating the Supreme Court decision in favor of Obamacare and same sex marriage. It's still an uphill battle – the struggle "for the minds of men," a phrase coined by Noam Chomsky, professor at Massachusetts Institute of Technology.

Before taking the blue MAX to the Lloyd Center, I had a bacon burrito at Don Pedro's and loaded it with all the extras including roasted onions and peppers, and wrote the checks to pay some bills. Jed always pays way before the rent is due. This check included the fifty dollar increase I asked for. On it he wrote "Rental freeze until 12/2017." When I raised the rent I told him I would not evaluate the rent for another two-and-one-half years. He's become more at ease, less defensive and more talkative ever since. My good fortune is that his passion, obsession with food is to my advantage. He'd rather spend his money on food than anything else. His other passions are music, the internet and gifts via AMAZON's Prime to his family members.

He was excited about doing steamed clams and invited me to share at 5:30 PM.

Got home in time. "I'm home early, Jed. Made quick connections. Green line came right away. Couldn't cut through the park to get it. A beer fest was there. The sign at the entrance said, 'Over 21! Need a glass and a wrist band.'"

"It's an international beer fest," Jed said.

Who's sponsoring it? I didn't see any names on the parked semis. Was setting up when I arrived – going big time – lots of people in their twenties, thirties."

Jed came in from the porch and pulled the screen door closed. He usually closes the glass door too. "Clams stink up the place so I'll leave this door open."

"This is a day to celebrate. Saw my doctor yesterday. My blood pressure went down to one hundred and thirty-three over sixty-nine. He was relieved. I had told him it went high when the republicans took over congress. It actually did go up then. Now the wooly Supreme Court delivers, for once in their lives, but Chief Roberts still opposes same sex marriage based on states' rights crap. Some states still use that excuse to practice all types of discrimination," I orated loudly.

I stay out of the kitchen when Jed is in there. It's a serious matter of territory when he's cooking. I sat on a stool in the living room, at the high counter with the cut out, facing him.

"A man from Texas said over his dead body. He's going to burn himself up. A Democrat said, 'Oh good, burnt bigots, no demand for,'" Jed said with a straight face.

"Gorgeous," I touted.

"A couple of others said they would burn themselves up too," he added.

"Donald Trump's a riot. Did you see where that South American singer has refused to perform at Trump's Miss USA pageant because of his put down of Hispanics," I offered.

Enough of that. Politics is not Jed's favorite subject. Food is. "Safeway had these for a dollar-ninety-nine per pound plus a manager's choice of additional fifty percent off so I got four pounds," he announced.

"That sounds like a lot," I told him.

"If they're as good as they should be we'll eat 'em all," he assured.

Jed filled my pasta pans with a sixteen ounce Rainier beer and two cups of water. He dumped the small raw clams, just over an inch in diameter, in an inner bucket with holes, then fit the glass lid on top. Quickly, it boiled over.

"Turn it down to eight," I quickly offered. "Once they're boiling, I always do my pasta and potatoes at eight but with plenty of water. I thought you just want to steam."

In just a few minutes, Jed announced, "Done. But I'll let them sit two minutes."

"What kind of clams?" I was curious, thought I might want to buy them again.

"Safeway calls them Venus, but I'm thinking they're Manilas."

"Not just baby? I have had them only once in my life. Mayetta Rocks fixed them in wine for lunch forty years ago. Those razor clams from Long Beach – large, all free – Trudy gave me, were so tough. They're tricky."

"Like I said, Clancy, you got to beat them with a mallet. Tenderize. Ready."

Jed dished up, putting the clam shells in one small dish. Spooning some of the butter garlic (he had melted in the large electric fondue pot his sister-in-law who works at Macy's gave him), he filled onto another small plastic dish, same size but different color. He reached in a sack to the right of the sink and pulled out a large soft roll. "These I got for us to use in the garlic sauce."

"You mean not your Texas Toast this time. Last time you ate four of them." (I caught myself trying to point out to him the sheer volume of food he eats – felt guilty – that's a no no, Clancy, live and let live. I'm too impulsive.)

I didn't want to bake in the oven, too hot today. Suppose to be one hundred and one."

"I was in Macy's today. They had specials on fondue pots and deep fryer. I bought a popcorn deep cup, plastic, on sale for my family for five dollars. It fell over in the shopping bag on the bus when it lurched, and cracked half way down on one side. Don't you think I can take it back?" I wanted Jed's opinion. I did take it back the following Thursday. The clerk explained. "It is hard plastic – will break just like pottery or porcelain." So I realized. "Soft plastic would absorb the salt and oil."

Jed didn't say a word. Dinner seems to put him into a séance. He loves to talk about food. His eyes light up. There's a higher pitched excitement and additional emphasis in his voice. "The Chinese know what to do with seafood. They're my favorites." He changed the subject to his one and only favorite.

I moved with him. "Your friend paid for all of it. That's fantastic. Even your drinks?" Two days ago he told me a friend took him to Wong/King's on Division for lunch. They had lots of dim sum, his favorite, tempura, sushi, kebabs, as appetizers followed by several entrees, "all sharezees."

I dished up. I found my son's stainless steel baby fork in the top drawer of the credenza to use as cocktail tines to pull the tiny clams out of the shells and dip them in garlic butter. Sitting at the dining table I looked out the wide window sporting my new two-sided red plaid café curtains Trudy stitched up for me which replaced ones I made ten years ago. As I feasted I became aware of a bee working the blossoms on the giant Linden. Right then I decided I better not replace that tree with a Red Bud even though the Linden is so messy.

Jed came back in from the deck to dish up seconds.

"It was absolutely superb, Jed. Thank you."

"I had thought about garlic bread but can't do it in the micro oven," he said.

"The roll sopped up the left over juice and butter, worked great," I said.

The mention of garlic bread made me rattle on about giving a loaf of it and pinto beans to the new family renting next door, listing how many lived there—six-- where they worked, the fact that the owner is in foreclosure, how much she owed the condo association, and on and on.

"They're real friendly," Jed said.

I shouldn't talk so much. For some reason that night I felt in an especially good mood – forgetting that Jed often has to read lips. Usually he gives me some indication that he can't hear me like, 'What did you say?' He seems more hard-of-hearing after recording one of his concerts.

When he was cooking today he wore suspenders for his Bermuda shorts. I have told him how "in style" they are. But the suspenders let the shorts drag, exposing three to five inches of bare midriff between his t-shirt and his hips. Gross. Why do some people, men and women, think exposing the split in their buttocks is attractive? The cheaper production costs of hip-width trousers, so-called in style, doesn't help. Have to be hiked up, constantly.

Jed lumbered back into the house, ran the hot water to rinse his dishes and utensils, then poured out the clam liquid in the pasta pan down the drain. Impulsively again, I suggested using the dish pan for soap and water.

"Want to get rid of the smell right away," he defended another of his habits.

Again I attempted to reinforce his efforts, "I see what you mean about clam stench." Occasionally I make the same suggestion regarding, "Isn't it time for a haircut? His thick white hair gets so long it curls up and under about mid neck, a very thick neck. The bangs on his forehead, with a broad face and fleshy jowls, make him look like he's imitating an aging Joan of Arc. When he avoids shaving for days, the brambles camouflage his eyes and nose. His pink mouth with worn-down teeth – one eighth left of what's normal – causes me to wonder how that man can chew the one and one-half pound steak he bakes by 5:30 PM Sunday evenings he doggedly shops for all week; claiming again and again, it was a reduction in price he "dare not pass over."

Just once, at Christmas time, I suggested he could hire as a Santa.

"I played with the idea at one time," he said then changed the subject. He wasn't flattered. He looks great after a haircut and a beard closely trimmed – takes ten years off him. But these days I find men don't seem to identify with clean-shaven and youthful, rather with the experience and wisdom of an elder?

It was so hot I was perspiring, so I ran water to fill another glass of it to drink. I looked to the left through the cut-out in the west wall at the two story window on the stair landing. The white shade now cuts the direct sun rays. "Thanks for pulling down the shade, Jed, when I'm not here. Glad I got it last September since I can't justify air conditioning. It cuts the heat. Keeps the upstairs cool."

As he headed up the stairs, leaving the pans for me to wash in my dishpan, I shouted, "Thanks Jed. Clams made it a perfect weekend – Supreme Court, et al – Safeway! Yeh! Yeh!"

The next morning, again in the kitchen, Jed shared his concerns about his forthcoming trip to an annual outdoor concert down in the valley, at Brownsville in July. "At this point I don't know who I'm going with. Richard's family, my usual camping fellows, has more complications with his diabetes."

"Richard's the one whose ninety-year-old mother just moved into their basement? You helped them ready it for her?"

Jed nodded. "Their autistic son moved out of it and is living with his girl he met on line. She moved here from the east coast at the same time Grandma arrived from Florida. Now, I'm afraid I'm in hot water.

"How?"

"Since my old friend, Richard, was iffy about the trip this year I made arrangements to camp with another couple, who it turns out, are at extreme odds with Richard."

"Why?"

"Some time back this couple's wife, Madera, had an affair with Richard. Now both couples want me to take sides. Richard's wife blames Madera. Madera's husband blames Richard. I try to avoid the entire discussion, but it seems Richard is putting me at a distance just because I'm friends of both families. At first, Richard told me they weren't going to the concert so I made these other arrangements. Now Richard and his wife, son and friend, and their two dogs, are all going. I expect fireworks."

That night Jed confirmed that he would be leaving Thursday morning and coming back Sunday evening. Clay, another friend, will deliver him, pick up his cot and sleeping bag he left at Richard's house last year, then join Jed with his camping buddies who have a tent Jed can use.

The last twenty-four hours Jed did three loads of wash. "I want matching shorts and t-shirts," he said. He did last minute scouting of the refrigerator and shopped for more food. Last year he provided all the food provisions for himself and Richard's family. In late June he ordered rib steaks, aged from Original Steer, to be ready for this trip. At that time they were for Richard, who likes Jed's cooking. Jed put the steaks in the freezer. They were no longer necessary, sad to say.

Martha is Still At It

In early June, a condo owner, recently widowed, and even more recently having to walk with the support of a cane, complained to Martha about the Stella d-Oro daylilies which spill over slightly onto the paved walkway and the two rose bushes that I put into an island on the south side of the parking lot. A hosta that I didn't put in, it moved in all by itself (the partial shade is perfect for it) also intruded ever so slightly onto the sidewalk.

I had a warning that someone didn't like the William Baffin dark pink roses. When blooming, it reaches four feet. Several days before, the long branches with full blooms had been cut and tossed askew over the bush itself and onto the spent Dutch iris, and the liatris just coming up. The perennials, like all else, I put in six years ago. I removed the tossed stems as soon as I became aware of the cuttings.

Martha was with her. She demonstrated how, with her cane, she was afraid there wasn't enough room for her to walk. The widow is a tiny, frail-looking lady and I, for one, realized that she could easily wobble and fall over, blame the plants, and sue the homeowner's association.

"The board will decide what to do about it," Martha said.

Further, the lady's parking space is next to the walkway on the west side, but she had demonstrated the danger of her walk on the east side, which was the only side where the hosta and daylilies hung over. I suggested that the hosta and daylilies could be trimmed.

The lady said, "How often? They would just grow back."

"You're so right," I said, "and they weren't meant to be trimmed, just thinned."

After that I shut up, let them stew, and removed myself from the scene. The next day the entire plot was nothing but dirt. Martha ordered with the Pacific people who garden once a week in season, the removal of the garden, and never ever reported it to the board and did not discuss it with me. She didn't even email us other board members and she sends emails about much lesser actions on her part, and always shares owners complaints.

I tried to bring up the subject before the last meeting with Martha by saying, "Good thing you removed everything, she could have sued."

Martha did not respond. Maybe she is developing a hearing problem like so many up in years.

The smaller rose bush, a shrub, Flutterbye, was delivered to my front entrance at my garden wall and just sat there, in its bare root which had been radically cut to get it out of the soil, dominated by a layer of rock approximately four inches down. I replaced a rose bush I'm not real crazy about and planted it in a protected area in an effort to save it. Now in the heat of early July, it's ninety-six right now at 4:51 PM on July 5th, 2015, it's leaves are dried up and brown but still attached to stocks, still green so far. Flutterbye, in a unique shape and shades of pastel pink, yellow, and white, lasts a long time as a bouquet in a small vase, won a ribbon for me my first year at the spring rose show. I took one stem of it to my writing teacher that first year in class because it's lovely and lasts so long.

Martha, our very efficient board member, made a snide statement to me as we traveled to the neighborhood center for a board meeting, the last Monday in June. Dotty was driving because Martha cannot drive at night anymore. To give you some background: Martha, Dotty and I, in the last four years, have attended EPIC. It's a program every other month, Wednesday at 6 PM, at the police precinct, open to anyone interested. It gives current information on police efforts. I have seen a police dog uncover a stash of drugs, another one for weapons and explosives. The riot squad has demonstrated for us in full regalia. The special gangs force often reports and the undercover prostitution wing has reported several times. Their current effort is to get the pimp and rehabilitate the prostitute as a victim rather than incarcerate.

EPIC is managed by Dave Smith, who is a police officer at Southeast Precinct on SE 106th, just south of Washington Street. A Portland police project Dave also is involved in provides police methods and organization guidance to a large city police department in Bangladesh, for several years now. Dave and his wife adopted two teenage girls and brought them to Portland to attend school. One of them is doing well at Mount Hood Community College and introduced herself in English at one of the EPIC meetings. The other girl returned to Bangladesh, probably homesick.

When I brought up the police department's prostitution redemption program, Martha said, "For all we know, you sleep with your renter."

She is critical of my garden, which all the neighbors tell me they enjoy, some love it. She doesn't like roses. Earlier I offered to give her my dwarf hydrangea, already potted, for her yard that faces west for the sun. Salty, another board member heard my offer and said she would love to have it. Martha said she hated hydrangeas too. She said the same thing when I offered a bouquet of lilies; long before that, when I offered dahlias. Although she did send me a note of thank you for the bottle of White Reisling I gifted her this Christmas holiday. She only likes Reisling and Gevurtztraminer wines and back when, she use to mention Rhine. She did give me a coffee cup filled with chocolates for Xmas the year before.

My first reaction was, how ludicrous. At first I didn't take it personally, tried to deal with it logically.

"I understand obese people have extra trouble doing sex with another. However, that said, your comment is an insult. Uncalled for. To alleviate your concern, tragically enough, I have only had intercourse with my husband. I'm real tough to love. That said, I am extremely particular." *You bitch.*

Finally, my sense of humor caught up with my outrage. "And extra cautious. At seventy-eight I'm still so viral I could end up pregnant or just come down with something worse. Who knows? My God knows. And my mother is up there watching my every move. I make an effort to keep her happy, maybe, laughing so hard, she would tear up. So maybe I need to know, What is your attitude towards unwed mothers?"

I got the last word in more ways than one. The William Baffin rose bush came back up. The gardeners just mowed it down, didn't uproot it. And Flutterbye likes its new home in a pot. It no longer has to struggle for space in the bedrock.

September 21, 2015 Dear Trudy: I apologize. I do remember you at my house and seeing my new faucet and updating my situation with my renter and my finances. I apologize for repeating information again and again. I don't see you often now that you have longer hours so can't play bridge. But, I do want to share with you.

You're going to be mad at me too, because again I gave away your gift to me. Hey! A gift belongs to the gifted. That's what I told my doctor when he asked me if he could give a rose I gave him in a bouquet to a patient of his who was distraught. I told my sister, Tilly (she prefers Matilda) about your wonderful bags. She wanted the gold one. "My color," she said. So I mailed it to her in a 9X12 envelope. She called me, "thrilled," as soon as she got it.

Tilly is very particular. For instance, buys nothing but Birkenstocks in summer and outfitted her kids with them as well. She gets tons of cream puffs from Costco for parties, etcetera, for her grandchildren. When she called to thank me they were going to Bend Country Club with another couple that Friday night "for their special clam chowder." I had a strong feeling she would love the bag. The gorgeous colors are my favorite, too.

"You're right. Your friend, Trudy, does beautiful work. Can't get this in a store." I had told her you sold twenty of them for $25.00 a piece at a bazaar, on the West side this time.

With your assistance we submitted all of my rose entries within the time limit, with time to spare, sans push and panic. Thanks again. I went back by 2:00 PM to see if any ribbons won – I definitely did not expect a trophy. None of my stuff was outstanding. I did get seven or eight ribbons which I was not expecting this time around. I wonder if the judges can tell I'm strictly organic? I stayed for the three o'clock awards ceremony and thanked Rich Baer for welcoming "my dear friend."

I told him about the rock Les Schwab was so generous to put in my garden in May of this year. Good thing I did. He advised against it for the roses in the ground: my two climbers, Altissimo (it placed this time) and Fourth of July (has won in the past), the Floribunda, Nearly Wild (I showed this year but a judge from Canada told me it didn't have enough blooms"three are required" which will help me in the future a great deal, and shrub, Carefree Spirit (a one stem spray won a trophy last year in 2014).

He said organic material necessary to the roses can't get through the rock. (I recall leaves that blow into the walled garden where these are, cover their roots, ground, even the pots all winter long.) So I have to remove the rock on them back away from their base at least eighteen inches. I'm frustrated...more time away from my book. Do you have a hoe I can borrow? – that would do the job the quickest. Mine disappeared during the move in 2000. With mostly my plants in pots due to the bed-rock in the soil, I didn't replace it. None of my neighbors use one either.

When the ribbons come in the mail, I will call you so you can see them. I left a message on your voice mail about your floribunda, Eureka. I saw it in the rose show Saturday. It's a beauty, designated color is Apricot, but it doesn't have a real high hardy rating so take extra care. How does it do? I already realize you probably won't sell it because it is in a pot and can go wherever you go when you retire big time to your dream home at Long Beach, Washington.

I don't think I woke Jake this morning at 5:20 AM, did I? I am proud of you for not giving up your fun and ultimate challenge, your persistent conditioning for the Hood to Coast run. Or is all that effort made for just a good and long life to see our grandchildren's children? Your description of your filling in for injured runners by making extra runs was amazing; in fact, phenomenal for your age, 64. Have you considered a marathon? Seriously! Do I sound like a grandmother? Let me remind you, I'm not old enough to be your mother but you treat me so good as if I was family. I treasure. And always, Clancy R.

Where Were You?

Brock didn't show for Bridge one morning. Tzok was in no hurry to finish his coffee and have another brownie provided by Neil. Our conversation started out sharing our mutual problem back when employed with a "family owned business." We agreed that was definitely "complicated."

I recalled a good son, the production manager, and a prodigal son, the bad one in my department – and with just the two of us in the afternoons he exploded with lots of complaints and criticism. After a short reprieve from his presence he would return with his five-year-old and turn to badgering his son instead of me.

"An unattractive redhead - he made me wretch in pain as he repeated over and over menacingly, "Don't color outside the lines, I've told you that a million times, stupid!"

"Years later I was told by an employer that I was "thin-skinned." I must be. That daily drama forced me to look for another job, an escape from the pain. I couldn't take it despite the fact I loved my job, loved my boss, Charlie Couche, the V.P., who obviously had to keep the owner's son in his department, so who had the power, Tzok?"

"Where were you when Kennedy was assassinated?" Tzok asked. "Everybody remembers. My son was born that day."

"The one in Seattle?"

"We're going there next week end. He's got a great house – a foreclosure –finished it themselves. Three story. On Lake Washington. View of the Sound and the city."

"Fantastic! But so much to manage."

"On one floor he has entertainment. His TV screen is as big as that wall over there," Tzok pointed to the huge back wall of the big open room we were in.

"Fortunately my brother was able to sell theirs to an attorney out of Connecticut – completely furnished, including the billiard table, even some of the art work. It was an albatross – for example, had to have the twenty-one palm trees on the property scaled once a year. Now they're in a two-bedroom condo, still with their own pool, but free to go."

"He's getting ready to sell."

"I don't blame him."

"He has to, his business is closing."

"Oh, how sad, Tzok, for him and you."

I was trusting Tzok for sharing what was important to him. I decided to share. How foolish of me. In addition, I didn't want to dwell further on his hurt, and me, always ready to change the subject. JFK's assassination was big for me too.

"When my supervisor, we called her MGM, because she was unofficially running the entire floor for her friend, the general manager, who had an undeclared illness which made it highly mysterious. MGM told me to stop sending blacks to her sales department, college graduates who merely wanted to apply for her temporary retail sales openings for the holidays.

"After all, my grandfather, out of Tennessee, was the attending physician to Jefferson Davis, president of the Confederacy."

"I guessed she was explaining her reason why I should not send them. I'll never forget the huge smile on her face when she informed me of John F. Kennedy's assassination.""Remember, the state of Oregon led the nation in equal employment opportunity laws, an outgrowth of shipyard, wartime days. Right there and then I decided to quit my job I loved with the state in work force. It was right down my alley, Economic History. It kept me in the thick of things. She didn't play by the rules. I went to grad school to teach in order to rid the world of her kind, that is, by providing adequate information. In my youth I had a habit of escaping from difficult, hurtful situations. I can't recall ever staying and tolerating much less putting up a fight, standing my ground. Yeh, that day was major for both of us. Good for you, bad for me. Cut my nose off to save my face."

This made me think of yet another job, 2000 to 2002, I quit – grunt work at a book distributor, fifty-seven hours per week. It was a subsidiary of a large British publishing company. We prepared six thousand new publications for shipment per week to colleges and universities in the US and the Commonwealth. The General Manager, female, happened to be from Idaho. The first round warning was when she removed a huge Jewish classic and the new biography of Thurgood Marshall, Supreme Court Chief Justice, from shipment. She claimed that these two new books did not meet bookbinding specifications. A real gruesome about the GM, an avowed vegetarian, was her excitement not only for Anthony Hopkins in Silence of the Lambs, but seeing him in Hannibal, not just one time. I still shudder when I recall her excessive enthusiasm for the carnivore in both movies.

Foolishly, still unsuspecting, I mentioned to her my suspicions of two publications; one of which I had purchased on discount. Another book on Nicaragua by Chomsky was definitely a counterfeit. It was definitely not written by Chomsky but listed as one of his many books. For footnotes it sent the reader to a website that didn't exist. The other was a thirty page *Little Red Book,* supposedly written by a black playwright which exposed him as a reverse racist, again obviously a counterfeit. I sent that one to a girl friend working for a law degree, for a second opinion. She never wrote back. The Chomsky book I placed with someone at Multnomah County Library, with a note of explanation regarding reasons for my suspicions.

At the same time, in my evaluation interview, she said, "I've decided there's nothing wrong with you except you could use some estrogen. I have hormones I can give to you." Her comment made me recoil. Of special note, a French savant, smooth-talking, wow-dressed, bon vivant, use to visit her. I interpreted him as a High-Class Pimp, nothing more, and did suspect she had her readers and evaluators of book binding, mostly struggling single mothers, needing extra cash nothing more, on her hormones.

The GM was especially influenced by James, another fellow peon, who wrote an essay to our writing group of how impassioned he was by Lisa, a Russian immigrant, who the GM fired. "I want her to have my baby," he wrote. When Lisa became pregnant and James abandoned her, her three brothers pummeled him. The GM testified his injuries occurred on the job.

At the same time one of her favorites, the computer tech, gave notice. Corporate replaced him with a new graduate from Portland State University. The six foot six black, named Oscar, was not allowed to roam free through the plant. Whereas the tech he had replaced had been given free reign and a friendly reception in all departments. We had to report PC problems to the GM and then she would consider whether or not to notify Oscar.

Kathi, my wonderful able and efficient coworker, most advanced of all of us on the PC – introduced us to Google at the time-- was suddenly fired Monday, after her son had applied for the shipping department, the previous Friday. The GM had given Kathi the go-ahead for her son to come in and apply. Needless to say, of course, he didn't get hired. He was black. Kathi is white.

May twenty-first. The last straw. At the usual weekly Approvals staff meeting the GM announced, with a huge grin on her face and joy in her voice, "Oscar won't be with us for a while. He's at the hospital. There's a problem with his new baby."

We said nothing, like in shock. She broke the silence by repeating the same great, emphatic announcement, with more glee in her voice. At 6 AM, May Twenty-second, I issued my written resignation to the receptionist at the front desk and returned home.

Kathi has remained a long- time friend. At that time her daughter, Ciera was ten. They visited me at my home and Ciera got an A for the story she wrote describing my decorated condo: curtains, area rugs, art and photos on the wall, and open shelves of fru fru with white walls and lots of color. By necessity Kathi has kept to the bare necessities. Just recently Kathi was able to get a jigsaw puzzle by an artist she likes at Fred Meyer at a bargain on coupons. She has fun assembling them, glues them together and places them on the walls of her apartment, which is in walking distance to that store. One can't get Kathi out of her car and on to a bus, and she is afraid to drive in ice and snow, so admits that she does miss work in real bad weather. "My arthritis flares up when I have to wait for and take a bus." Understandably, Kathi is not in tip top physical condition, but there's nothing wrong with her work ethic.

With the loss of the book Approvals job she ultimately lost her house just a short distance from my condo. The next years she worked as the primary inventory record keeper plus retail clerk for a popular second-hand equipment and general junk dealer, still on minimum wage. A family business, naturally the wife finally decided she wanted Kathi's job in 2008, at the downturn of the economy.

For the past three years Kathi, still in her fifties, has been a volunteer for not one but three nonprofits and now a government agency, on the computer learning their programs. How this system is supposed to work is you volunteer, learn the job, and when the budget allows a new hire, she will be hired. The budgets have not come through and ultimately the nonprofit locations were shut down. To me it looks like those organizations cash in on a lot of expertise which doesn't cost them much. But she is still optimistic. Last time she talked with me, she explained how much she learned about the nonprofits she worked for, like Make a Wish, to raise funds. One was making quilts from old wedding dresses that sell for one thousand dollars.

As Kathi just told me today December, 2015, she "works her fanny off" hoping to get hired and intends to work until she is seventy-two. Ciera is a serious and gifted student in advanced placement. As a soprano in the high school's Concert Choir, they performed at the Christmas Tree concert at Hope church and at the Grotto this season. Ciera has wanted to go to Reed College ever since she was in the eighth grade. Her mother doesn't know what Ciera wants to major in and wisely does not speculate.

When I filed for unemployment in May 2002, the hearing officer challenged my reasons for quitting. I asked him what his credentials were. First he said that was not my business. I immediately questioned his response so he said he was an attorney. I drove to the Oregon Bar Association and asked about him. I was told he was disbarred and had not applied to challenge and get reinstated.

I reported that information to the Employment Department. Their first response was that the adjudicator position did not require a law degree. I didn't settle for that. Ultimately an interviewer admitted that this particular hearing officer was hired because he was an attorney and accepted my claim. The British Publisher who was the holding company of the book distributor closed down its operations and vacated the building by mid-summer of that same year for the purpose of displaying new books for approval on the internet.

I fell into police volunteer effort and finally found a real job in 2004 as a cell phone customer service person. There was an underground war between drug users and dealers versus what I call clean personnel. The bad guys tried to recruit me like they did everybody else. Management and personnel were finally hauled into a Multnomah county grand jury hearing shortly after I left in 2006.

I'M BACK IN THE BALL GAME NOVEMBER 2015: But Change is the name of the game.

This weekend I caught up on my reading, *MidCountyMemo*. The Northeast Portland newspaper published by Tim Curran, has hired my friend, Jim Stewart, as a reporter. The November issue was Jim's second effort. He has three articles, all very important, and two of them are scoops, literally – investigative reporter style. I sent an email to him congratulating him, calling his articles "bombarding the city fathers" with critical, until now undiscovered, information. For one, a blind man explained that the Braille instructions on a corner sidewalk on NE Glisan, gave dangerous instructions to persons like him intending to cross the street.

He's so honest. He wrote back, "Bombarded, hah ha, I love it. No feedback yet but from my singular fan, you. And Chief is glad/lucky to have found me...jimmie O."

I had worked with Tim Curran in the early 1990s at a group of citywide neighborhood newspapers owned by Pry Publishing. Tim was in charge of the advertising for Mid County Memo which targets outer northeast Portland and purchased that newspaper from Marcia Pry before she sold her package (including the *St. John's Review*, *Sellwood Bee*, *Hollywood Star*, and one of the two Slabtown (NW Portland) newspapers and several others, to Treasure Island.

No wonder Jim's stories are so formidable. Confronted by his firm's reduction in force in the downturn of 2008, a patent attorney by trade, he has been freelancing ever since; felt saved by ObamaCare and his wife's willingness to open up a beauty shop in their garage. There are opportunities in other cities but their home, families, friends and heart are in Portland. We had last talked after his story in his first issue of the Memo. He said, "I call my new boss Chief. He loves it so he calls me Jimmie."

"Good. At AAR Western Skyways I wrote The Wind Soc, an employee monthly. I put in the column, The Chief calls 'em, for my CEO, Dennis Nichols. He loved it but had me write it for him most of the time because he had to be out of town a lot. "Tim's a survivor, so are you – you gotta be to be in newspapers."

"There's so many organizations I've got to find out about," Jim said.

"One for sure. Lori Boisen, director of the Midway Division Street projects – great gal – I'll ask her to put you on her email list. She's up-to-date
on most everything east of eighty-second and south of Burnside – she's
also plugged into the immigrants - will keep you posted."

"And attend E.P.I.C. at the precinct on 108th, south of Washington,
every other month, Wednesday, 6 PM. I'll give your email to Dave Smith
the next time he sends notice of the next meeting," I added.

I met Jim and Amity at Cleary's Bar and Grill where my friend,
Maddi was bartender. I went there on Wednesday nights five years ago
before I went to the police department on 106th for the citizens meeting sponsored by the Commander. When I started taking Cindy Hiday's
writing class Wednesday nights at Mount Hood Community College
three years ago, I stopped to visit with Maddi, Jim, and Trudy and her
husband, before I caught the 5:11 Number 71 that takes me to 102nd
and Prescott, the Maywood campus, in the old St. Rita's grade school
building.

Maddi always poured me a glass of house white wine that her husband treats me with, because he and I care about the same things, the
same ideas and the same people. In management at a window manufacturer, he works long hours and has a glaucoma condition, so he is rarely
at the bar. He treats me in absentia. We even root for the same basketball
and football teams. He's my soul mate, whereas Maddi turns intellectual
on us and makes effort to argue both sides. She rarely takes a position.
She insists on sitting on the fence.

Her father was from Norway. In 2014 she gifted me with a calendar
from Norway she brought back from her visit to family still there, which will
hold far beyond its printed year. Maddi is well read and ventures into publications when they are offered at a bargain for a short time. Her favorites
are *The New York Times*, *Rolling Stone*, *Atlantic Monthly,* and she liked
Foreign Affairs I gifted her when that was made available to me. "Who I
vote for is none of your business," she has said. She has always made her
subscriptions available to me. It was my first exposure to Rolling Stone. I

love their political editorial, intensive research. I love Maddi. She consistently challenges.

But I'm gearing up for changes. Cleary's was purchased by a couple of brothers who don't speak English. They ceased to advertise. Tears in the seat cushions were merely repaired with colorful mending tape. The wonderful longtime chef decided to return to Mexico. Staff's hours were cut. One could see the writing on the wall. Maddi, with seniority, stuck with it, but finally switched to a more stable situation elsewhere, six months ago. That turned out to a great move for her – more money, bigger tips, and a class clientele in St. John's. Maddi use to live in St. John's and swears by their soil, far superior to our southeast's bedrock. Yes, she's a gardener, vegetables and peppers. Blond and stately and always a lady she quickly reminds anyone who knows her, "Don't dare underestimate a bartender." I'm reminded. One of our finest mayors in my time was a bartender and great inn keeper.

Bridge City Tap Room, opened by a former steak house owner of forty years in Portland, is located across from the popular Don Pedro's restaurant and the library. Cleary's faithful began to gather there, attracted by the gourmet food, attractive Brazilian woods interior, and efficient management one could count on. Now Trudy and her husband, Jim and Amity, and even Cleary's daytime bartender, can be found at Bridge City. In fact, Maddi, well known in east Portland, is old friends with the owners of Bridge City.

I met the bartender from another local bar who has lunch there. She told me she just found cheaper rent in somebody's house. "I've never had to live with someone before, always had an apartment, but I only get ten dollars an hour." Her brother joined her that day and said he was on his way to court to take custody of his roommate's daughter's new baby, "if the girl refuses to finish high school. She doesn't want to leave her baby," he said.

I took the opportunity to tell him about St. Helens school for unwed teenage mothers. They take their baby to school where there is full baby care plus required classes to finish. The number seventy-one bus takes them there. "Have talked with lots of girls taking advantage of the program." He had me write the name of the school on a lottery ticket for him.

In February, 2016 Maddi gave me ride home from Fred Meyer early Sunday morning. She is no longer sitting on the fence. Madder than hell at the Republicans she is glad her tugboat and other industrial customers, so called blue collar, are too. "They're a breath of fresh air from the hate brokers and fear mongers, hell bent for election at any price," she exclaimed.

◆ ◆ ◆

At Mountain View, Tzok, without warning one Friday morning decided that Bob, the other substitute, also a tennis player, would be the fourth man for bridge. Brock let me know. It wasn't a surprise to me. Tzok and I had some meaningful conversations prior to that, which I have shared with you. But the very last exchange gave me foreboding. On a morning that Brock didn't show for a game, Tzok and Paul both asked me what I thought about the "trillion dollar debt?"

Without hesitation I rolled out, "When companies and individuals are making billions in profits and, of course, keeping moneys abroad big time, paying little or no taxes, a trillion dollars makes sense. Two American Nobel prize winning economists, Krugman and Stiglitz, say that these extremes in income can be solved by human action and legislation, which is what caused the debt to begin with. That and war and wartime graft. After all, even congress has borrowed from the social security fund and never paid it back."

They were speechless, but Tzok looked fit to be tied, furious. They had wanted to set me up and I disappointed them. I guess they wanted to make me speechless with their big so-called overwhelming earth-shaking question. So I tried to change the subject, "I hope Brock's leg gets good enough soon to play tennis again. He lives for his game with you two."

Paul said, "I'm going to take a shower since we can't play," and took off. Tzok didn't say another word and also vacated the premise.

I went back to the main reception area to see if there was an *Oregonian* to read and finish my coffee, decide what to do with the rest of the morning before lunch, and watch CNN on one of the televisions. As I took a deep breath, a woman in workouts approached me and said, "I heard what you said to them, I agree with you."

I was shocked by her statement because inside I was pretty riled up but said, "Thanks." If I wasn't so distraught I would have exchanged introductions, but she caught me more off-guard than I already was. Eventually her comment gave me hope, encouraged me.

Now, Rei, Brock, Gerard and I play bridge usually every other Thursday at noon at her house or mine. We prepare appetizers, salads and easy to eat entrées. Gerard is a vegan, an obsessed one, so Rei has prepared grilled mackerel, cod, salmon, shrimp, and a fish I've never heard of – the last five times for him. I fill in with deviled eggs, turkey meatballs in a cherry sauce, and a great chipotle black-eyed pea dish. We munch for hours. One time we played until nine PM. Gerard's all time favorite was my date-nut macaroons and chocolate macaroons made with Eagle brand condensed milk. Rei makes a great almond sliver cookie, so light and crisp, called Tuile. Irresistible sushi is a regular, a specialty by both Rei and Ito.

Since Neil bakes goodies for Fridays, I will bake banana nut or zucchini bread or peanut butter cookies, or little red potatoes with cream cheese and chives, and something pumpkin (I did bars last year) when I have time on Tuesdays for their Wednesday bridge games, when Pat O'Reilly plays with his oxygen tank attached.

Brock keeps me posted on everybody's health. A good friend, he confirmed for me my major faults and reason for my removal from the foursome. "In the Navy, Clancy, first rule of thumb given us was, 'Don't talk politics or religion.'"

Laughing, I completed the last of his words with him and added, "or Money. Money, not good cooking, is the major concern of men, not mice."

♦ ♦ ♦

Gerard is in demand at bridge tables citywide. A dear friend, he sponsored me for the duplicate bridge at Holiday Park retirement center which meets Saturday afternoons. Devoted to the written word, he was a former editor at a respected publication in Kentucky, and then with an internationally distributed tabloid out of London. After he retired early, he wrote plays produced in northern California community theatres. He had worked in theatre in New York City after college.

From New Orleans originally, he haunts Powell's Books, listens to many book readings, and attends movie festivals in downtown. His recent favorite is Spotlight. His view condo is convenient to the Yellow MAX. He uses Tri-Met buses and their trains without complaint. But Gerard recently is experiencing "no control" over his legs so he has invested in expensive crutches and is now considering a lightweight wheelchair to shop for groceries "since it's impossible to shop with crutches."

He has calculated his condition via books and internet independent of medical personnel. In fact he avoids doctors because he does not want to subject himself to examinations and extensive medical treatments, most of which he figures will be just experimental. Drawing from others with the same condition, he has become familiar with the usual routine treatments applied to his case. He does not fear death. He has not experienced any symptoms of depression like panic attacks, or insomnia or weight loss or extreme gain. "I'm good from the legs up," he says, "Have total control, otherwise."

He lives a full life away from home and especially enjoys mornings and evenings at home with his three cockatoos, all adopted from owners who had to give them up due to changes in their lives. A vegetarian, Gerard highly recommends delectable crock pot dinners out of his favorite cook book, *150 Indian, Thai, Vietnamese & more Slow Cooker recipes.*

Gerard describes a condition of financial security. His four year old condo on the fourth floor with view and skylights on North Killingsworth has doubled in price. He got in on it tax-free for a number of years to go yet. For eight years he has been writing a book about a family in Montana surviving the famine of 1917. So far, he has read three rewrites of the first chapter to me over the phone, each one of them more sensational, more extreme. Keeps putting more emphasis on the father's horrendous jaws – leading me to believe that the story resorts to cannibalism, but I hesitate to tell Gerard so. I don't want to give away his story before he has a chance to tell it.

He avoids Windows and WORD. Two years ago he met with Jed who gave him some advice on investment and use of electronic equipment. Needless to say he's not close to publication. He refuses to use a credit or debit card on line and sees no reason to invest in a PC or cell phone. Uses the Multnomah Public library to do research on internet and keep an email.

When Gerard shared with me his reasons for his major choices regarding his health, I told him how unique and yet practical they were and asked him if I could tell about him in my book. He gave me the go ahead. Prior to his explanation of why, as a friend I had been very concerned. I am no longer worried about Gerard. I'll still pray that it goes the way he anticipates. He is only seventy-two.

I'm flexible too, rarely hold a grudge. December 10, 2015 Brock called to ask me to be a fourth for bridge at Mountain View, with Tzok and a new tennis player named Tom, 8:30 AM Wednesday morning.

"I'd love to. Thanks for calling."

Tom and Brock thoroughly trounced us. Brock became actually giddy over their great hands. I liked the friendly and comfortable demeanor of this new guy, Tom. Close to the end of our disaster I impulsively said, "You're regular people. I like you."

"I'm what they call balanced....back when, well rounded."

I laughed, "Well rounded. I remember that term – try the fifties – maybe sixties. Now the kids have to be volunteers – give freely of their time – looks great on a college application."

At the end of the game I shook Tom's hand, then Tzok's.

No wonder he's open, unafraid, and a happy guy. Tom is much younger and employed full time. A new member, he's rarely available to play.

Encounters Worth Celebrating

For years I have chatted with Karl while waiting for the bus at the corner of 122nd and Division, a chef with two jobs: Sanford's and a Denney's. Clean shaven and pleasantly well fed, he sends his money back to Budapest. The last time I saw him he said he had reason to celebrate. "I'm retiring after twenty-seven years, on social security and savings, with my family in Budapest. I will leave my roommate and her kids to join my wife and family, but I will take trips back to visit."

• • •

After lunch recently, I boarded the Division bus at Gresham transit center. Seated behind the back exit was a lovely girl in a beige fitted Hijab, using an iPad. I figured she was a student at Mt. Hood Community College and just might speak English. I'm glad she did.

"Motivated by Malala," she is majoring in Political Science and plans to work in an organization that encourages education for girls. From Kenya, she learned English in school there. She purposely chose a local college. "A girlfriend went east to school and had a nervous breakdown. She had to come home." She was coming home from school to visit her father who is working in a shop on SE Division in the city. "I am close to him like Malala is to her father. He encourages."

• • •

There was a long line at the bank so the manager was helping the tellers by filling out the paper work for those of us who were only depositing. A woman behind me said to him, "I'm so glad you're at my bank. You make me feel better. My son is in prison. My fourth son, I have five. He was my smartest – graduated from high school. What's your name?"

"Jamal," he said.

"I bet you played football or basketball, both!" she said.

He said, "Football."

I joined in, "What school?"

"Portland State."

"Their football is in contention,"

"We go to all their games." he offered.

I said, "What position?"

"Safety….(something?)" he explained, but I'm not up to date on the names of the positions anymore. Secondary? I'm still trying to figure out the term.

The lady behind me asked him if he was married and had family. He answered in the affirmative, then asked her why her son was in jail.

"His girl worked for a bank so he dreamed up a scheme and got caught right away."

The teller was ready for me. She is a beautiful blond from the Ukraine.

The lady behind me opening up her grief and Jamal are both black. He accepted her anxiety and treated her with, "I'm Okay, You're Okay," not at all stiff or formal or noncommittal. It seemed she was so relieved to see her people there. She was a loving black mama spilling out what burdened her, unrelenting.

♦ ♦ ♦

Last minute holiday shopping at Fred Meyers, a female checker I was familiar with checked me out. She is the daughter-in-law of Frances, an old timer who uses a modified motor scooter, a WWII vet who wins contests for her hats at Meals On Wheels at East Portland Community Center for Easter bonnet and Halloween costume contests. "The store is having a wonderful Christmas, but never have to wait in line. Do you get a bonus when it does?" I asked her.

"Never."

"How long have you been here?"

"Twenty-seven years. My husband, head of paint – twenty-five years."

"I know and like him. You two don't look that much mileage."

She laughed. "Thanks."

"You met him here then. Isn't that wonderful?"

The next time I saw her in February she couldn't hold back her tears. Frances, on her scooter, driving in the bike lane on the four lane Division Street, was hit by a van and killed instantly.

♦ ♦ ♦

"Where are you from?" I asked a handsome fellow with two children who got on the bus and sat across from me.

"Afghanistan," he said.

"You speak such good English," I said. "How long have you been here?"

"One month. I was eighteen years with the U.S. Army. Decorated."

It was December 20, Sunday, 9:20 AM on the bus 71. I had two bags of cans to go to Bottle Drop. He was fit, well built. He said his daughter was ten and the boy, eight. They smiled and nodded. I stood and reached across the aisle and shook his hand, "Welcome," I said. "Thank you for what you have done for our countries. Good luck to you."

We were at my stop. I waved goodbye to them. They waved back, all smiles.

The *Bloomberg Business Week*, in December 2015, pointed out that since 9/11 only forty-five persons have been killed by Islamic terrorists in these United State of America. Someone is barking up the wrong tree.

♦ ♦ ♦

The *Columbian* is running a feature about an outstanding gentleman in his struggle in the last stages of multiple sclerosis. It makes me think of Sharon Beauvais, a friend of mine in high school. Their mother gave twenty-four-hour home care to their father with MS. At that time he was totally dependent on her for living one more day.

Sharon never expressed to me or anyone the sacrifices she and her two brothers, who supported the family, had to make. I recall as an adult being ashamed of myself, when questioned by Sharon at the reunion, regarding the state of my life. I had always looked up to her levelheaded seriousness and sense of responsibility. And she was such a little thing. I had to look down to her, even though I actually looked up to her. She majored in Food Science at Oregon State University and had a career with the Oregonian's very active test kitchen and six page "Food Day" in its heyday. Married to an engineer she has a good life – above all people, she deserves it.

Dick Franzke's dad was like a mummy in a wheelchair when I met him at their home as a freshman in college. His dad had been a republican independent journalist in Montana until he became ill. The family with four boys moved to Portland where Mrs. Franzke became the Human Resource Manager at Meier & Frank. There she graciously hired Dick and his friends, students at Portland State College and other local colleges, as Transfer Boys, Stock Clerks and Sales, especially in sporting goods, all part time to pursue their education.

Dick and his girlfriend, Marla became friends of mine at Portland State. His older brother was an engineer with IBM, so Dick started out to major in engineering. But Dick loved Debate, was a devout republican, and switched to pre-law. Accepted at Willamette Law School, I loaned him the portable Smith-Corona typewriter I got for high school graduation. Three years later he returned it. It had gone the journey full-force for Dick. He won the national Torts Mock Trial and graduated with a Doctor of Jurisprudence. Offered huge salaries by East Coast firms, they decided to join Stoel-Rives, the largest law firm in the Northwest, based in Portland.

When he graduated I wanted to treat him and Marla, it was her victory too (she worked to put him through and brought forth three children, too boot) to a steak dinner. Palaske's had just opened up on Barbur Boulevard on the property of a defunct bowling alley. It got notoriety. They featured a huge aquarium in the lounge downstairs. We waited in the bar two hours for a table. A memorable evening for sure, we could groan about years later.

Summers Dick had worked building curbs for Goldie Construction and developed expertise with construction. He became the attorney for General Contractors Association and, ultimately, Kiewit. With Stoel-Rives his first account was Union Pacific. In those early days, Dick traveled only by train. He feared flying, he said, which later disappeared. He and Marla built a home with a view of Mt. Hood and an indoor swimming pool on ten acres of walnut trees on Bull Mountain. He designed, did the contracting, but most of the work by himself. Marla was his runner for materials and tools, making trips down Bull Mountain Road thousands of times.

In Phoenix he had the new surgery for short-sightedness so as to remove the need for glasses. It was not a success and Dick fought off poor eyesight from then on, and in later years resorted to a reader to execute. I loved Dick and Marla. I wanted good things to happen to them.

My joy with Dick was many a debate regarding politics. Marla was from a democratic family. Her father was a skilled laborer and union and her mother was a retirement home official and designer, a Canadian Nurse. In graduate school I read The Conservative Mind by Barry Goldwater, Dick swore by. It gave ride to long-running, never-ending debates between us. I have some fond thoughts of the then. Before her mother died of throat cancer she was unable to speak, so Mrs. Denton and I wrote notes back and forth to express our political feelings.

◆ ◆ ◆

Kalli O'Keefe came by to see me before Christmas. She looked great – her hair and face again stunning, her old self. She was keeping house for Darren's folks. His father broke a leg taking the turkey out of the oven at Thanksgiving. "Darren loves my ten thousand dollar face lift." She is having second thoughts. Will she quit boxing? Now she's got money, bargaining power, choices; she's taking it in her stride. Kalli is not finished, not by a long shot.

Our last conversation was in January, 2016 from her home in the Sierras. "Maybe one thousand people in my world now, who all claim to know all about me. Church every Sunday is all day…breakfast, lunch, and dinner," she shared.

Kalli, someday you will discover it's not a good idea to sleep with business partners. Now that you're safe and sound, thank goodness, and paying your dues, I can tell you: Holding garage sales to move stolen goods is a crime, my dear-- no matter how neighborly, no matter how good the cause. Or is love still blind? Or easy money irresistible? In retrospect, I have no problem with thieves stealing from thieves. Who should the police charge with a crime?

A recent medical report shows a high rise in venereal disease among the elderly. There's more elderly females than men. Foolish women.

◆ ◆ ◆

Leonard Pitts, one of my favorite "national columnists," out of *Miami Herald*, (the other, Paul Krugman of the *New York Times*) saw the new movie, '*Creed*' so headed his column "Reminds that we're in long fight against time." It ran in The Columbian December 7th 2015. Following are excerpts:

"…time is a thief. Yes, it steals your legs and stamina, your quickness and strength.

"But that's just physicality. Time takes more. It takes the places you used to go and things you used to do. It takes memory. It takes loved ones. Eventually, it takes you.

'Life' – and '*Creed*' – are about how you respond as time does these things.

"So much of what time steals, we have no choice about….*Creed* tells us 'the thing inside that makes you get up from every knockdown is different. Its loss is not predetermined by age. Rather, it's a choice. You decide to let time take that thing away from you. Or not.'"

I am grateful for all the persons in my life, including Jedediah Hildebrog. He contributes to my well being, my survival. Almost fifteen years younger, he's not in as good a shape as I am so he might not last as long as I do. I hope that is not the case. At last report Jed and his friend, Richard, are fast friends once again. All is forgiven.

My mother fretted about the capacity of the medical profession to prolong life – even as a vegetable – "which isn't living."

But – these days, the power to sustain, continue, and/or end life, Mom, have ended up in the wrong hands. They use ancient weapons to justify their use of the tools: anger, fear, falsehoods, hate, promised land lost, conjured enemies to maintain their greed.

The ancient Greeks and Romans examined oratory of those seeking leadership, or rather, power, on basis of their use of appeals: ethical or logical or emotional. They concluded demagogues resort only to emotion.

Fear and hate doesn't feel good in my belly, Mom. Aren't there more important things to be done with my life?

Part Six

The Biggest Chunk of Me

Dear Emily:

Although I avoid organized religion, the habits of my youth find me making the sign of the cross followed by Hail Mary and the Our Father to talk to my Lord, to thank Him and also ask for help. Your mother's commitment to her faith and your gratefulness to your Creator keep me humble, as did my mother's undying devotion. The intellect He gives us and my unique experience in the world tells me most of the religious of the world reach for the same God. The variations in socio-economic and physical conditions cause us to interpret His intent askance, bringing war, poverty, ignorance, and what my mother called "man's inhumanity to man."

My beautiful granddaughter, exterior and interior – you're not only a work of art but a gift from God. I know you will not obliterate your beauty with piercings, tattoos, artificial trappings, or cosmetic surgeries. Keep the package God provided you with to face the world's haunts and taunts.

Via your art work and studies and activities you searched for self. I hope you continue to find yourself as the self-motivated, disciplined, hard-working student, athlete and caring big sister, a role model for two amazingly energetic brothers, also full of promise. Most of all, you are loved and will continue to be loved on your journey. When you have had choices, you have applied tools you've developed to select those that work for you – you could live with. When there have been road blocks (walls seeming too high to climb), you have sought counsel and a way to cope or find options, another route to realize your innate urge and passion to learn and acquire expertise. Personally I consider you already in possession of the scientific methodology.

You have willingly acknowledged the support of your family, who are pathfinders and achievers in their own right. Your mother and father are carving unique contributions of their own. Others' expectations can be overwhelming. You take it in your stride. You don't let them dominate. You were more than just curious when you were only three. Always investigative early on, you could see the relationship between causes and results, and continue to do so. You are applying it to your choice of goals.

Self-aware of your exceptional characteristics, you treat others, some less fortunate, as equals and participate with them to achieve mutual goals. "But for the grace of God go I." You have accepted the leadership which is your destiny to take yourself and others to another level. You're practical, a problem solver, always with your flat feet firmly on the ground (except when they are jumping sky-high to spike). Speak up, although you seem to know when it's best not to.

Sometimes that journey can be lonely, difficult and sometimes futile, even remote. "Don't give up the ship" of God, country, self, family and team, not necessarily in that order. "Live well, love much, laugh often." And don't resent your tears. When life gets too complicated, KISS, "Keep it simple, stupid." Pan Am people (an international motley crew) used to say "Play it by ear," that is, listen with your brain and heart in your belly. Go with what feels good – gut level. If it works, don't fix it. It is apparent, Emily, that you work hard to reduce the margin of error that is inherent in all human endeavors. Don't punish yourself too harshly.

It sounds like you want a school in a city? I don't blame you. Consider Portland State! Seriously, it's moving up in academic circles. I wish I would have stayed there. U of O incurred an economic burden. My initial goal was a PhD, but my life became a greater and grateful journey in neglected furrows, so my education has served me well. Find a love and associates who make you feel beautiful and whole, rather than ones that make you unsure and overly critical of self. You deserve all that life and love can provide.

Continue to be your forthright and honest self. Continue to be true to yourself. Don't relinquish your high ideals and concrete goals for anyone or anything. Stay as strong and courageous and persistent and in search as you have always been.

And always, With love and great pride in my family and a joyful life given to me by a good God,

Grandma Clancy

HAPPY FIFTIETH, my son.

You've always been here for me. At one time I feared that you would interpret me the way your father decided to color me. He did not like me. I was merely a meal ticket. He didn't seem to aim beyond that...so I feared that you would take up where he left off and put me down too. Whereas, I recognized your embrace of me as a valuable human being. We have grown up together.

But you were so self sufficient and self-motivated, so you shared your discoveries with me: Frankenstein, Dick Gregory's *Nigger*, *Sports Illustrated*, Led Zeppelin, The Who, even now, Cold Play and Sleater-Kinney, your dreams and your goals, and your friends and fears. Actually every musician's efforts are safe with you.

You scored in the 98th percentile in mathematics on the SAT but wanted to be a journalist. I found journalism school with a possibility of scholarship for you. I'm sorry I couldn't afford Oregon, your first choice.

You were so wanted with hope and promise when I ate seven delicious apples a day from Washington State in Houston to nourish you. I concocted a lot of lasagna and talked to you, to be sure you thought good thoughts, for you to arrive happy and healthy, and you did all of those. Feel fortunate that I insisted in returning to God's country, the great Northwest.

When I lost work so late in life, without question you paid my mortgage to save my life's investment ... of major, it told me you believed in me as much as I believed in you. Along with my beloved brother and sister you have never let me down.

You fought back and reclaimed your life big time after sudden death – June 5, 2000. You must have decided – "life is good – worthwhile. I want to live some more of it, Lord."

I have lots of acquaintances. You have close friends, including fellow editors, who have marched beside you, who share your exploration into every odd corner of music and expression, who venture into the unknown with you, who share your dedicated, endless search for a better way.

I grasp your undying commitment to wife, family, the printed effort, God and country. You stayed with the ship, never doubted your choice of journey necessary to express your dependence on truth-finding, honesty and your need to love, laugh, think, and tell it like it is. Your father was convinced that "What appears to be is more important than what is." You prove to me and the world that WHAT IS, IS MORE IMPORTANT THAN WHAT APPEARS TO BE. What is must be uncovered, discovered, and communicated. Every day I thank God for His gift to me – you and yours.

You have always been careful to choose what you share with me – and your readers – and I appreciate your reticence, your reserve. Au contraire, I have to spill and spill to finally find my target, my voice...please, bear with. Like you have said, I meander like a rambling rose. See me as still in flux, on the road. Hence, I write more books, because they seem to fall short of what's in my heart and gut...but so grateful you're here. You're my life – the biggest reason I am on earth. Above all, I have prayed never ever to let you down. You hear what I hear.

Still, I make a lot of people smile, maybe feel good – on the bus, next door, old timers and volunteers at Meals on Wheels, bridge, pinochle, eye-to-eye, and seekers for goodness and beauty like me-- even on internet, when I sign my name to a meaningful petition – even when I tell my doctor, "I don't hurt anywhere," and I don't, maybe because you're still here and doin' it big time. You qualify for your friend O.B.'s, and now that of your youngest, the six-year-old's "AWESOME."

Love, and always, Mom